The wide variety of techniques and activities systematically described in this text have been designed to assist the classroom teacher and his elementary school pupil in creating and constructing instructional materials. Adaptable to each child's individual learning style, these techniques and activities are directed toward stimulating verbal learning within an existing curriculum.

The authors utilize a decision making model as an aid in selecting a learning approach for each child. The model also demonstrates how an educational program can be modified to deal with individual learning problems.

Section I presents a detailed discussion of learning theory in relation to the child's developmental stages, learning style, types of learning, and instructional techniques. The purposes of education, as well as those principles which guide the learning process, are discussed in relation to the curriculum. A rating chart, which helps the teacher to evaluate the pupil's progress, is further utilized in the decision making model.

Section II describes specific techniques that can be used singly or in combination to develop instructional or learning materials. These challenging activities require planning, cooperation, sharing, problem solving, evaluating, explaining, summarizing, and synthesizing from the child. Such techniques as layouts, lettering and manuscript writing, sketching, bulletin boards and displays, and printing are described. The authors stress the importance of field trips, role playing, dramatization, puppet shows, and discussion. Particular emphasis is given to various types of construction—paper mache, frame, and solid block. After explaining each technique, the authors demonstrate the application of the various activities to social studies, science, mathematics, and reading and the language arts. They then offer suggestions for introducing these techniques and activities into the curriculum.

ues and
ities
late Verbal
earning

rence of
ed in the
ents and
ciples is
the op-
demon-
tools, as

bed are
how to
program
articles
m, mak-
to pro-
onomies
conven-
stem. A
sources
is also

h chap-
ties fol-
nctional
add im-
rstand-

today
dividual
oaches
uggests
mulate

sociate
on and
Mate-
at The
rned a
nnecti-
Univer-

culum
versity
she re-
brings
rience

Tech-
niques and Activities to Stimulate Verbal
Learning.

Techniques and Activities to Stimulate Verbal Learning

Clarence R. Calder, Jr.
University of Connecticut, Storrs

Eleanor M. Antan
University of Connecticut, Storrs

THE MACMILLAN COMPANY/COLLIER-MACMILLAN LIMITED, London

THE MACMILLAN COMPANY
866 THIRD AVENUE, NEW YORK, NEW YORK 10022

COLLIER-MACMILLAN CANADA, LTD.,
TORONTO, ONTARIO

Library of Congress catalog card number: 79–91025

First Printing

PREFACE

The tenth Annual Phi Delta Kappa Research Symposium was planned to attack one of the most resistant problems in education: why schools persist in emphasizing verbal mastery of subject matter when they have known for years that such mastery has little effect on the quality of the lives of children. For example, the ability to repeat principles of democratic citizenship in the classroom by no means guarantees success in the examinations of life.[1]

Much criticism is prominent in the educational press today of verbalism in learning, of failure of instruction to affect behavior, and of the inability of many programs to reach a large proportion of pupils.

We feel that too little attention is given to the learning styles of individual pupils. Lecture, recitation, conversation, and discussion have an important place in education, but these should not be relied on exclusively. Constructing, manipulating, viewing, and demonstrating are techniques that do not depend on verbal facility. It is our contention that these learning styles should be utilized in a variety of ways and in varying degrees for all pupils. They should be utilized in accordance with an individualized plan for each pupil. In the hands of an imaginative teacher they can help each child reach his self-fulfillment goals in his own way. They also can give the teacher a broad basis for evaluating each child. Not only his attainments, but the processes he employs and the attitudes and values he demonstrates can be assessed.

We believe it is of particular importance for undergraduate students in education to learn to perform the techniques suggested in this book and to put them into practice as extensively as is consistent with the program when they work with elementary children as student-teachers. We are convinced

[1] *News, Notes, & Quotes.* Phi Delta Kappa. Vol. XIII, No. 2, November 1968.

that they will be better student-teachers because they have these skills and knowledge and that they will be better prepared teachers because they will be able to apply a variety of approaches to learning in their student-teaching experiences.

We recommend that every elementary teacher become proficient in the skills and activities suggested in this book. We hope that the teacher will use them, and teach his pupils to use them, to attain the aims of a tailor-made plan for each child.

The writers are grateful to their students, to authors and publishers, and to business organizations for their willingness to make contributions to the content of this book, and due credit is given in the footnotes.

We especially appreciate the assistance of the students in "Education 210" who experimented with the techniques and who produced the models and devices shown in the photographs. We wish to thank Dr. Suleiman Zalatimo, Dr. W. Howard Martin, and Mrs. D. Rose Calder for their technical assistance and constructive suggestions.

C. R. C.
E. M. A.

CONTENTS

PART THREE

Tools, Materials, *and* Supplies

PART ONE

Theory *and* Rationale

The setting for this book is the elementary classroom. Its environment should be extended and enriched to provide a variety of paths along which individual children may travel toward the accomplishment of learning tasks. Each of the pupils through an admixture of background, experience, aptitude, abilities, and disabilities comes to the classroom with his own particular learning style. The environment should provide the stimulus and the means by which the learner can utilize his own level of the learning process and his own capabilities and interests to advance toward educational goals. To set the background for this classroom environment of interaction of people with people and of people with materials, a general look at the educational process is summarized in Chapters 1 and 2. Chapter 1 discusses the learning setting, the learner, the teacher, and the concerns that they properly pursue. Chapter 2 looks at learning principles, the kinds and stages of learning, and the ways in which these precepts can have direct bearing on the learning process. To assist the teacher in planning and evaluating learning tasks tailored to learning styles, a decision-making model, a chart depicting learning levels and styles, and a pupil's record sheet are included.

CHAPTER 1

The Need *for* Learning Activities

The assign-read-write method no longer has a dominant place in education. It was a simple method, easy for pupil and teacher alike; but its results were woefully inadequate. At best it gave a fragmented segment of knowledge and understanding; often it was merely rote learning without a grasp of underlying principles or even sometimes without actual understanding of the meaning of the words involved; usually the material was quickly forgotten after the test. The method presented little challenge to the pupil to develop an understanding of the relationships and the dynamics of knowledge.

Today the means of education are under careful scrutiny, and a multiplicity of methods have been brought to the problem of providing the best possible education. Various ways of organizing schools, grouping pupils, and restructuring content have been submitted to trial and research; and ways of reaching all pupils have been given careful attention. No small part in this vitalization of education has been played by the emphasis on a broadened concept of a variety of resources, which may turn the classroom from a dull, stereotyped situation into a laboratory of growth and learning, and which may contribute to the development of learning centers equipped with an ever-increasing number of instructional materials and devices helpful in the solution of meaningful problems.

Multiple Learning Materials

Textbooks are no longer the only important instructional materials available to the child. Today's classroom has become a laboratory—a learning

3

environment replete with visual materials and manipulative devices. The environment is ever changing as learning progresses in the room. Every learning device or activity must be just what the name implies—an aid to learning. Excellent commercial aids of all kinds have been developed to make the learning environment a laboratory. Some of these are the motion picture, the teaching machine, language laboratories, science kits, closed-circuit television, and reading laboratories.

These, excellent as they are, have two principal drawbacks: they are expensive, and they are not developed in the classroom. It is not implied that these fine commercial aids should not be used whenever they are available and whenever they pertain to the learning problem at hand. But in the many other situations when the right commercial aid is not at hand, much can be done to charge the environment with impactful devices simply by making them in the classroom. And in the making—designing, planning, working according to plan, correcting errors, finishing neatly, decorating attractively—children learn much, not only in solving the problem at hand but also in building work habits and self-control that will contribute to success in school, home, and community activities.

The activities and techniques described in this text were designed and planned to help the classroom teacher and elementary school children create and construct instructional materials and equipment. The writers realize that it is seldom possible to have on hand or readily available all the instructional materials and equipment needed in a learning situation. The task would be insurmountable even without school budget limitations, supply ordering procedures, storage space, and the other obstacles that frustrate educators. However, the techniques described in this text can help the classroom teacher overcome these frustrations and can assist in making the learning process much more flexible. The teacher who is willing to develop a degree of proficiency in these techniques and is willing to try these techniques with children can circumvent many school limitations. These techniques and activities can help create an atmosphere that is in accordance with the learning style of each child. They can be carried on within the framework of the present curriculum and can be used as adjuncts for establishing new approaches to learning. They should be developed to implement a carefully thought-out system of planning and organization. The pupils should be made aware of this planning and organization so that they will know what to do, what their purpose is, what framework they must operate in, and what the guidelines are.

A brief explanation and illustration of learning theory is presented here so that the reader will understand the rationale for the approach recommended in this text for helping children learn. A decision-making model is also presented to clarify for the classroom teacher some of the alternative approaches he can use with children. It presents the rationale for developing a program that considers instructional techniques and learning styles as important ingredients to the solution of learning difficulties.

Criteria for Classroom-Prepared Materials

The following criteria have been applied to all of the techniques described in the text:

1. *Purpose:* The devices suggested must be a means of solving some problem or developing an understanding of meaning in line with the teacher's and children's educational objectives.
2. *Ease:* The devices must be quickly and easily constructed so that the time spent on them will be commensurate with the purposes they are designed to achieve.
3. *Inexpensiveness:* The cost of the article must be a mere fraction of what a similar commercial article would cost. In the majority of instances, the cost can be figured in pennies.
4. *Immediacy:* Because of (2) the devices can be planned so that they are available when needed. It is important to have the right device on hand at the right time to clinch a problem before the threads are lost. The teacher does not have to say, "You'll be able to understand this better next month when our globe arrives."
5. *Durability:* The articles made are firm and strong. They can be manipulated frequently by the children without fear of breakage.
6. *Permanence:* This criterion need not be applied to all the devices, but many will be made through the course of the year that can be set aside and used again in another year when they become appropriate to a problem faced by a new group of children. The teacher can, in this manner, build up a collection of models and diagrams that grows year after year. Perhaps a permanent exhibit or museum can be developed over the years. Many other devices, because of their passing value, can be disposed of easily because their cost was so low initially.
7. *Adaptability to learning style:* The individual characteristics of the materials should be diverse enough to encompass learning styles of children who need practice with verbal learning, who require alternative routes to a learning goal, who must deal with simplified learning materials, who are highly organizational, who are challenged by creativity, and who combine many variations and gradations of approaches to learning.

Specific Techniques

With these criteria in mind, the authors have suggested some basic understandings needed in the development of instructional materials. The first is a detailed explanation of the term *layout* and the concept it implies. Emphasis is placed on tools, equipment, and techniques that simplify the layout process. In Chapter 3 is explained how a careful use of this technique in constructing materials saves time and money and brings home to children a valuable lesson with many lifetime applications.

Many times well-planned instructional materials are spoiled because of poor lettering. Emphasis is placed on the importance of lettering in communicating ideas and on the variety of lettering devices available in assisting teachers and pupils in their learning activities. Lettering is so important in the school that not a day goes by that it is not employed in some way. Techniques and rules for lettering are explained in Chapter 4 as well as the important points needed in the teaching of manuscript writing.

Sketching is a valuable tool for both teacher and pupil. How quickly a teacher can sometimes explain a point by a brief sketch on the blackboard! If he knows how to do this well, his point will be more meaningful because no time or attention need be lost through inept mechanics. The pupil enjoys sketching; and, if skilled in it, he can use it to illustrate his written work and find satisfaction in employing it in creative activities. The essentials of good sketching are given in Chapter 5 in step-by-step order so that only a little practice is needed to become a skillful worker in this technique.

The use of bulletin boards and display cases in the learning process is given much prominence. These displays are not designed as decorative adjuncts to the room but must be utilized as functional devices that, because of their visual impact, make a point clear and meaningful in a direct way. In Chapter 6, ways in which many techniques—lettering, sketching, design, and color—can be combined to make a striking and attractive educational device are described.

The various types of printing techniques are described in detail in Chapter 7, with stress on their use with pupils in the development of instructional materials. It can be readily seen by the information presented that great variety and originality can be expressed through these techniques. Their practical value, too, must not be lost sight of in teaching. Printing is a real boon to the teacher of reading readiness, early developmental reading, and remedial reading, because of the instructional material that can be developed quickly with this technique.

A variety of techniques that are common to the construction of inexpensive instructional materials are explored in Chapter 8. Several ways of working with papier mâché are described in detail. Papier mâché is a strong, inexpensive material that is employed in making models, exhibits, toys, puppets, and other objects useful in the teaching-learning process.

Frame construction is still another versatile operation that can be used in the development of instructional materials. Houses, barns, stores, and puppet stages can be constructed in the primary grades; greenhouses, workbenches, and flats for scenery can be built in the intermediate grades.

Solid block construction represents another medium for making three-dimensional instructional materials. Historical villages, homes around the world, and community redevelopment are only a few ways in which it can be employed. This technique enables pupils to construct buildings, trucks, boats, and other types of models that can withstand the punishment meted out by pupils in the elementary grades. Solid block models can be handled and manipulated by pupils, thus becoming more than a visual display.

In each instance, after the technique is explained, attention is turned to the areas where the technique and activity can be employed. Various suggestions for meaningful, impactful use have been made. Many additional applications and variations will occur to the teacher.

The hand tools needed to make three-dimensional instructional materials and objects are discussed in detail in Chapter 11. These are common tools that everyone is called on to use sometime in life. It is surely an asset to learn how to use them safely in school. It can be noted that even some of the necessary tools and equipment can be constructed at little cost in the classroom.

In Chapter 12, the basic materials and supplies needed to conduct an effective activity program are discussed. The materials and supplies described are common to the building trades and can be purchased at hardware stores and lumber yards.

These materials and tools are then ready to be utilized by the children in all areas of the curriculum. They can provide nonverbal learnings and stimuli for verbal learnings and the environment for social skills and relationships. They also provide an opportunity for children to develop new instructional materials.

Curriculum Trends

The writers are aware of the argument that learning by doing is time-consuming, often wasteful of time and materials, and inclined to get out of hand. It should be pointed out that in the classroom setting advocated in this book, most learning can still take place through the verbalized methods of lecture, discussion, question and answer, demonstration, reading for appreciation, writing, and reciting. Indeed, many of these are suggested as activities that may be enhanced with the described techniques.

But two developments in education today are challenging the classroom of textbooks, workbooks, recitations, and lectures. They are the reintroduction of the Montessori [1] methods into early education and the *integrated* or *free day* approach utilized in the British Infant Schools and developed in Leicestershire County, England.[2]

The Montessori method stresses appreciation of the individual child, sensitivity to growth patterns, freedom within limits, child development toward self-motivation and self-discovery, a prepared environment, free choice of material appropriate to the child's level of understanding, self-correction of errors, sensory-motor training that includes sensory discrimination and motor coordination, and reliance on devices to stimulate learning. The fact that the Montessori schools are growing in numbers testifies to their efficacy in helping young children. The Montessori methods are now

[1] Maria Montessori, *The Montessori Method* (New York: Schocken Books, 1964).
[2] Mary Brown and Norman Precious, *The Integrated Day in the Primary School* (London: Ward Lock Educational, 1968).

beginning to take hold in the upper grades with children more than 6-years old.[3] Teachers are using the Montessori theory and applying it to the development of materials for older children to supplement verbal learning.

The British Infant School is beginning to receive attention in this country. The schools of Leicestershire County have been freed from the pressures of the English examination given to children at the age of 11 to determine their educational future. The overpowering importance of this examination has made teaching in England almost exclusively a determined effort to teach for this examination to the detriment of many other important learnings. Now in Leicestershire County, and increasingly in other parts of England, children of ages 5 to 7 in the Infant Schools are being educated through exposure to a rich environment that meets the needs of individual children in a relaxed atmosphere. It includes a profusion of materials for children to explore and experiment with: scales and weights, potted plants, woodworking tools, sewing materials, cooking materials, boxes of art materials, beads for counting, and a variety of other types of scrap materials. Prepared materials are also available for children to work with in any way they desire. Children are treated as individuals, progressing at their own rates, moving about the building to develop their interests. Materials are arranged in the classroom, but they also spill outdoors where children work with building blocks, tools, and easels; the corridors are beehives of activities, learning materials, and interest tables. The children are free to work according to their interests and there is no separation between activities that are "work" and those that are "play." There is no pressure to make a child read or do anything else by a certain age. Teachers usually manage classes of forty pupils. This program was started experimentally in 1946, but has been so successful that it is being extended to the junior schools (ages 7–11), which are also part of the primary school system. The rich environment, the individual and group activity, and the interaction of pupils are aspects of the British Infant School that these writers feel can be implemented through the activities and techniques suggested in this book.

Techniques Applied to Subject Areas

Various techniques and activities are suggested in the book to enrich and improve the learning of subject matter. The teacher should always attempt to select materials and activities according to the learning styles of the pupils.

In mathematics, devices are suggested that will simplify number concepts, set theory, fractions, and geometry. They also will provide experiences by which the child can approach the solution of problems with a wide variety of alternatives. The writers believe that manipulative devices are most important in understanding meaning. No matter what method is used in

Theory and Rationale

[3] Shirley DeLeon, "Imaginative Learning Aids," *Children's House,* 2:11–15 (Winter 1968).

teaching mathematics, meaning is of paramount importance. These aids, therefore, can be used to supplement any program.

In science, devices that will contribute to the understanding of the body, to the beginnings of the development of knowledge of physics, to the furtherance of nature study, and most of all to fostering an inquiring mind and an experimental attitude have been suggested. These writers believe that science is a most fertile field for the use of tools, materials, and equipment. Teachers, especially, often fearful of science, can learn with the children through many experiments and models easily constructed with the techniques described.

In social studies, the understanding of our heritage and our environment is often fostered through the use of a variety of models, maps, globes, charts, bulletin boards, and exhibits. In language arts and foreign languages, too, many of the same kinds of devices can be used to illustrate literature and to inspire creative writing. Puppets made of papier mâché with a frame construction stage can be used to dramatize historical or literary episodes, to point out social relationships, or to give a lesson in economics. Stick figures can be used to vitalize grammar or a foreign language. The writers have pointed out only a few of the ways homemade instructional devices will bring interest and color to the learning act.

In art and music, the use of the devices is more obvious. The subject of art is filled with uses of the techniques that have been described. The making of musical instruments has been a favorite activity for many years.

Industrial arts in the elementary school is not a separate subject but is considered an integral part of the total elementary program. However, it does possess individuality and makes its own unique contribution to the total education of the child. Industrial arts in the elementary grades should be interwoven into the study of our material culture. It embodies a universal study of shelter, furnishings, utensils, instruments, tools, weapons, vehicles, clothing, foods, and other goods, conditions, services, and necessities of life.

Industrial arts, economics, social studies, and science are examples of subject areas concerned with the significant highlights of the ways and means by which man has satisfied his material needs and wants. The extinction of the home industries and the dwindling number of neighborhood shops and small factories make it imperative for the schools to teach something in this regard if each generation is to acquire adequate insight into this important phase of life. General education is not complete until students develop concepts, understandings, and appreciations of industrial society and its influence on the total culture.

The study of industry is really an investigation of one reflection of man's struggle to adapt to his environment. Much can be revealed of the character of a people by their industries and by the products they produce and consume. Folkways, customs, and standards of living of people throughout the world can be studied through a knowledge and understanding of their industrial development.

Techniques Applied to Developmental Stages

The writers advocate the development of instructional materials and constructional techniques that they believe are essential to a curriculum that works toward clarifying, expanding, and enriching the child's understanding of his environment and culture. Emphasis in the curriculum areas is placed on the theory that, when words, pictures, and ideas are given form, detail, and color, learning activities, by the addition of this third dimension, are highlighted, and concepts can be grasped more rapidly by children. It is important to stress that these learning activities are much more than recreational experiences. They are of such a nature that they add to the total development of the child's imagination and interest.

Piaget,[4] through careful, detailed observations of children, has described their mental development in six segments. The first three stages can be grouped as the prelanguage learning of infants. The next large grouping (ages 2–7) is a period of intuitive intelligence and spontaneous social relationships. The child can handle verbal representation for the first time; that is, he can reconstruct the past and anticipate the future. He begins to internalize words (produce thought) and internalize actions (produce intuition). He cannot differentiate between the internal or subjective world and the physical universe. He wants to know why things are so but is inclined to explain things intuitively without proof and in terms of himself. His intellectual acts are accompanied by feelings of sympathy or antipathy. Interests become very important as extensions of needs and as activities that have value for him. Symbolic play is enacted in an effort to assimulate the real world. "It can be maintained that the child of this age is unable to verbalize his thought and that his real domain is still that of action and manipulation." [5]

The next stage of development (ages 7–12) is a period of concrete intellectual operation and of moral and social feelings. It is preponderantly a period of the development of logic. It is characterized by concentration, collaboration with others, mutual respect, rational operations and the disappearance of egocentric language. Respect for others makes possible productive interaction. Games are played according to rules. Concepts are developed through rational operations. "Interest . . . is an astonishing regulator. It suffices to be interested in work in order to find the necessary strength to pursue it, whereas disinterest curtails the expenditure of energy." [6] Will power is now developed as a regulator also. It strengthens weak tendencies (toward duty versus play) so that they prevail. "Up to this age (11–12), the operations of intelligence are solely 'concrete,' i.e., they are concerned only with reality itself and, in particular, with tangible objects that can be manipulated and subjected to real action." [7]

---

[4] Jean Piaget, *Six Psychological Studies* (New York: Random House, 1967), pp. 3–69.
[5] *Ibid.*, p. 29.
[6] *Ibid.*, p. 59.
[7] *Ibid.*, p. 62.

Theory and Rationale

10

The fourth stage is that of abstract intellectual operation and formation of personality. It is the period of adolescence.

It can be seen that the latter part of stage two coincides with kindergarten and grade one and that all of stage three is in the province of the elementary school. The developmental aspects of these stages are suitably fostered through the techniques advocated in this book. Their emphasis on concrete materials, on group projects, on individual interests, on activity according to rules or standards, on exploration of the environment, and on dramatization and role playing are in accordance with Piaget's description of the natural interests and talents of children of these ages. It is the writers' contention that the manipulation and the use of the concrete materials advocated in this book—putting some things together, separating and re-grouping other materials, structuring and ordering with others, and questioning and experimenting with still other objects or living things, working together and assisting one another in group projects—can be of enormous help to the child in progressing successfully through the two stages of development that fall within the years of the elementary school.

THE ELEMENTARY CLASSROOM

Concerns of the Teacher

Manolakes [8] has set up guidelines for the good elementary school. Many of them are functions of administrators, but those that are the concern of the classroom teacher are these:

1. Effective group living by interaction
2. Respect for individual
3. Self-concept
4. Fostering creativity
5. Individual differences
6. Learning experiences related to the world children know
7. Responsibility in planning and organizing
8. Learnings appropriate to particular community setting
9. Evaluation as an integral part of learning

These writers believe that through the use of the techniques and activities suggested in this book, many of these concerns can be provided for.

EFFECTIVE GROUP LIVING. The elementary classroom is an excellent place to practice group living. In the planning of an activity that utilizes child-developed media, group living is a natural aspect. In the primary grades, the construction of a community facility—for example, a store—provides for harmonious cooperation. As the children plan, they assign the various tasks

[8] George Manolakes, *The Elementary School We Need* (Washington, D.C.: Association for Supervision and Curriculum Development, 1965).

of assembling the store to individuals. As each fulfills his task, he has contributed to the finished product. The concepts of dependency on others and division of labor begin to take form. With the finished product, role playing can be employed to show the functions of the proprietor, the clerks, the cashier, and the customer. The children have an opportunity to practice social relationships as well as to develop language, economics, hand craft, and arithmetic skills.

In the planning of any activity, it must be decided how tools will be shared, how materials will be apportioned, and how responsibility for the various segments of work will be taken. The interdependence of the group makes possible an appreciation of human relationships. Should harmony break down, an analysis of the situation can bring out the factors mitigating effective group living.

RESPECT FOR THE INDIVIDUAL. As group living progresses, children can learn that each individual is contributing to the desired whole. Appreciation of the individual contribution is developed. Individual activities can also be engaged in. As these are shared with the class, children learn to recognize that each person has abilities and contributions to make, but all need not or should not be of the same character. Each person is appreciated for the worth of his activity, whether it is a part of a large project, a clarification of a difficult point, a demonstration of a process, or any of the many facets that are open to the individual's talents.

Learning through self-discovery is enhanced by individualized or small-group explorations. Construction activities provide an opportunity for pupils to begin with those experiences that are commensurate with their ability and to progress at their own rates into more complicated realms of ideas as questions are answered and new questions evolve from the old.

BUILDING A SELF-CONCEPT. Both the individual activities and those that contribute to a large-group project reveal to the child his importance to society. He plays a satisfying role, one for which others depend on him, and little by little, he learns to appreciate his own worth. Because his learning and activities are geared to his own rate of progress and to his own interests, he is not apt to meet with repeated failure. The child is not competing with anyone else, nor is he left out of the group. The teacher is able to observe him in his relationships with the group and to draw him out or suggest subtle changes or developments that will help him grow in social stature. His concept of himself, through satisfying relationships with the teacher and with his peers, is nurtured toward a positive, healthy development.

These writers believe that teachers are sensitive to the needs of the pupil for self-discovery. The techniques and activities presented in this text emphasize an approach to learning based on the child's need to develop at his own pace in a program tailored to his individual interests. A child's curiosity or inquisitiveness is a force for maintaining interest, the best form of motivation. This curiosity is nourished through the techniques and activities suggested in this book. Children probably solve problems best in situations requiring the use of concrete materials from which perceptual learning accrues. As children continue in a program that utilizes constructional materials, the intellectual processes of explaining, comparing, classifying, measuring, and forming conclusions evolve progressively.

FOSTERING CREATIVITY. Just as the child develops a favorable self-image in the modern classroom, so does he have an opportunity to create. A wealth of materials is at hand. He discovers how to combine and assemble them. In his planning process, he may give free reign to individual ideas. In seeking to understand a social problem or to create a design, he can give full play to new ideas for utilizing the materials to his purpose. Divergent thinking has a vital place, for no set patterns have to be followed except as agreed on by the children in the planning. Different approaches to problem solving are encouraged, and the lack of rigid structuring by the teacher gives scope to the child's ideas.

Inquiry is a creative process. A child encounters something that puzzles him or something that does not fit his picture of what the world is like. For example, the question, "Why does a balancing clown stand up?" arises in his mind. He wants to know why the clown balances. The process has begun. Using the teacher as a resource person, he discovers that in the science corner of the room are directions for making a balancing clown and the needed materials. He constructs his clown with movable weights as directed. He then experiments with the weights and observes their effect on balance. He asks questions about the causes of the various positions of the clown as he adjusts the weights. He draws conclusions as he experiments. He eliminates possible solutions, such as leverage, and comes to the conclusion that a properly located center of gravity is the answer. When he arranges the weights equally on both arms, he realizes that he has placed the center of gravity in the correct place for an erect position. Thus, inquiry has been a quest for understanding and has led one child to construct a testing device that provided a solution to his problem. Further research into the force of gravity might be the next step in the learning process.

INDIVIDUAL DIFFERENCES. Individual differences then are given full sway. No one has to conform to a set standard. No one has to be penalized for failing to demonstrate coverage of a block of material at a specified rate that is the same for everyone. Individualization of learning is the goal. Each child's constructional tasks are part of a plan of which he has shared in the making, and the portions assigned to him are in accordance with his needs and interests.

The early childhood years are too precious for the teaching of skills alone; they must be used to teach inquiring and critical attitudes as well. With the understanding and cooperation of parents and administrators, teachers can provide experiences that will allow children to use materials, tools, and equipment to invent and to explore their environment on an individualized basis.

A specific application of individual development is in the field of special education, a field particularly highlighted in education today. In the past, many mental laggards were shunted into an opportunity room where too often the curriculum was mere busy work or a custodial arrangement. Many were labeled retarded who had never been given a chance to develop mentally. It was not deemed necessary to put thought and planning into a developmental learning situation for these children, for they were believed to be incapable of learning.

Modern research has shown that the custodial and "hands-off" approaches to dealing with the mentally retarded have been entirely wrong.

Johnson maintains that "the basic characteristics of the mentally retarded . . . are in all probability the same as for normal children of approximately the same mental age." [9] He has found no data to support the contention that the mentally retarded require more time to learn a task, more repetition or practice, or that they grasp concepts slowly or learn a task slowly. The difference is one of intellectual development. Their developmental rate is only a fraction of the normal rate. When their mental development has reached the mental age appropriate to the learning of a task they can learn it as well as any other child.

These writers believe that the techniques and activities described here can also improve results in a program built for the mentally retarded. These advantages are available in such a program:

1. The child can derive quick and satisfying success in the construction of an item simple enough to be appropriate to his stage of development.
2. He can express with his hands and with materials what may be denied to him because of lack of verbal facility.
3. He can proceed at his own rate in accordance with a plan geared to his ability.
4. Reading skills can be developed through a motivated situation. Simple directions or work sheets written in his vocabulary are the means to his goal—a model, toy, or device. Therefore, by utilizing reading, he improves in it and reinforces the skills he has learned in a natural way.
5. Similarly, arithmetic skills can be strengthened through planning, measuring, and projecting the constructional activity.
6. Social skills are a part of every activity in planning, cooperating, executing ideas, and evaluating.
7. Discovery through devices and models makes possible the same kind of concept building open to all children.
8. Work habits can be fostered and evaluated and some basic occupational skills can be taught at various levels.

LEARNING APPROPRIATE TO COMMUNITY OR SETTING. Because the school's setting—the area or section of the community served by the school—has a bearing on the individual child, larger aspects of inquiry may be provided through construction activities. Understanding the area and its contribution

[9] G. Orville Johnson, "Psychological Characteristics of the Mentally Retarded," in *Psychology of Exceptional Children and Youth,* edited by William Cruickshank (Englewood Cliffs, N.J.: Prentice-Hall, 1963), p. 461.

can be developed through models and charts. Problems and sensitive spots can be identified and examined in relation to other parts of the community. In deprived areas, the child desperately needs much individual attention paid to the development of a wholesome self-concept. Through individual activities that utilize his strengths, through the statement and solution of problems he recognizes, through satisfaction of accomplishment and contribution, the child constructs a belief in his own worth. This recognition of personal value is at least one positive step in mitigating unfortunate environmental influence.

Today the Federal Government is allotting large sums of money to improve education. Experimentation and innovation are sought to promote better results in the educational program. Those children who do not have a satisfactory home environment are considered with special care so that the differences between their backgrounds and that of the schools can be ameliorated. One great difficulty has been found to be the lack of communication between the child and the teacher and others in the school. Verbalization by the teacher, however well-intentioned, cannot be understood by the child in many instances. Vast differences in vocabulary and in ability to relate to oral instruction can exist for the child. The British Infant School program provides an opportunity for real communication to take place. Sponberg testifies to this statement:

> "We must also give people chances to examine what they've done and communicate their failures and successes." This statement confirmed another observation about English education: there seems to be real communication between teachers and teachers, teachers and pupils, pupils and pupils. And perhaps here lies the ultimate strength of the integrated of free day concept.[10]

The techniques discussed in this book will provide ways to get away from verbalizing and establish communication in a visual or tactile manner. Meaningful verbalization can come about through planning and sharing comprehensible techniques.

Although there are no clear-cut methods that have been established successfully for teaching the disadvantaged, two points of view exist with regard to emphasis. In one, the cognitive aspects of learning are stressed; in the other, the affective aspects. Both are important, and these writers are convinced that the techniques described here will help develop both aspects. For example, in cognitive learning, content can be developed through such activities as puppetry, diorama construction, chalk talks, and many others. In working with creative techniques, the mutual assistance, planning, sharing, and evaluation that go on continually provide development in the area of affective learning.

President Johnson's National Advisory Council on the Education of Disadvantaged Children, in a report based on a survey of 116 Title I (Elemen-

[10] Ruth Ann Sponberg, "New Kind of School Day," *The Instructor:* **78**:14–15 (December 1968).

tary and Secondary Education Act) projects in 39 states, presented a list of what it considered misdirections in policy. One of these states:

> Most projects are disregarding the belief of modern education theorists that the disadvantaged learners need "an abundance of sensory and motor experiences dealing with concrete objects before they proceed to abstract learning." These experiences may be with construction toys and games, simple science gear, pegboards, or any of a number of manipulative objects around which language and arithmetic abstraction can be built.[11]

The suggestions in this book have the potential to make learning both purposeful and personal for the disadvantaged.

EXPERIENCING RELATIONSHIPS TO THE WORLD IN WHICH WE LIVE. The elementary child as he grows older must increase his understanding of his environment. He must go from understanding his immediate locale to grasping some of the broad concepts of the earth and the universe. The making of two-dimensional and three-dimensional representations of the concepts and relationships of mathematics, science, and social studies will contribute to the assimilation of ideas gleaned from reading and viewing. What the child learns in the elementary school must not be simply an additive process but one of assimilation and integration. He is not going to remember details, but he will gradually build broad concepts of scientific and social relationships that will help him understand the world in which we live.

In the laboratory situation, the children should be encouraged to become critical thinkers, efficient collectors and recorders of data, originators of ideas, proficient users of measurements to test accumulated information, and appraisers of assumptions that condition the accuracy and acceptance of information.

Each day's discovery challenges thinking, values, and the nature of our laws. Society is imposing demands for the teaching of subjects relevant to today's needs. Technological, sociological, and geographical changes are causing an expansion in man's need for knowledge of the world and are requiring special skills to master and utilize this information. The discoveries of science and developments in technology require a variety of approaches to teaching children about their world. Scientific and technological changes are being brought about through interdisciplinary activities in society. The same interdisciplinary action must result in new methods in our teaching if children are to know more, make better decisions, and adapt to a constantly changing world.

DEVELOPING RESPONSIBILITY IN PLANNING AND ORGANIZING. Personal habits that will stand the child in good stead all through his life should be developed in the elementary school. Many, of course, have been made in the home and in his early contacts with his environment. Many more, however,

11 *Washington Monitor*, "Education U.S.A." (February 5, 1968), p. 125.

are the responsibility of the elementary school. Planning work and organizing work, habits too often overlooked, are important to the individual as he goes through life. With the use of a variety of materials to construct meaningful objects, the child learns to plan and organize. The child must decide on the best use of materials, the time when he can take his turn with tools and equipment, and the effect he wishes to produce. He must organize and synthesize his knowledge and ideas to create an impact with a bulletin board or in a diorama. He learns to economize his time and to put forth his best efforts in order to make a maximum contribution.

Children should have a prominent part in the development of the classroom laboratory. They should plan demonstrations, experiments, organizational charts and exhibits, scripts, settings, and properties for dramatizations and puppet shows. All these will require the collection of materials, the development of techniques, and the making of models and devices, some of which may be added to the learning center to be utilized by others.

EVALUATION AS AN INTEGRAL PART OF LEARNING. The child learns to evaluate himself, his efforts, the use of time, his display of originality, the effectiveness with which he communicates, his relationships with other members of the class, his skill, ingenuity, and creativity. He can compare his efforts with those of others and with his own previous work. With the help of the teacher, he focuses on weak spots to eliminate or correct them. He can try again when something does not turn out right. He learns to accept criticism and suggestions from his peers. He learns to help others without being officious and boastful. He learns to evaluate a product without evaluating a person. He learns to face the consequences of his own ideas and opinions, not to rely passively on the teacher's. A group project or an individual project can be criticized objectively because it is a product of many skills and ideas. Evaluation of a child's work will not rely solely on tests of work covered. It will be more truly an understanding of how he is solving his problems and how he is progressing in the formation of broad concepts and mature relationships. Achievement of high academic standards was never a product of some "get-tough" policy, but rather a result of meaningful inquiry in line with the student's own experiences, perceptions, and reactions in order to build greater self-direction, responsibility, and understanding.

IMPLICATIONS FOR EXTENDED USE

Advanced and Specialized Programs

THE SECONDARY SCHOOL. The secondary school can utilize in a more sophisticated manner many of the same techniques. Although the secondary school deals less with concrete objects, many devices are appropriate. The science and mathematics courses, with their need for models and equipment, provide a wealth of opportunity for constructional techniques. Literature, particularly dramatics, can suggest many more. Certainly the social sciences can become far richer courses with the appropriate use of models, dioramas, and exhibits.

A PROGRAM UTILIZING TEACHER AIDES. The provision of teacher aides and/or teacher teams is a means commonly sought to develop conditions for better instruction. These aides and teams will find many uses for the techniques in this book. The aides are usually paraprofessionals who work under the direction of a teacher. They can readily learn the techniques these writers recommend and can assist or instruct and supervise pupils in a purposeful use of media. An arrangement based merely on verbalization can thus be avoided in the best interests of a meaningful program.

TEACHER TRAINING. Teachers in training need to become familiar with both the theory and practice of the skills and techniques described in this book. For them, these skills will provide a facility with well-planned, carefully constructed, adroitly utilized teaching techniques that will be of untold value in their teaching careers.

If the student-teacher has not experienced this approach to learning, he will probably find it difficult to understand and translate it into a program for use with children. The student-teacher needs to feel comfortable and secure with these activities and techniques if he is to become an important part of the instructional program. The student-teacher who does not have this feeling will probably cling to a series of textbooks and assignments in workbooks for his instructional methods and thus become a supervisor of busy work rather than a guide to children with a variety of learning styles. Student-teachers in their training programs need an opportunity to learn in an activity-geared environment. Students preparing to teach have remarked along these lines to these writers about their experiences in constructing various types of instructional materials:

> When I constructed that papier mâché model of the upper portion of the human body I finally learned the shapes and location of the heart, lungs, intestine, and diaphragm.
>
> As I planned that bulletin board I learned about my topic. It was difficult to select, from all the material collected, the right materials to relate this story to others.

One student was amazed to find out that the seeds from string beans actually come from the inside of a dried bean shell.

Students in the School of Education, University of Connecticut, working in the Instructional Materials Development Laboratory are fascinated with the type of objects that can be made with a few simple hand tools and scrap materials. They enjoy using power equipment: jig saw, sabre saw, and drill press when they find out that these tools save them time and make their work easier.

After they gain skill in construction they are given the opportunity to work with children utilizing these activities and techniques in a learning situation.

They are usually surprised to find how easily children learn to work with tools and materials.

The teachers or student-teachers who can relate these activities and techniques to their own experiences will have a greater awareness of their contribution to the learning act and a more realistic expectation of the classroom management problems they will encounter in this type of program. They will also learn that relating to children is more than being permissive or authoritative. They will learn that the teaching act is a complex role that calls for different patterns of behavior from both the teacher and child in different situations in order to obtain a degree of success.

The Teacher's Role

The teacher's part in support of inquiry encompasses four roles. Role one requires that the teacher create a free and open environment that stimulates and sustains free inquiry. This environment permits the learner to examine his ideas and test them against available data. The learning center, with its tools, materials, and equipment is as important as ideas to a program committed to learning through inquiry.

Role two requires that the teacher become a storehouse of ideas. Children cannot be expected to originate all of the ideas that will be utilized by them in interpreting their environment. It is not important that each child invent for himself every idea used in the inquiring process; it is important that the teacher stimulate the learning experiences of each child.

The third role requires that the teacher coordinate the activities brought about by the ideas, theories, and plans of attack suggested and used by children. The teacher must also support and encourage the child in his pursuits. He must be careful not to be the authority always ready with the right answers. The teacher must not tell the child his idea is wrong before he has a chance to test it out. On the other hand, he must not let the child become hopelessly bogged down with an idea that cannot be worked out. In role three, the teacher oversees the smooth running of the classroom laboratory.

The fourth role requires that the teacher plan and evaluate the children's activities. He must diagnose the learning problems and decide on their possible solutions. The teacher needs to decide what is to be taught, how it should be presented, and how the learner should be evaluated. The program recommended in this text requires that the teacher explore learning experiences that go beyond those suggested in the child's books or in the teacher's guides. It is suggested that alternative learning styles and instructional techniques be used to meet the needs of children. The teacher has the responsibility for evaluating the child in terms of the behavior changes stated in the instructional objectives. When the desired behavior changes are not obtained, the teacher's job is to analyze the reasons for failure and select an alternative approach to the child's learning difficulty.

CONCLUSION

New trends in education involve major changes or modifications in three areas: the curriculum presented to the students, the methods or procedures by which this curriculum is presented, and administrative arrangements and organization. The material presented in this text is closely related to the first two trends. Our elementary classroom is the center for learning. It is a classroom with equipment and materials appropriate for children's use. These materials are vital because the teaching-learning process has become one of inquiry rather than one of telling. Even though telling takes less time and provides more coverage of subject areas, it is well to remember that "talking is not teaching," and "listening is not learning." When the teacher allows the student to guess, experiment, observe, and draw conclusions about ideas and perceptions, then learning by discovering is in force in the classroom.

Woodruff asserts that it is "extremely important for the teacher to understand just how a person gets his actual personal knowledge of the things of this world." [12] He believes teaching is relatively ineffective when teachers talk to or tell a class something instead of showing it. He states that contacts through the sensory organs must be made with objects, events, or circumstances in the environment. This object, the *referent*, is perceived by the brain of the learner and a concept is formed, the components of which have meaning or understanding, feeling or preference, and symbols or language. "Each person has to make his own concepts. The easiest way for him to make them is through directly perceiving the thing itself, not through listening to someone else's words." [13] Concepts are combined with other concepts from past experience and become predispositions for future behavior according to the value or feeling inherent in them. In the areas explored in this book, the teacher will find many suggested direct contacts with the environment and he can help the child to form concepts from their perception.

In learning experiences, instructional materials of one type or another can be required to assure maximum learning. If these instructional materials are not available to children and teachers, consideration should be given to the possibility of constructing them. The teacher must realize the need for the materials and must have confidence in the fact that these techniques and activities can be performed successfully by children. The creative and inventive teacher can work wonders in helping children fabricate the objects and instructional materials they need to improve the learning process.

The techniques and activities presented in this text can be constructed within the four walls of any classroom with a minimum amount of supplies, tools, and equipment. However, the program does require careful planning

[12] Asahel D. Woodruff, *Basic Concepts of Teaching* (San Francisco: Chandler, 1961), p. 88.
[13] *Ibid.*, p. 81.

and effective organization in order to insure its success. The skeptical teacher can start on a small scale and increase the scope of the program as he gains the confidence needed to direct this type of learning experience. For the inexperienced teacher, small exploratory experiences should probably precede any large-scale activities. Initial experiences can be started with a few children and then expanded to include the entire class.

There are certain pitfalls inherent in the type of activities suggested in this textbook. Children can flounder and waste time and materials if they do not understand their roles or tasks. An insufficient and inappropriate number of tools and materials can cause frustration. These pitfalls can be avoided through careful planning with children. Proper organization can provide the framework within which the program will function. The purpose of the program should be explained in detail and instructional objectives established as guides for the learning experiences.

Teachers should not underestimate the capacity of children to execute the techniques and activities suggested here. They should also have faith in their ability to perform the activities required to make the suggested program a success.

The reader should try the techniques and activities recommended for stimulating verbal learning: make a globe of the world, a model home, or a puppet stage and discover how easily these items can be constructed. The important factors in success are following the instructions correctly and understanding the characteristics and properties of the materials being utilized. When the opportunity presents itself, these techniques and activities should be tried with children. The excitement that can be generated in the learning act will bring its own reward.

REFERENCES

BROWN, MARY, AND PRECIOUS, NORMAN. *The Integrated Day in the Primary School.* London: Ward Lock Educational, 1968.

BURTON, WILLIAM H. *The Guidance of Learning Activities* (3rd ed.). New York: Appleton-Century-Crofts, 1962.

CRUICKSHANK, WILLIAM M. (ed.). *Psychology of Exceptional Children and Youth* (2nd ed.). Englewood Cliffs, N.J.: Prentice-Hall, 1963, pp. 448–479.

DeLEON, SHIRLEY. "Imaginative Learning Aids," *Children's House*, 2:11–15. (Winter 1968).

FROST, J. L. *Early Childhood Education Rediscovered.* New York: Holt, 1968.

JOHNSON, G. ORVILLE. *Education for the Slow Learner.* Englewood Cliffs, N.J.: Prentice-Hall, 1963.

MANOLAKES, GEORGE. *The Elementary School We Need.* Washington, D.C.: Association for Supervision and Curriculum Development, 1965.

MONTESSORI, MARIA. *The Montessori Method.* New York: Schocken Books, 1968.

OHLSEN, MERLE M. *Modern Methods in Elementary Education.* New York: Holt, 1959.

PIAGET, JEAN. *Six Psychological Studies.* New York: Random House, 1967.

ROGERS, VINCENT. *The English Primary School.* New York: Macmillan, 1970.

SHUMSKY, ABRAHAM. *In Search of Teaching Style.* New York: Appleton-Century-Crofts, 1968.

SOWARDS, G. W., AND SCOBEY, MARY-MARGARET. *The Changing Curriculum and the Elementary Teacher* (2nd ed.). Belmont, Calif.: Wadsworth, 1968.

SPONBERG, RUTH A. "New Kind of School Day," *The Instructor,* **78**:14–15 (December 1968).

TAYLOR, CALVIN W., AND WILLIAMS, FRANK E. *Instructional Media and Creativity.* New York: Wiley, 1966.

THOMAS, GEORGE L., AND CRESCEMBENI, JOSEPH. *Individualizing Instruction in the Elementary School.* New York: Random House, 1967.

ULIN, DONALD S. "What I Learned from the British Schools" *Grade Teacher:* **86**:100–103 (February 1968).

Washington Monitor. "Education U.S.A.," (February 5, 1968), p. 125.

WOODRUFF, ASAHEL D. *Basic Concepts of Teaching.* San Francisco: Chandler, 1961.

CHAPTER 2

Learning *and* Its Implications

Teachers and pupils in our schools are involved for the most part in verbal learning. Reading, listening, writing, and speaking are the processes of education. Yet there are many pupils who daydream when they are supposed to be reading, who tune out instead of listen, and who will put only marginal effort into writing or speaking. These are the people who, through lack of interest, are not reaping the benefits of verbal learning. There are many other pupils who sit in the classroom without sufficient skill to profit from the level of verbal learning taking place. These are the pupils who are below grade level in reading, or who come from homes where there is no conversation or where a foreign language is spoken, or who for various physical, psychological, or other reasons have not developed verbal facilities.

To these pupils more verbal learning using the same abstract stimuli at a higher level simply puts them further behind until they give up school in their minds and just put in time until the day they can legally quit. Or, they make sporadic efforts, and with insufficient help, they are passed along from grade to grade without having received any real education.

Verbal learning—reading, discussing, demonstrating, organizing, analyzing, synthesizing—is the stuff of education. These writers contend that a variety of approaches and activities, many of them nonverbal, can—by the very fact that they involve the student, catch his interest, and provide satisfaction in a task well done—stimulate and provide readiness for verbal learning. In certain instances learning through these techniques can take place without verbalization.

23

To provide a rationale for these various learning approaches an examination of the research on learning, what it is and how it is accomplished, and of the goals of education is in order.

GUIDEPOSTS TO LEARNING. Bloom defines learning as the "changes due to experience in a student's way of thinking, feeling or acting"; education as "a system of learning experiences which bring about desirable changes in students"; and a learning experience as "an interaction between the learner and his environment." [1] He points out that not all learning experiences are educational. Random life experiences, which are occurring all the time, are not necessarily educational. Educational experiences should be planned. They should start with the learner, with his capacity at the moment, and advance him to a new level of competence or maturity. They must be in accordance with his characteristics, must be based on an understanding of the learning process as well as the means by which the individual learns, and must be pointed toward objectives that are specific statements of characteristics to be possessed.

From these statements the teacher may develop these guideposts:

1. Learning results in a change in behavior.
2. Educational experiences should be carefully planned to promote desirable learning.
3. Planning entails
   a. Knowing what the teacher and pupil wish to accomplish (the objective)
   b. Knowing how to proceed (the learning process)
   c. Knowing the characteristics of the learner, his capacities, his state of readiness, and the ways in which he learns (the learning style)
   d. Providing an environment in which interaction can take place
   e. Providing a way to assess the value of the activity in terms of the objective

These guideposts will be explored throughout this chapter and throughout the book. They are important elements of the learning process and should be considered when planning a learning task.

EDUCATIONAL OBJECTIVES. Bloom [2] and Krathwohl, et al.,[3] have classified objectives in a hierarchy of difficulty. They bring home to the teacher the vast range of concerns that must be his in planning for his pupils. They mention a third domain, still unclassified, the manipulative or motor-skill

---

[1] Benjamin S. Bloom, "Teaching Cognitive Ability and Achievement," *Handbook of Research on Teaching,* edited by Thomas Gage (New York: Rand McNally, 1963), p. 386.

[2] Benjamin Bloom (ed.), *Taxonomy of Educational Objectives,* Handbook I: Cognitive Domain (New York: McKay, 1956).

[3] David R. Krathwohl, Benjamin S. Bloom, and Bertram B. Masia, *Taxonomy of Educational Objectives,* Handbook II: Affective Domain (New York: McKay, 1964).

development, which they imply is more in the realm of the elementary school than in other educational levels; thus, it becomes a prime concern in this book.

The six major classifications of cognitive, or intellectual, objectives are in the order of complexity: (1) Knowledge, (2) Comprehension, (3) Application, (4) Analysis, (5) Synthesis, and (6) Evaluation. The reader may note that the mere acquisition of a fact or facts is only in step (1). The other steps represent conceptualization, understanding, and application of the facts in higher and higher orders of thinking. Even though the more complex categories (4–6) are usually in the province of secondary and higher education, they are not without relevance for the elementary school. Treating knowledge in these complex ways can be begun in the elementary school. Any step taken beyond (1) is an improvement over the mere acquiring of facts, which is still the ultimate goal in too many classrooms.

In dealing with feelings and attitudes, the authors of Handbook II of *Taxonomy of Educational Objectives* [4] found that they encountered intensity as a factor that must be taken into consideration. They therefore subdivided each major category, already arranged for complexity, into degrees of intensity. They thought of qualities such as attitude, feeling, interest, value, and appreciation in this hierarchy:

1. Receiving
   1.1 Awareness
   1.2 Willingness to receive
   1.3 Controlled or selected attention
2. Responding
   2.1 Acquiescence in responding
   2.2 Willingness to respond
   2.3 Satisfaction in response
3. Valuing
   3.1 Acceptance of a value
   3.2 Preference for a value
   3.3 Commitment (conviction)
4. Organization
   4.1 Conceptualization of a value
   4.2 Organization of a value system
5. Characterization by a value or value complex
   5.1 Generalized set
   5.2 Characterization

The last two categories are based on much experience and maturity and are therefore probably not pertinent to the elementary field. The first three are the concerns of the elementary teacher and must be planned for in relationship with the cognitive goals. Affective objectives are difficult to teach; they cannot be graded or marked; they often escape evaluation; they have emotional complications; and they can be highly controversial. Certain

[4] *Ibid.*, pp. 36–38.

attitudes, such as religious beliefs and political leanings, are not the business of the school. But the teacher must foster the emotional as well as the intellectual development of the child.

A child comes to school with many attitudes, feelings, and values, already formed and in varying states of intensity. Some of these, for example, racial prejudice or "the world owes me a living" attitude, are not socially acceptable. Some, such as interest in late-night television or too great a liking for sweets, are physically harmful. Other feelings, such as inadequacy, bashfulness, or braggadocio, are harmful to a sound self-image and therefore are in conflict with healthy emotional development. To change formed or partly formed attitudes; to avoid conflict with established home values; and to plan experiences that will create receptiveness, a willingness to respond, and a satisfaction or commitment in attitudes, interests, appreciations, and values that the teacher and the school feel are desirable are indeed difficult tasks. There is a strong Judeo-Christian tradition in this country with an accepted ethical code and there is also agreement that appreciation of artistic and literary achievement broadens self-development and promotes understanding of others. So the teachers must work toward these goals in the affective domain, giving the children a chance to work together in ways that will help them learn and intensify healthy attitudes, interests, and values. The writers believe that many experiences in this book, based as they are on sharing, on valuing individual contributions, on interests of all kinds, on prideful achievement for each pupil, and on attention to the individual, will bring rich rewards in emotional health, ethical development, and understanding and respect for one another.

THE LEARNING PROCESS. There is much research on learning and there are many learning theorists. Each describes learning in his own terms and with his own emphasis. Hilgard [5] states that the relationship between learning theory and educational practices is the same as that between pure science and technology, between Einstein and Edison. He points out several false conclusions to be avoided when considering learning. One of these is that because learning theorists cannot agree we cannot have scientifically based instruction. The trouble with this statement, he says, is that their disagreement is only in ways of interpretation, and learning theory alone is not the entire basis of educational practice. He also says it is false to assume that should the learning theory be presented in perfect order, principles of instruction would flow from it. Theory, he says, deals with fundamental principles that practice cannot violate, but theory certainly does not dictate practice entirely.

The implications to be drawn from these statements are that the teacher, although well-informed in learning theory, cannot look to it as to a cookbook, to find out how to proceed with instruction. But within the framework

[5] Ernest R. Hilgard (ed.), *Theories of Learning and Instruction,* The Sixty-third Yearbook of the National Society for the Study of Education (Chicago: University of Chicago Press, 1964), pp. 402–415.

of the suggested principles, he can try various procedures and methods that seem suitable to the situation and the child. He can experiment and innovate and, so long as careful evaluation is employed, he can be creative in trying to meet the educational goals for each child.

LEARNING PRINCIPLES. Based on the principles summarized by Wallen and Travers [6] the precepts and guidelines that the teachers should keep in mind are the following:

1. Behavior that represents achievements of objectives should be *reinforced*. The weakness of the lecture method is the fact that no reinforcement is provided for. Praise is often used as reinforcement as is a quick knowledge of results and comparison with standards. The reinforcement that is built into many of the activities in this book is the intrinsic kind, the sense of accomplishment, the joy in a new ability.

2. *Cues* that arouse motivation toward achievement of objectives will increase the effectiveness of the attainment. The teacher supplies such cues, but all pupils are not able to accept them or catch them. Anxiety can be a motivating force and reduction of anxiety a reinforcer. However, too great a degree of anxiety can inhibit learning. A rich environment can provide cues. It is this method of motivation that strongly recommends the activities described in this book.

3. Practice in *applying* a *principle* to the solution of problems will increase the probability of transfer to new problems requiring the same principle of solution. This principle has long been utilized. It is not clear in the research whether self-discovered principles are more useful than those supplied. The writers contend that self-discovered principles are more useful because they involve the learner more completely in the learning task. The reader will find that the equipment, tools, and materials suggested in the later chapters will inspire much discovery of tested principles.

4. Learning geared to the capacity to acquire new responses is most productive. It is difficult to assess the capacity of the learner. In the absence of a thorough assessment, different teaching methods must be tried so that the pupil can attain his goal. Many different learning experiences are pointed out. Even the self-selection of methods and materials, which has possibilities for success but which has had insufficient research, can be tried in the classroom geared to the suggested techniques.

5. If a pupil has had training in imitation he is capable of learning by observing demonstrations of the skills to be acquired. Imitation is a learned behavior tendency. Many opportunities for learning imitation are suggested. Role playing, puppetry, and learning to work with tools are all occasions where pupils practice imitation.

6. The learner will learn more effectively if he makes the responses to be learned than if he learns by observing another or makes some related

---

[6] Norman E. Wallen and Robert M. W. Travers, "Analysis and Investigation of Teaching Methods," *Handbook of Research on Teaching,* edited by Thomas Gage (New York: Rand McNally, 1963), pp. 494–501.

response. This is the old "we learn by doing" rule. These writers still believe in its efficacy, particularly in the elementary classroom, and this book is dedicated to the principle.

TYPES OF LEARNING. As previously pointed out, the environment and the learner must be considered in planning educational experiences. The teacher is aided in these considerations if he understands the kinds of learning that can take place. Gagne [7] posits that there are eight types of learning, and he arranges them in the order of their complexity. These types will be considered in the light of their relationships to the activities and techniques of this book. The eight types are (1) signal learning, (2) stimulus-response learning, (3) chaining, (4) verbal association, (5) multiple-discrimination, (6) concept learning, (7) principle learning, and (8) problem solving.

Signal learning is that exemplified by Pavlov's dog as he learned to salivate in response to a buzzer. It relies on a natural reflex such as an emotional response (fear, anger, pleasure). The conditions for learning are contiguity and repetition.

Stimulus-response learning is similar, but it is not dependent on a natural response. It is difficult to find a pure example of this type in human learning. Probably the infant learns to hold his bottle through this method. The learning is similar to trial and error, but is more nearly a procedure of successive approximations. A set of stimuli becomes connected to the right response, which is satisfactory. The response does not have to be innate as in type (1), but does have to be a reinforcing one (satisfying). The conditions for this learning are reinforcement, contiguity, and repetition. The function of repetition is to provide for the selective process previously noted. Much of early childhood learning is a result of types (1) and (2) and they may well be basic steps of the other types to be described.

Skinner's [8] shaping of behavior might be mentioned here. *Shaping* is bringing about desired behavior by allowing repeated trials at a task and reinforcing trials that approximate the correct response. The reinforcement is applied to progressively finer distinctions of behavior until all behavior that is not near the mark is eliminated, and finally the closest possible approximation to the perfect response is the one rewarded.

The teacher may find valuable opportunities to shape behavior and to reinforce a desired response as he observes children manipulating tools and materials. An attitude toward a task or toward others may be shaped by quick recognition by the teacher of a response that is an improvement over a previous response, a show of patience where none existed previously, for example.

The third and fourth types of learning are built on the first two. They are a series of stimulus-response actions in a chain. The first is the motor type of chaining. It may have a verbal stimulus, but the response is motor. It is

[7] Robert M. Gagne, *The Conditions of Learning* (New York: Holt, 1965).

[8] B. F. Skinner, *The Technology of Teaching* (New York: Appleton-Century-Crofts, 1968), pp. 66–67, 222–223.

exemplified in learning to use a tool, for example, a screwdriver. The child learns to follow a sequence of inserting a screw in a small prepared hole, applying the screwdriver to the slot at a 90° angle, holding the screw properly, turning the right amount, and finally seating the screw in its place flush with the wood. Each link of the chain provides the stimulus for the next link. The young child learns a number of these motor skills: using a pencil or crayon, erasing, drawing lines, throwing a ball, kicking a ball, and the like. Verbal instructions can smooth the learning path but they are not essential. A great many of these motor skills that will be learned in the classrooms are geared to the instructions in this book. The handling of tools, nails, and templates, measuring with instruments, and projecting and drawing are all motor skills learned through chaining.

The fourth type of learning is called verbal association. It is chaining on a verbal level. Linking foreign language words to comparable English ones (*feuille*-leaf) is an example of simple verbal association. In the learning of paired associates there is apparently an intervening link that codes or in some way links the meaning of the new word with some helpful clue. An example would be in learning that the word *terminal* is a connector on a battery. The intermediary step might be to think of terminal in reference to a bus terminal, the end of a bus route. The idea of *end* is established. Thus, the paired associates can be a three-link chain. Chains can be of any length, but seven, plus or minus two, is given as the maximum for any single event. Longer chains can be broken into pieces. Interference in the chain presents various degrees of forgetting or extinguishing previously learned responses. Teaching any process in the activities used to stimulate learning presents too long a chain. When the whole process is taught in one lecture or demonstration, the learner tends to forget one or more of the operations. The teacher should carefully assess the learning span of his pupils and teach them a portion of the process at a time. Five to seven steps (links) would be a maximum for one session.

Memorizing the alphabet or a multiplication table or a poem is chaining. It does not receive today the high degree of attention it once had in education. Memorizing still has some place, however, as when a child learns his part in a play, or works with puppets.

Further up in the scale of complexity are steps (5) and (6), multiple discrimination and concept learning. Stimulus-response connections, rather than being put together chain fashion, are here put together in diverse and complicated ways. In multiple discrimination the learner might be provided with a collection of objects or events as stimulus. In the example of the tools, a tool kit might be the stimulus. The learner must perform a different response for each tool. In type six, concept learning, the responder would make a response to the set of tools as a class; that is, he would develop a generalized statement about them, or a generalized response, such as keeping them on a panel in a handy place.

Both multiple discrimination and concept learning are very important in the elementary school. In the activity program suggested, multiple discrimination, in terms of materials, tools, size, shape, color, and texture, is constantly brought into play. And concept development is one or more of the objectives of all the activities.

The learning of principles and problem solving—steps (7) and (8)—are highest-level learning. Gagne [9] calls principles chains of concepts that make up what is generally referred to as knowledge. They also entail relationships among concepts. They are interwoven with problem solving in that they can be used to solve a problem or can be developed as a result of problem solving.

These high-sounding types of learning appear at first glance to belong only in secondary or higher education, but such is far from the case. With constructional techniques and activities, as with the verbal learning in the elementary school, the child will discover and work with many principles, and problem solving will be an everyday occurrence.

The writers believe that if the child is having trouble understanding principles or drawing conclusions from the problem-solving process he may have to go back with regard to a particular area of learning to multiple discrimination or to concept forming. Even going back to motor or verbal chaining may be needed in some instances. The approaches and techniques in this book are so varied in complexity that it would be possible for a child to try an easier learning type with an entirely new activity. In that way, the fact that he was simplifying his learning task for the time being would not be an ego-damaging development. He could try verbal chaining with object clues and then proceed to the higher types of learning without having felt any inadequacy or shame. Reinforcement of lower types of learning is often essential to working with the higher types. This reinforcement can usually be planned for through a new technique.

Skinner [10] has experimented widely with operant conditioning. Instead of a stimulus in the environment eliciting a response in the behavior, the individual initiates a behavior in order to cause a change in the environment. For example, a child may raise his hand in order to attract the attention of the teacher. His behavior causes a change in the environment; that is, it puts into action certain movements by the teacher. Should his original behavior (hand raising) be reinforced by a pleasant response from the teacher, or by notice from his peers, he will be inclined to use again the same method to gain attention. Much of the behavior in the classroom is of this type. Certain actions are initiated by teacher or pupils in order to promote environmental change or change in other individuals. Should the resulting change in behavior be reinforced positively, with rewards of satisfaction (or negatively, with punishment or scolding), the tendency for the behavior to be repeated (or avoided) will be strengthened. This action is not as clear-cut as it appears to be. What is meant to be negative reinforcement, such as scolding, can turn into positive reinforcement if it brings admiration from

[9] Gagne, *op. cit.*, p. 141.
[10] Skinner, *op. cit.*, p. 61.

other children. Immediate and consistent reinforcement is most effective. Large tasks, like a perfect arithmetic paper, are not easily reinforced. Each arithmetical operational detail needs immediate reinforcement for maximum learning. This is an advantage of the teaching machine, which provides immediate reinforcement (the satisfaction of being right) for each segment in the development of learning.

In working with materials to construct models and objects, the manipulation of the environment is in itself a satisfaction and therefore a reinforcement according to Skinner.[11] He further states that a small amount of reinforcement can be effective.

In addition, the opportunities for sharing and for group projects made possible through the techniques described in this book provide many opportunities for operant conditioning of social relationships. Helping to erect a store or to produce a drama, sharing tools, showing another how to perform an operation, appreciating with others a fine design or display, or realizing the values of interdependence are all examples of reinforcement of the constructive interaction of human beings. Aversive behavior is also strengthened when materials are spoiled, things do not fit where they should, tools are broken, or accidents occur.

Implications

THE LEARNER. The teacher is obligated to treat each child on an individual basis. This means that every child does not receive the same educational experience as every other child. It requires an educational program that provides learning experiences that are unique to each individual. These experiences should be planned to take into consideration the way in which the child learns best, the way that will enable each child to utilize his innate ability to the highest degree.

Educators have little difficulty in putting children into different categories (slow, average, gifted) based on their ability to learn. However, they then find it difficult to develop a program geared to the various learning styles. If a child learns best from concrete materials, he should be afforded the opportunity to utilize these materials when undertaking any learning tasks. But if he learns best from verbal abstractions, the program should be geared to accommodate this style. It is easy to say that a child just does not have the ability to learn or is not interested in school. Not many, if any, children start out disliking school. In fact, most children are tremendously excited in their first weeks and months in school. The question that arises is, "What happens to make children lose their enthusiasm for school and certain subject matter?" The answer could well be related to the fact that much of what goes on in the classroom lacks relevance for the child and confines him to inactivity. The writers hope that this text will suggest a scope of learning experiences that can challenge a child to work purposefully in line with his interests and

[11] *Ibid.*, p. 20.

learning style and find satisfaction in a developmental program geared to his individual requirements.

ALTERNATIVE LEARNING STYLES IN ACTION. The conventional approach to solving a learning problem is to present the task to the child at a slower pace, to use a different book, or to give him some individual help. Many remedial and tutorial programs are built around the same approach that caused the original learning difficulty. The writers would like to suggest an integrated program that would introduce a number of alternative learning styles to be substituted for the one causing the original learning problem. Direct experiences, role playing, concrete materials, visual materials, and symbolic representation of verbal abstractions are examples of experiences or materials that could be introduced into a learning situation to simplify or enrich the learning process. An educational program that is built on learning alternatives could be planned and organized by the teacher, but the selection of the learning style could be left up to the child. He could be introduced to the choice of learning a concept through verbal abstractions or through manipulation and demonstration with concrete materials or real objects. Both learning processes would be planned and organized to allow him to achieve the same learning goals.

Ability grouping, commonly employed in our schools today, is not successful in providing for individual differences. Ability grouping must be based on some measure of ability. IQ's have been found unreliable. Achievement in one subject area does not necessarily match achievement in another. Too much variation exists in children to allow for any but the most transient type of grouping.

Once the group is set up, however imperfectly the arrangement is made, differentiation of instruction is still apt to be varying degrees or different timing of the same activity. Group I of the reading groups might be on page 30 of a grade 3^2 reader; Group II might be just starting the same book; and Group III might be in the last half of the 3^1 reader. Perhaps one or two lagging children are referred to a special teacher who might try to close the gap, usually with more abstract stimuli of the same type that has already given those children trouble.

The program suggested in this textbook would enable the children to work according to an individual plan that would try different approaches to reading skills. Some children might be reading and evaluating a script for a play; some might be preparing to share a story through a homemade movie; one or two might be working on vowel principles through the making of charts; and another group might be playing a game, constructed through a printing device, to reinforce visual discrimination. All these and other reading or discussion groups could be working simultaneously. A variety of learning styles would be operating according to individual needs.

Many children can learn to figure the area of certain geometric shapes, such as rectangles or triangles, through the use of verbal abstractions. However, some children may have difficulty learning to make generalizations about the areas of these basic shapes. Other children may have problems transferring this learning to other situations. The latter group has not reached the principle-learning stage and the former has not achieved concept formation in the categories of learning types. An alternative approach may help the child learn the task and reach the conceptual level. A peg board with rubber bands could be used by the child to learn the areas of the geometric shapes. The use of this material will move the learning from the verbal-abstract to the concrete. A third technique could be through the use of layout tools to develop a verbal-pictorial learning approach. These examples are by no means the only alternatives to teaching the concept of area. But they do represent various ways that could be used in a classroom without any expensive or elaborate equipment or materials.

Another example could be drawn in the area of language arts. A hobby show or a series of reports on hobbies could be planned. Each child would demonstrate his hobby in accordance with his own abilities and talents. Oral expression would always play a part, but it might be through description, dictating directions, presenting a puppet show, or dramatizing a sports event. The interest in the hobby would provide reinforcement for the task of oral reporting, which otherwise might be an occasion for anxiety with faltering results.

The story that comes to mind when discussing creative writing concerns the fifth-grade child who was sitting in his room doing his homework two weeks before school started. The child was asked why he was doing homework ahead of time and how he knew what the assignment would be. His reply was that for the past two years on the first day of school the teacher had had the pupils write a story about what they did during the summer. Even young children have learned to anticipate this hackneyed activity. Have you ever thought of some of the limitations this places on some children? What does the little boy from the inner city write about compared with the child that spent the summer at camp or the family's summer home? How humiliating to have nothing but family problems to draw from for a recital of summer activities! In Part Two of this textbook some alternatives that can be used by children to stimulate their writing are presented.

An example of a child's frustration with learning can be shown in an assignment to learn the names of the fifty states and the capitals of each. If the first step is to learn fifty names and the child learns only twenty-five, how can he be ready to learn fifty more names that must be paired with the first fifty? In this chaining, the first set of links must be learned in order to present the stimulus for the second link. If the learning of states and capitals is important, then those children who cannot accomplish each step through verbal means should be given alternative ways to learn the assignment. Puzzles, games, and pictorial material could be added to the learning environment. Reinforced repetition and practice should be used to ensure learning and retention. But repetition and practice can become a burden if alternative experiences and materials are not used in the learning process.

The classroom teacher should try to teach skills and concepts insofar as possible through socially meaningful situations.

TRANSFER OF LEARNING. Any program predicated on alternative learning styles needs to be planned to encourage transfer of learning. It would be impossible to set up any educational program that was constructed with all the identical elements needed to live successfully in a complex society. Therefore, the program must have built into it activities and techniques that enable children to learn concepts and generalizations that can be transferred to solve the problems of everyday life. The program needs to be highly organized and the learning activities systematically utilized to accomplish the desired outcomes and goals.

Woodruff [12] describes the process of teaching concepts. The first step is to perceive something in the environment, called the referent. The referent can be experienced either by direct contact or vicariously through stories, pictures, models, and the like. It then should be considered in its specific details, differentiated so that it is understood in the mind. This is a specific concept. Events of the past can be brought to attention; then their relationship to the specific concept forms a more complex understanding. Relationships between processes or complexes are integrated in the mind into concepts of principles. Concrete concepts with common characteristics are organized in the mind into generalizations and thus become higher-level concepts. Then the qualities of the referents that make up concepts can be thought of by themselves and abstract concepts can be formed. Still higher levels of concepts can be formed from the processes of integration, generalization, and abstraction. Democracy, friendship, and philosophy are examples of these higher-level concepts. Woodruff suggests that concepts are formed with the assistance of such verbal processes as discussion, lecture, conversation, special reports, and questions and answers. These processes aid in differentiation, in practicing the new terminology of the concept, and in understanding attendant functions. The testing of the principle or generalization must be made in the environment and can be well planned for through many of the activities suggested in this book. The testing of a principle in a new situation is a transfer of learning, and a generalization or abstraction that becomes established can be used subsequently as a guide for behavior.

The essential verbal character of Woodruff's process can be stimulated and varied in working with elementary children by using the various techniques in the book. For example, discussion, special reports, and question and answer techniques can be enlivened by sketching, can be highlighted with displays, can be classified with charts, and can be dramatized with settings made of frame construction. The writers contend that the motivation provided through this type of variety will more effectively engage each child in active participation in the verbal components of concept learning.

[12] Asahel D. Woodruff, *Basic Concepts of Teaching* (San Francisco: Chandler, 1961), pp. 155–213.

NONVERBAL LEARNING. The significance of nonverbal learning and its relationship to the learning act is an idea that is growing in importance. As teachers look for new ways to improve the teaching act, nonverbal learning and its implications for use by the child cannot be overlooked. This type of learning has direct relationship to the techniques and activities that stimulate verbal learning. The Montessori and British Infant School programs would both provide the environment for a great amount of nonverbal learning to take place.

Nonverbal learning is behavior that conveys ideas and meaning without the use of words. The process can use symbolic or nonsymbolic action and can be spontaneous or managed. Nonverbal learning can be expressions that transmit emotions or information. It can be as specific as a gesture or as general as the atmosphere of the classroom and is either dynamic or static.

Nonverbal communication can take place between two children using facial expressions, posture, gestures, or movement, or by the arrangement of objects in a space. As children work with materials and tools they will communicate with one another without speaking or making any sounds with their mouths. While children work they will be conveying information about the activity, tools, and materials that they are using. One child needs a tool that another youngster has near him. Instead of verbally asking for the tool both communicate using facial expressions and gestures. The child that needs the tool may reach for it, while the second child nods his head to respond that it is all right to take it.

Teachers also communicate with children through the use of nonverbal behavior. A frown or a stern look can often prevent an infraction of discipline. A smile or a nod is a potent form of reinforcement. Teachers and children both should become conscious of the power of nonverbal learning. It provides important clues of awareness, acceptance, and understanding. It also may indicate a lack of interest or motivation. It can provide rapport, confidence, and trust when verbalism is inept or inadequate. Its values can often be realized in the construction and manipulation of materials, and the mastery it brings can be utilized as a step toward improved verbal learning.

THE LEARNING ENVIRONMENT. A learning environment is considered to be inclusive of any specifically designed and comprehensive set of materials, techniques, equipment, and activities that will stimulate and encourage learning. These materials, techniques, equipment, and activities could also be called educative agents. Educative agents include all curriculum materials plus the total environment of the classroom, school, and community. Books, magazines, pamphlets, charts, posters, pictures, clippings, bulletin boards, chalk boards, records, movies, slides, displays, drawings, models, tools, benches, school grounds, equipment, and the lighting, temperature, ventilation, color, and condition of the room are all factors that modify learning and are educative agents. They may also provide the referents needed to start the process of concept formation described here. Some of these educative agents can be controlled by the classroom teacher, whereas others cannot. In Parts Two and Three of this book the writers point out many suggestions for changing the classroom environment to make it a laboratory of learning. Ways of utilizing the community as the learning environment are also indicated.

EVALUATION. So far in this chapter the broad meaning and the principles of learning, the objectives of education, both intellectual and emotional, and the types of learning the teacher must distinguish have been discussed. The importance of planning for learning with the objectives, the process, the learner, and the environment in mind has been stressed. Some of the acts of learning in process have been shown. Now the final step of the learning act, in many ways the most difficult, the evaluation, must be considered.

In the evaluation process it is necessary to keep in mind the objective. Because learning results in change in behavior, and because the objective was stated in terms of the new behavior desired, it would seem to be a simple matter to observe and record the change. However, although this is the principle of evaluation, it is made extremely difficult by the complexities both of learning and of the child. It has been pointed out that learnings are built on a series of other learnings, that they are generalized and synthesized into complex concepts and principles. It is known that a change in behavior can be shallow and fleeting, or it can be intense and permanent with infinite gradation in between. A change can be overt or it can be internalized, it can be a change in thought processes or attitudes. So the difficulties of evaluation become apparent, and it is evident that any method devised must be imperfect. The best course seems to be the employment of as wide a variety of techniques as is feasible. The limitations of testing are known: verbalism, imperfect sampling of knowledge, misunderstanding, emotional affect, and many others. However, tests can be constructed to measure judgments, attitudes, values, applications of knowledge, transfer of knowledge, logical thinking, and a host of other qualities beyond the mere sampling of facts. These, of course, should be utilized. But, remembering the nonverbal emphasis stressed for many children, the reader can utilize many of the techniques in the next section as evidence of behavioral change. Demonstrations, charts, bulletin boards, and dioramas are examples of nonverbal evaluative devices. Careful records kept by the teacher of observations and conclusions drawn as objectively as possible about the outcomes of specific tasks become a telling body of evidence of progress.

Implementation

CONCRETE TO THE ABSTRACT. Participation in an experience with concrete materials does not insure that learning will automatically improve over the learning that was undertaken with abstract materials. In any learning situation the move from the concrete to the abstract cannot be overemphasized in altering the learning experience for any child. Piaget in his writings emphasizes the school's role as one of enriching the normal development of the child as much as possible and of making instructional decisions with the child's developmental stages in mind. These writers believe that the role can be implemented if the child is provided with the opportunity to perform real actions on objects and materials as well as to read or to hear how others perform. Opportunities should also be provided for children to work in group activities that free them from their egocentrism and allow them to interact. The chart presented in Figure 2–1 illustrates levels of abstraction of instructional materials. The instructional materials listed under each heading have no order of significance with respect to their effectiveness with children in a learning situation; they are presented to help the reader organize in his own mind the types of instructional techniques that could be used to move the child from the concrete to the abstract experiences according to his developmental level.

The key to success for the learner depends to a great degree on how these levels of abstraction are interpreted and how they are integrated into the teaching-learning process. At the vicarious-learning-through-constructional-technology-and-verbal-representation levels of abstraction the way in which instructional materials are used in the learning process is much more important then the fact that all of these are used. The child can listen to an

Figure 2–1. Levels of abstraction of instructional materials.

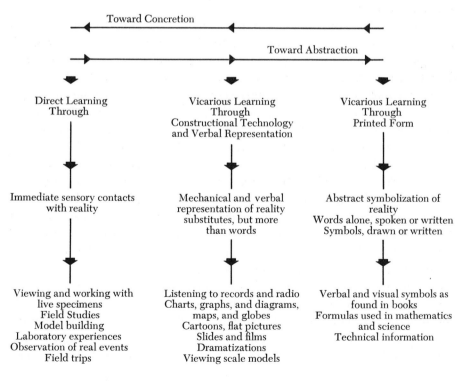

Toward Concretion

Toward Abstraction

Direct Learning Through	Vicarious Learning Through Constructional Technology and Verbal Representation	Vicarious Learning Through Printed Form
Immediate sensory contacts with reality	Mechanical and verbal representation of reality substitutes, but more than words	Abstract symbolization of reality Words alone, spoken or written Symbols, drawn or written
Viewing and working with live specimens Field Studies Model building Laboratory experiences Observation of real events Field trips	Listening to records and radio Charts, graphs, and diagrams, maps, and globes Cartoons, flat pictures Slides and films Dramatizations Viewing scale models	Verbal and visual symbols as found in books Formulas used in mathematics and science Technical information

audiotape or view a series of slides, but if the principles of learning are not made an integral part of the design of the instructional materials, their use will not assist the learner in obtaining his desired developmental stage. Does the material provide the learner an opportunity to be active? Does it provide for the child's response to be reinforced at the correct time in the sequence? Does it provide an opportunity for the child to progress at his own pace?

Instructional materials at any level of abstraction will not answer a child's learning problem. However, if they are in accordance with the principles of learning and within the range of the child's developmental stage they probably will contribute extensively to the teaching-learning process. The move from the concrete to the abstract or from the abstract to concrete is not something that automatically takes place in the learning act. When the child is working with concrete experiences the teacher should provide him with an opportunity to make generalizations about what he has learned rather than elicit simple statements of fact. The child starting with generalizations should be encouraged to make specific and concrete responses that exemplify the generalizations. The teacher should keep the child's developmental stage in mind when selecting experiences from various instructional levels as designated in the chart. The teacher needs to evaluate constantly to determine if the child is experiencing difficulty with a concept at the abstract level or if he needs reinforced practice at the concrete level. The teacher is responsible for selecting instructional techniques based on the child's responses to the level of abstraction.

DECISION-MAKING MODEL. The decision-making process of the teacher is described in Figure 2–2.

RATIONALE. We continually hear about the large number of children who are labeled nonverbal, nonreader, culturally deprived, or disadvantaged, children who are lost to the productive process and to society because they do not learn in the present educational system. The classroom teacher, working with twenty to thirty elementary school children, has a difficult assignment in trying to plan learning experiences that will meet differences in ability, interest, and needs. This decision-making model presents a graphic illustration of one approach that can be used to attack the problem.

USING THE DECISION-MAKING MODEL. In utilizing the model, the teacher first considers the child. He thinks about his developmental stage, his intellectual and emotional development, and the problem to be attacked at this particular time. He then makes the following decisions: he must decide what to teach (objectives) and how the child learns (instructional techniques and learning style). He must also determine to what extent the desired changes in behavior have taken place (evaluation). All the decisions are interrelated and interdependent. Failure of the teacher to make good decisions affects the total learning process. Many teachers have only one program available for children with widely varying abilities, interests, and needs. The program often exposes a child to information that he has already mastered or for which he is not adequately prepared. The purpose

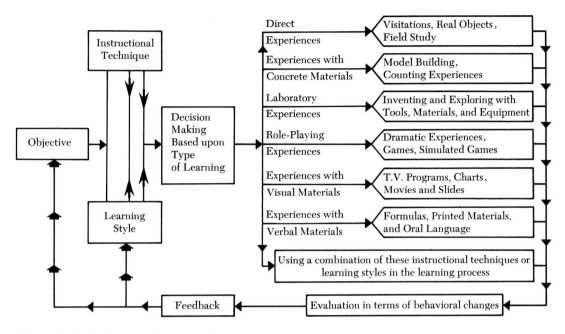

Figure 2–2. Decision-making model.

of this model and this textbook is to illustrate how a conventional educational program can be modified to meet the individual learning problems of all children.

Once the instructional objectives have been stated for any phase or unit of work, the next step in the educational process requires that a decision be made on how the learner can best achieve these desired goals and outcomes. Many times we think of the teaching act as presenting information or the imparting of knowledge. In other words, we consider the teaching act to be the only important function in the learning process. The decision-making model is constructed on the premise that an equally important function of the teacher is deciding which instructional technique or learning style will help the child reach his fullest potential.

In deciding on the type and complexity of the learning task to use for each child, the teacher should use the valid diagnostic instruments at his disposal. Diagnostic tests are helpful in deciding the educational level of the child in language skills, reading, mathematics, and other basic subjects. Informal reading inventories give needed information. A combination of informal tests, conferences, and observations might be needed to diagnose the child's need. The teacher should constantly evaluate the diagnostic methods used and not try to depend on any one method for the subject being considered.

PRINCIPLES TO GUIDE DECISION MAKING. The following list of principles should be considered when making decisions with regards to the learning tasks:

1. The child should be ready to learn the task.
2. The task must have value and meaning to the child.
3. The task must be of interest to the learner, because interest can facilitate the learning act.
4. The task should be simplified to the learning level of the child.
5. The learning of any task should start with familiar materials or experiences and proceed to new materials and experiences.
6. The task must be within the learner's capabilities, and must provide an opportunity for him to experience the reward of success and satisfaction.
7. The learning of a task should take place through the use of concrete, socially meaningful experiences and materials whenever feasible.
8. The learning task must have a plan or a way proposed for carrying it out. As far as possible the plan should be initiated and executed by the learner.
9. The task must have flexibility through differentiated assignments in order to provide for individual differences.
10. The task should provide for reinforced repetition and practice to insure retention.
11. The task should be planned to encourage transfer of learning.
12. The learning task should be highly organized and systematically presented.
13. The task should enable the child to experiment with new learning styles.
14. The task should provide for self-evaluation by the pupil.
15. Provision should be made for feedback to be used as a basis for the assignment of the next task.

This process requires a careful analysis of the various instructional techniques and learning styles that can be used to facilitate the learning act. Selection must be on the basis of how effective the experience is in obtaining the desired behavior change in the learner. Each one of these instructional techniques and learning styles presented in the model must be understood by the teacher in relationship to the learning theory and learning process.

The teacher must determine how well the desired behavior changes have taken place with each child. If the evaluation indicates that the child has fallen short of mastery or some lesser standard of achievement, one or all of the components of the model may require adjustment. The feedback loop indicates how the information obtained is fed back to the various components.

Pupil's Learning Record Sheet. The Pupil's Learning Record Sheet, Figure 2–3, should be used by the teacher to keep a record of each child's learning styles. The record sheet is set up to enable the teacher to assess learning difficulties in various areas and diagnose possible solutions. In column 1 broad areas, called learning areas, can be listed by the teacher for each unit of work or other time segment of the curriculum. Each area encompasses several learning tasks according to the needs of the child at the particular time. These are listed in column 2. These become the objectives to be accomplished through the learning styles in columns 4 to 10. Column 3 states the number of the learning style to be used to accomplish the task. Columns 4 to 10 are numbered according to the learning styles from verbal abstractions to real experiences:

1. Verbal
2. Visual
3. Role playing
4. Laboratory
5. Concrete
6. Direct
7. Combination

Once the solution is tried a plus or minus sign indicates success or failure in that particular style of learning. When a plus is attained in any one column the task has been deemed accomplished. Provision is made in column 11 for brief evaluative comments.

The Pupil's Learning Record Sheet can be used as a guide to how the child learns best. It uses a diagnostic and evaluative approach that requires no complicated statistics to find out what alternative learning style is the most effective with each child. A child may have to try many learning styles before a *plus* is accomplished for that particular task. As the record grows, the teacher develops a running account or inventory of the child's learning progress and learning styles. Figure 2–3 contains a few examples of a possible record.

The chart will provide systematic evidence of a child's progress toward the objective of any given unit of work. It will enable the teacher to plan for each individual and to keep track of his work in a simple but comprehensive manner. It will show whether he is being given the opportunity to take advantage of many learning styles. It will provide a meaningful body of evidence of the child's progress that will be impressive to both parents and child.

The record will be motivational and encouraging to the child. He will realize that his needs, motives, and interests are being provided for, and that his time is spent in doing what he needs and wants to do for his own advancement. Self-evaluation will be made easy for him, and consultation between him and the teacher to plan further work will be facilitated.

The teacher will find the time well spent if he uses these planning and recording devices. An individualized program based on a variety of learning styles brings a challenge to the teacher's organizational and supervisory abilities. A smoothly working system of record keeping will go far toward maintaining balance.

Pupil's Learning Record

Name _____ to _____

Date _____

Grade Level _____

Age _____

Learning Area	Task to be Learned	Diagnosis	Instructional Techniques and Learning Style							Evaluation and Comments
			1 Verbal	2 Visual	3 Role playing	4 Laboratory	5 Concrete	6 Direct	7 Combination	
Reading	Consonant Blends C1 S1 P1	1, 2, (1&2) 1, 2 1, 2, (1&2)	— — —	— + —					+ +	Learned through the use of a game that combined the visual and verbal
Math	Area of Rectangle Triangle	1, 2, 5 1, 2, 5	— —	— —			++			Used a peg-board with rubber bands
Social Skills	Share with Other Children	3, 3, 4			—	+	—			He has improved since working with other children to construct a puppet stage
Language Arts	Oral Expression	1, 3	—		+					Liked working with other children in the play. *Shared* some clothing brought from home for costumes. Became less tense

Figure 2–3. Pupil's learning record.

CONCLUSION

A knowledge of the research on all the factors of learning and the learner can serve as a testing ground for instruction. But a capable, imaginative, and inventive teacher is needed to set the conditions for learning in the classroom. Unable to turn to any certain guide for a prescription for teaching a certain task, the teacher must, with whatever knowledge is at his command and with whatever insights he has concerning his pupils, and with his goals in mind, determine the best procedure to follow. The composer of a symphony must know the properties and capabilities of the instruments of the orchestra (learning theory), the sounds and effects that are possible to each musician on his particular instrument (the student), and the over-all effect he wishes to express in his symphony (the goal); but the artistry of the symphony reflects much more than these components. It reflects the originality, the inventiveness, the power, the subtlety, the emotion, and the understanding of the composer. So when we compare the teacher to the composer, we realize that his art transcends all the knowledge discovered so far of learning. It is up to the teacher to innovate, invent, and try various approaches to facilitate learning.

REFERENCES

BIGGE, MORRIS. *Learning Theories for Teachers.* New York: Harper, 1964.

BLOOM, BENJAMIN S. (ed.). *Taxonomy of Educational Objectives,* Handbook I: Cognitive Domain. New York: McKay, 1956.

DeCECCO, J. P. *Human Learning in the School.* New York: Holt, 1963.

GAGE, N. L. *Handbook of Research on Teaching.* New York: Rand McNally, 1963, pp. 386–392, 494–501.

GAGNE, R. M. "The Implications of Instructional Objectives for Learning." In C. M. Lindvall (ed.). *Defining Educational Objectives.* Pittsburg: University of Pittsburg Press, 1964, pp. 203–240.

GAGNE, R. M., and BOLLES, R. C. "A Review of Factors in Learning Efficiency." In E. Galanter (ed.). *Automatic Teaching: The State of the Art.* New York: Wiley, 1959.

GAGNE, ROBERT M. *The Conditions of Learning.* New York: Holt, 1965.

HILGARD, ERNEST R. *Theories of Learning* (3rd ed.). New York: Appleton, 1962.

HILGARD, ERNEST R. (ed.). *Theories of Learning and Instruction.* The Sixty-Third Yearbook of the National Society for the Study of Education. Chicago: University of Chicago Press, 1964.

KIMBLE, G. A. *Hilgard and Marquis, Conditions and Learning.* New York: Appleton, 1961.

KRATHWOHL, DAVID R., BLOOM, BENJAMIN S., AND MASIA, BERTRAM B. *Taxonomy of Educational Objectives,* Handbook II: Affective Domain. New York: McKay, 1964.

SKINNER, B. F. "Why Teachers Fail," *The Saturday Review* (October 16, 1965).

SKINNER, B. F. *The Technology of Teaching.* New York: Appleton, 1968.

TRAVERS, JOHN F. *Learning: Analysis and Appreciation.* New York: McKay, 1965.

TRAVERS, ROBERT W. *Essentials of Learning.* New York: Macmillan, 1967.

WIEHELMS, FRED T. (ed). *Evaluations as Feedback and Guide.* Washington, D.C., Association for Supervision and Curriculum Development, 1967.

WOODRUFF, ASAHEL D. *Basic Concepts of Teaching.* San Francisco: Chandler, 1961.

PART TWO

Construction Techniques *and* Utilization

Part Two is concerned with specific techniques that can be utilized singly or in combination to develop a variety of instructional materials or learning materials. These techniques are

Layout
Lettering
Sketching
Bulletin boards
Printing
Papier-mâché
Frame construction
Solid block construction

As these techniques are described, the writers have a dual purpose in mind: the mastery of the technique by the teacher so that he can utilize it in the preparation of materials and the teaching of the technique to the pupils so that they can make models, art objects, scenery, posters, diagrams, and countless other real or representative constructions of ideas.

Careful directions in the performance and mastery of each technique will be given; the usefulness of each will be pointed out; and suggestions for bringing it into the curriculum will be offered. It will be up to the reader to go on from what he reads to apply the techniques in many creative ways suitable to his own situation.

CHAPTER 3

Layout, A Basic Technique

Layout is a planning technique. It is also a representation of an existing order, design, arrangement, or configuration on another scale, larger or smaller. Its key is accuracy and its purpose the visualizing of an idea in its relationships.

A playing field, such as a baseball diamond, is a layout. The bases have been placed in position, the foul lines marked, and in general the field has been planned in accordance with the rules of the game. A map is a layout. It shows a certain region with its features in their relative positions so that the relationships within the area are apparent.

In modern industry the drawing board is the symbol of the layout. A plan, blueprint, or design is made in advance of every operation and every product. These designs are the means of the communication of ideas so that the relationships between the parts and processes can be understood before they are put to the actual test. Once tested, the layout can be used as a set of directions to communicate the process to the worker—the cabinetmaker, the machinist, the builder, and so on. A technical or industrial society could not exist without a visual communication system to supplement the verbal system.

Teachers too need a visual communication system to supplement their verbal approach to working with children. In fact, there are some concepts in science and mathematics that cannot be taught through the presentation of verbal stimuli alone. For example, if children were asked to draw an animal that they had never seen from a verbal description read to them directly from a dictionary, the finished drawings and the representation of the characteristics of the animal would probably vary with the number of children in the class. This is chain learning. Without one link in the chain—the picture—learning is difficult if not impossible.

There is no question that more information can be covered by lecturing or telling children what they are expected to learn. However, the learning styles for some children require visual or other stimuli to be introduced into the environment if any degree of successful learning is to take place.

The success of television as a teaching tool is a result of its visual appeal. The teaching-learning process can be enriched when visual representations of the ideas and constructs that are to be presented are utilized as an integral part of the instructional program. This approach allows for a meaningful interplay to take place, combining listening, reading, and/or viewing, and discussion to relate ideas and experiences and promote the generalization and synthesis that is learning.

This chapter will give the teacher some layout techniques that can be used to create graphic materials. It will also point out and describe the tools needed to prepare the layouts. It should be noted that the process and the product are unified. It is not possible to discuss them separately. The tools and techniques used in creating the layout determine its form. A layout is considered to be a chart, a diagram, a picture, or a map. As the tools utilized in preparing these visuals are discussed, the type of visual aid appropriate to the tools will be pointed out. These techniques will free teachers from dependence on inadequate, ready-made materials and enable them to fit the visual technique exactly to the problem.

The following example illustrates the need for visuals in the communicative process: In defining a word such as *cat*, the background of the pupils determines their response to a great extent. "A small four-legged animal with fur" might be the definition from an American, whereas an African or an Indian might define it as a large animal. Furthermore, a construction worker would use the term to define a large caterpillar-type tractor. However, aided by selected illustrations, such ambiguities could be clarified or eliminated.

The first step in transferring an idea to the visual representation is the selection of the appropriate layout technique. The medium to be used, the space available, and the purpose of the visual presentation are all considered in the planning. With the principles of good design (see Chapter 6), an optimum use of space is decided on and the layout, or plan of space utilization, is made. It is important to remember the functions of the material being designed. For example, in the preparation of murals, charts, bulletin boards, transparencies, and chalkboard illustrations, consideration must be given to the size of the space, the arrangement of the material, and the placement of the detail. The picture or chart to be reproduced may have to be enlarged or reduced. The details may have to be placed with accuracy and care to insure easy readability and interpretation. The design may have to be sketched in a new dimension. These changes from the original concept can be accomplished by using one of the layout techniques to be described subsequently.

It is important to emphasize that these techniques are not only for use by the teacher, but also by the pupils. The writers have seen first-graders and older slow learners at the primary level copying materials that an overhead projector reflects onto a bulletin board. Squares laid out on a surface to form a grid are used by children as a layout technique at various levels in our elementary schools. Templates and various kinds of patterns have been used by children as soon as they can hold a pencil or a crayon.

These tools can be used by the classroom teacher to develop a learning style for those children having difficulties with abstract learning. For example, "How do we add angles or subtract one angle from another?" The child can actually lay out these angles with a T square and triangles. This type of experience moves the child out of the verbal-symbolic learning situation into a graphic-manipulative situation. The graphic-manipulative experience can and should lead the learner to the outcome desired. All children, not only the slow learners, can profit from a graphic-manipulative technique.

Although this chapter is devoted to layout techniques, no attempt will be made to cover the total field. Those techniques most applicable to classroom teaching and the clearer conveyance of ideas will be emphasized here.

Layout with Drafting Tools

For graphs, charts, or diagrams, children can cover a sheet of paper with 1-inch squares. If they were to use a ruler or a yardstick, this operation would require two marks on the paper for every line. It would also require an accurate measurement at the top and bottom of the paper. These tasks could be simplified by the use of layout tools (T square, triangle, and drawing board). It is not the purpose of this section to make experts in the area of mechanical drafting, but familiarization with simple application of these tools can facilitate layouts considerably.

DRAWING BOARDS. A drawing board is made of a soft wood such as basswood or white pine. The surface should be smooth and the edges straight. A piece of ½-inch fir plywood will make an adequate drawing board for use by elementary school children. A coating of shellac helps protect the surface of the board.

PENCIL. The pencil is the drawing tool that makes the actual mark. For best results, the pencil should be held freely (not too tightly) about an inch from the point. It should first be held at right angles to the paper, then tilted slightly in the direction in which the line is being drawn, and then have pressure lightly applied. See Figure 3–1.

All pencils have the grade of hardness stamped on one end. They should be sharpened at the opposite end, thus making it possible to identify the degree of hardness for the life of the pencil.

All drawing pencils are graded by letters ranging from 6B (very soft and black) to 9H (extremely hard). The ordinary pencil, which is used for most schoolwork, is a No. 2 and is about the same grade as an HB. The grade of the pencil to be used depends on the type of work being done. Too soft a pencil might smudge or blur, whereas too hard a pencil might cut grooves in the paper. In general, the 4H should be used to draw lines and either

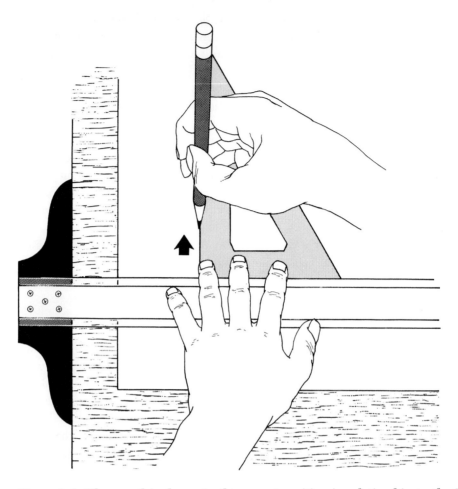

Figure 3–1. The pencil is shown in the correct position in relationship to the T square and triangle.

the 2H or H for lettering and sketching. Drawings are usually made lightly with a hard pencil and when completed are traced with a soft pencil. This procedure is followed so that mistakes can be erased without marking the paper and drawing.

After a pencil has been sharpened, any excess dust should be blown off because, if allowed to remain on the paper or if wiped off with the hand, it is liable to smudge and be difficult to remove. Draftsmen usually use a brush for this purpose. For this same reason, a pencil should never be sharpened over the drawing board.

No matter how carefully the pencil is used, the drawing will not be accurate or neat if the pencil point is not kept sharp. The professional draftsman sharpens his pencil every few minutes. There is a special sharpener that points a pencil to look like the pencil shown in Figure 3–2(A). A penknife can be used to sharpen it in this manner.

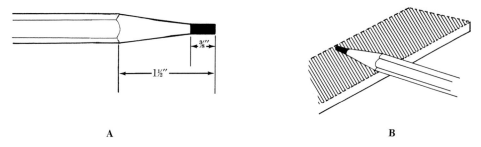

A   B

Figure 3–2. (A) shows the wood removed from a pencil point, while (B) shows the point being rotated on a piece of sandpaper.

The pencil is sharpened to a needle point by rotating it on the sandpaper pad as shown in Figure 3–2(B).

Whenever the pencil dulls, it should be rotated a few times on the sandpaper pad to obtain the needle-like point.

Pencils will last a long time if care is taken in their use. They should be replaced if difficulty arises, and not dropped or stored carelessly.

ERASER. There are two principles of operation concerning erasers, depending on the type of eraser being used. The very soft gum eraser used for cleaning and erasing light lines works on the principle of absorption, giving a clean erasure without marring the surface of the paper. Most erasers are abrasive, however; that is, they not only take away the lines, but also some of the paper. The abrasive eraser must be used for heavier pencil lines.

To scratch out a line with a knife or a razor blade, or to use the so-called ink eraser, is not recommended because of the damage to the paper.

When an eraser gets dirty this dirt is rubbed into the paper. An eraser should be kept clean by rubbing it frequently on a rough surface, such as a piece of wood.

COMPASS. The compass is used to draw circles with radii from about ½-inch to about 6 inches. Smaller and larger circles are usually drawn with special types of compasses. The *bow compass* is used for small circles, whereas a *beam compass* is used for large circles. A string and pencil can also be used to draw large circles.

To draw a circle the legs are squeezed apart with the thumb and forefinger, the needle point placed at the center of the circle, and the compass adjusted to the required radius previously set off with a ruler on the center line. See Figure 3–3(A). The points are set after first marking off the distance directly on the sheet of paper or on a piece of scrap paper. It is difficult to set accurate distances directly from a ruler without marking off first. Start the circle by holding the compass handle between thumb and forefinger (see Figure 3–3(B). The compass should be leaned slightly forward and the circle drawn in a clockwise direction with the handle rotated between the thumb and forefinger. See Figure 3–3(C). Left-handed people should hold

*Layout,
A Basic
Technique*

51

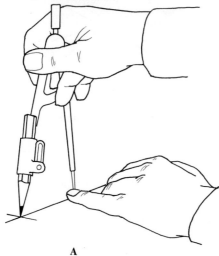

Set compass
point at center,
with one hand adjust
to required radius
previously set off.

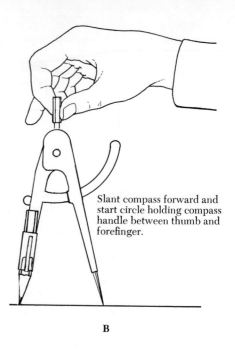

Slant compass forward and
start circle holding compass
handle between thumb and
forefinger.

A   B

Complete circle
revolving handle
clockwise between
thumb and forefinger.

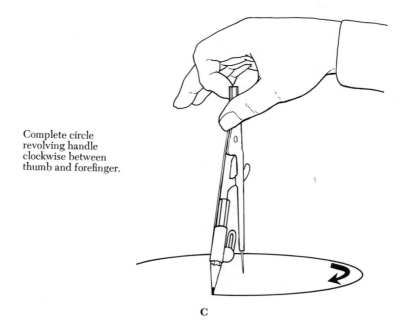

C

Figure 3–3. Directions for using a compass.

the compass with their left hand and draw the circle counterclockwise. Care should be taken not to disturb the setting between the legs.

T Square. The T square is used principally for drawing horizontal lines, as a guide for the triangle, and for aiding in "truing up" the paper on the drawing board. The head of the T square is placed on the left edge of the drawing board, thus forming a right angle to the edge. It is held firmly in place while the line is being drawn. By holding the head of the tool, the worker can slide it along the edge of the board to any desired point. In drawing vertical lines by the use of the triangle, the T square is held in position against the left edge of the board by the left hand, and the triangle is adjusted with the right hand. The vertical edge of the triangle is always facing to the left and the line drawn upward from bottom to top. If the worker is left-handed, the head of the T square should ride against the right edge of the drawing board.

The head of the T square is fastened securely to the blade at right angles to it. The head is the part that should always be snug against the edge of the drawing board to insure the drawing of a horizontal line.

The blade is the part of the T square that is used for guiding the pencil. It is also the part on which the triangle rests. Horizontal lines are drawn by using the upper edge of the blade as a guide.

Hardwoods, steel, and celluloid are common materials used in making T squares, with wood the predominant material. Transparent celluloid or plastic is often used on the edges of better blades.

Almost all T squares come with a hole bored in the blade that enables them to be hung on a nail or hook in some prescribed place. T squares come in sizes ranging from a 15-inch blade to a 72-inch blade. The 24-inch blade is recommended for use with elementary school children. The blade can be kept clean with soap and a damp cloth. It should always be wiped dry before using.

TRIANGLES. A triangle is a guide tool that has three sides and three angles. In mechanical drawing (drawing with the aid of guides or instruments), the triangle is used as a guide for vertical and inclined lines. There are two kinds of triangles used in drawing rooms and shops. One is called the 45 triangle. It has two angles of 45° and one of 90°. The other triangle is known as the 30–60 triangle. This triangle has one angle of 30°, one of 60°, and one of 90°.

USING THE DRAWING TOOLS

1. *Horizontal Lines:*
   a. The head of the T square should be held firmly against the left edge of the drawing board with the left hand.
   b. The pencil should be held about an inch from the point and inclined slightly in the direction in which the line is being drawn. Figure 3–4 illustrates the correct method of drawing horizontal lines.
   c. Care must be taken to keep the line parallel to the guiding edge.
2. *Vertical Lines:*
   a. Hold the head of the T square against the left edge of the drawing board. Move the T square into a position just below the start of the vertical line.

Figure 3–4. Drawing horizontal lines with a T square.

b. Place a 30–60 or 45 triangle against the T square blade and slide it along to the desired position.

c. Keep the vertical edge of the triangle toward the left and draw the lines from the T square toward the top of the paper.

d. Incline the pencil in the direction in which the line is being drawn. Figure 3–1 illustrates the correct method of drawing vertical lines.

3. *Inclined Lines:*

a. Slanted or inclined lines of 45° are drawn with the appropriate triangle held against the T square blade.

b. Slanted or inclined lines of 30° and 60° are drawn with the appropriate triangle held against the T square blade.

c. The T square and "30-60" and "45" triangles can be used in many combinations to draw horizontal, vertical, inclined, or slanted lines. Figure 3–5 illustrates some of these combinations.

Transferring or Laying Out Irregular Designs

In the following section three techniques that can be used by teachers or pupils to transfer or lay out irregular designs are described. These techniques will assist the teacher or pupils in enlarging or decreasing the original size of pictures, illustrations, and diagrams found in books, magazines, posters, or other sources. The grid square, projection, or pantography technique gives the teachers and pupils greater latitude in the development of visual or graphic materials.

CHANGING THE SIZE BY MEANS OF PROPORTIONAL SQUARES. In many in-

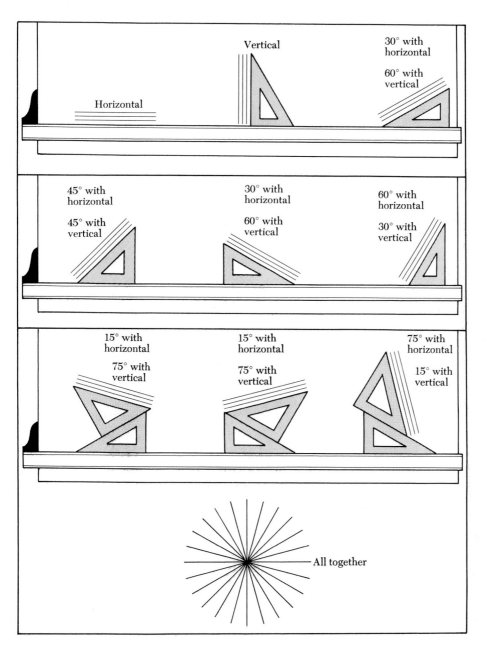

Figure 3–5. Combination of lines and angles drawn with 45° and 30–60° tri-angles and the T square.

stances, it is necessary to change the dimensions of a particular design because of its inappropriate size. One of the easiest methods is the use of grid squares. The following material illustrates the square method of enlarging or decreasing the size of objects:

1. Select a design and estimate the size to which it should be enlarged or reduced.

2. Mark off the original drawing with ¼-inch squares for small, complicated objects, or ½-inch squares for larger objects. The squares on the original drawing should be small enough to aid in the drawing technique.

3. Select the appropriate materials and the correct size on which the enlarged drawing is to be placed. If the copy is to be twice as large as the original, make the same number of squares but with the dimensions twice as large on the copy. Thus, if the sides of the square on the original are ¼-inch, those of the copy will be ½-inch. Number and letter the squares as illustrated in Figure 3–6, starting in the lower left-hand side of both the original and the copy. Letter on the side A, B, C, D, and so on; then number across the bottom 1, 2, 3, 4, and so on.

4. Locate the points where the lines of the design intersect those of the squares and mark these points on the copy. It is important to connect points as they are transferred, as shown in Figure 3–6. When sketching the copy, it is necessary to keep referring to the original design so that the lines will be transferred accurately.

5. If the original design is a symmetrical one, such as a circle or square, copy only half of the design and fold the paper down the center. See Figure 3–7. The second half of the design can be cut or traced using carbon paper.

6. Refine the completed design and transfer it to the desired surface.

7. To make a design smaller, the reverse procedure can be used.

Figure 3–6. Transferring irregular shapes by the grid-square method.

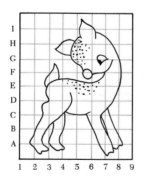

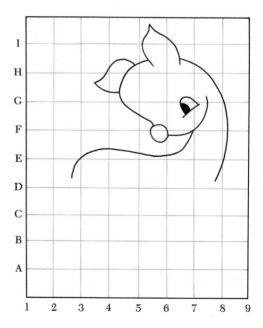

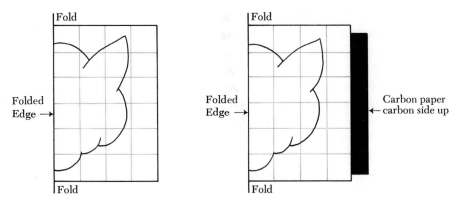

Figure 3–7. Cutting and tracing symmetrical designs.

PROJECTION TECHNIQUES FOR ENLARGING MATERIALS. Several types of projectors can be used to increase the original size of an object, picture, or illustration. The original to be reproduced must be the correct size and must be made of the appropriate material for the projection device being used. Examples of these devices are as follows:

1. *Opaque Projector:* The opaque projector can be used to produce enlarged illustrations from any opaque materials. Illustrations for posters, murals, cut-out figures, and bulletin boards can be enlarged by following a few simple steps. Teachers or pupils can use this technique to enlarge materials for their classrooms.
   a. With the projector in place, set the materials to be reproduced on the platen as shown in Figure 3–8. Materials are placed face up with the bottom of the picture toward the front of the projector.

Figure 3–8. Using the opaque projector to enlarge a picture.

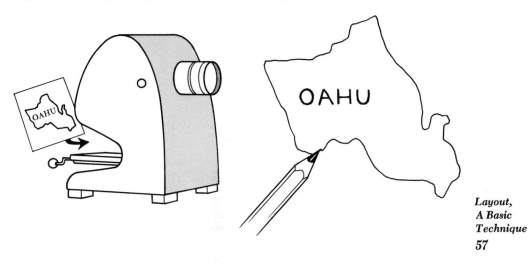

Layout,
A Basic
Technique

57

b. Secure on the wall the surface on which the image will be projected. Newsprint or wrapping paper requires a solid backing to facilitate the reproduction of the original illustration. The chalkboard can be used for this purpose.

c. Turn on the motor and lamp, and adjust the front legs of the projector for the proper spacing of the projected material. Position the projector to give the desired visual size. Move the projector toward or away from the surface to be reproduced to obtain the desired picture size.

d. With the room lights off, trace the projected image on the selected surface. Chalk, crayon, felt pen, or a soft pencil can be used. Figure 3–8 illustrates the tracing procedure.

2. *Overhead Projector:* The overhead projector can be used to enlarge illustrations for bulletin boards, posters, murals, and cut-out figures. In order to use this technique, materials to be projected must be transparent and small enough to fit on the projector.

3. *Filmstrip and Slide Projector:* These projectors can be used to enlarge pictures found in filmstrips or slides. These projectors can, of course, be used to provide all types of illustrations on a screen or other surface.

The writers wish to call attention to a recent development in projection: the overhead projector transparencies. These are made through various technical processes including photocopier devices. The machines and materials for making these transparencies would probably be available in the media center of a school or community. A description of these processes can be obtained in texts on audiovisual materials.[1]

The overlay, or multiple-layer, method of projection is a process by which a basic image can be altered by the addition of successive layers of transparency that are flipped into position as needed. This process allows an image to be changed by simply adding or removing a transparency.

PANTOGRAPH. The pantograph (see Figure 3–9) has been specially designed for proportionately reproducing enlarged or reduced drawings, maps, and pictures. It is easy to operate and will copy material swiftly and accurately.

1. Select a map or design and determine the size to which it should be enlarged or reduced.

2. Set the correct proportions on the bars of the pantograph. Each bar has two sets of markings, one for proportion and the second for position. The lower set of markings, ranging from 1⅛ to 8, represents the ratio of the new size to the original size. The upper set of markings,

[1] Carlton W. H. Erickson. *Fundamentals of Teaching With Audiovisual Technology* (New York: Macmillan, 1965). On pages 301–316 there is an excellent description of transparency making.

Construction Techniques and Utilization

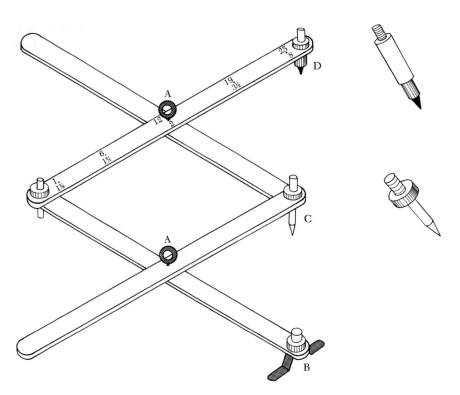

Figure 3–9. Parts of the pantograph.

from 1 to 25, is an arbitrary set that corresponds to the proportions below. These numbers are used only for quick reference when locating the screw eyes that hold the bars in position.

Example: To enlarge 2¼ times, screw eyes are placed in position number 14 on all four bars.

3. Secure the pivot shoe (B) to a table or drawing board with masking tape.

4. With a piece of fine sandpaper, sharpen the lead point, which is held in a small chuck.

5. Locate the position of the design on the original blank material. Position can be located by tracing around the original copy with the scriber point (C), and allowing the pencil point to move without pressure on the blank material. Both the original and blank material can be adjusted to the desired position.

6. Secure the original and the blank material with masking tape, as shown in Figure 3–10.

7. Apply pressure to the pencil point and allow the scriber to follow the pattern of the original. It is important that the scriber be held up off the paper so as not to tear the original.

8. To reduce materials, the positions of the pencil point (D) and scriber point (C) are reversed along with the original and blank material.

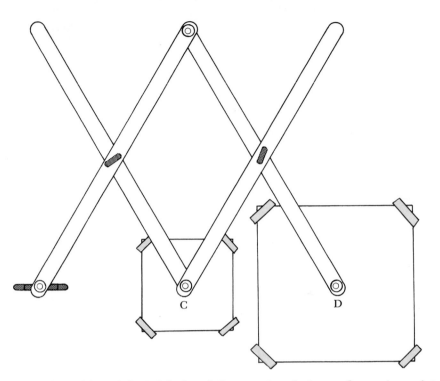

Figure 3–10. Position of the original and the copy in relation to the tracing point (C) and the copy point (D).

9. When copying materials from a text, the blank materials and the pivot shoe may require that the height of each is at the same level as the original. This can be accomplished by using drawing boards to raise the pivot point and the blank material to the proper height.

Templates

Templates (see Figure 3–11) are outlines of basic shapes useful for the tracing of designs that are going to be used more than once. Permanent templates can be cut from a durable material and then used with some degree of speed and accuracy for tracing objects for which multiple copies are needed. Geometric shapes, outlines of animals, plants, parts of the human body, states, countries, and continents are examples of templates that will be found useful by teachers. Not only do templates save time, but they insure the worker exact and matching parts. The following steps describe the procedure for making a template:

1. Select the desired material (Masonite or plywood for a permanent template, or cardboard for a temporary template).
2. Select and lay out the desired design using one of the techniques described earlier in this section.

Handle

Space Ship

Cloud

Face and Arm

Globe (Black areas are cutout)

Figure 3–11. Various examples of template shapes.

3. Cardboard templates can be cut with a pair of scissors, whereas Masonite or plywood templates are cut with a coping saw or jigsaw.
4. With a wood file and sandpaper, smooth the edges of the template. Rough edges will interfere with the tracing process.
5. Select a piece of soft pine $2 \times 1 \times 1$ inch for a handle and attach it with glue, working the glue back and forth to increase its holding power. (Figure 3–11 illustrates how the handle is attached to the template.)

Pattern

This method of reproducing graphic or visual materials is sometimes referred to as the punch, or pounce, technique. It is used to draw those graphic or visuals that are to be used more than once. Semipermanent patterns can be made from a durable material (cardboard, plastic) and then used with a reasonable degree of speed and accuracy by teachers and pupils to reproduce objects or illustrations.

Outline maps, geometric shapes, and drawings of plants, animals, and the human body suggest a few patterns that can be used in a classroom. The following procedure describes how a pattern can be constructed:

1. Select the desired material (cardboard, wrapping paper, plastic) for the pattern.

2. Select and lay out the desired design or shape using one of the techniques described in this chapter.

3. Cut a series of holes around the outline of the design with a leather punch and mallet. A ⅛- or ³⁄₁₆-inch punch can be used to cut the holes. The distance between holes should vary from ¼-inch to 1 inch, depending on the contour or complexity of the design.

4. Fasten the pattern against the chalkboard and rub a dusty eraser firmly across the perforated section of the outline. This procedure should result in a series of chalk dots on the selected surfaces.

5. Connect the dots using a sketching technique. It is important to check the original as dots are connected to make sure lines are accurate. Some lines may be straight, whereas others will be curved.

APPLICATIONS

Although any of the layout techniques under study can be adapted to a variety of uses, each one also has a particular application. The grid-square technique is best used for enlargement, reduction, or transferal of material that involves a somewhat limited intricacy of detail. For small-scale enlargement or reduction that requires a greater degree of intricacy, the pantograph is most useful. The projection technique is invaluable for enlarging materials for bulletin boards and murals or for activities requiring the enlargement of small images onto a large surface. In every subject area there are many ways in which these techniques can be employed. The following applications will give the reader some insight into how they can be utilized in the learning process.

Social Studies

DRAMATIZATION. The overhead projector can be used to flash appropriate background scenes on a wall while children are dramatizing a historical event in their classroom. Scenery will make the dramatization seem more realistic and help reinforce the concept being developed. This simple technique requires only that each scene be placed on a transparency or series of overlays. Transparencies will make possible minor additions or deletions to a scene. For example, an animal could be added to a barnyard scene and then removed by adding or deleting a transparency. A total scenery change requires additional transparencies. Creative dramatics helps the child:

1. *To understand himself:* The child in a dramatic play has an opportunity to become a person, animal, or object that is of interest. A star athlete, an unusual animal, or a spaceship are some of the characterizations that the child could portray. These characterizations enable the child to understand what he is like in comparison to others.

2. *To understand others:* Participation in dramatic play allows the child to assume many roles, through which he develops a feeling of empathy for others.

3. *To develop poise and confidence:* The child can become so engrossed in the character he is portraying that he will forget himself and his learning problems. Poise and confidence are important ingredients to speech improvement. The child, because of his interest in the characterization, will listen more intently to mistakes in speech and usually will try harder to correct them.

4. *To cultivate his imagination and improve his process of concentration:* The child needs to gain an understanding of the character that he wants to portray in the presentation. Involvement in the characterization should help him develop imaginative detail about the personality and actions of the character. The intensity of his involvement should insure his concentration in the period and environment represented in the dramatization.

5. *To understand subject matter:* Dramatic presentations can be used to integrate various aspects of the curriculum. The presentation can be about a historical event, for which the children make the props, write their scripts, set the time and place, bring in the music and artifacts of the period, and thus evolve a series of generalizations about a period presented through their combined efforts and interest.

IMAGINARY COUNTRY. The child's understanding of longitude and latitude can be reinforced by having him locate an imaginary country on a grid sheet of paper. Pupils lay out latitudinal and longitudinal lines on a sheet of paper. (The size of the paper and grids can vary.) The lines are properly labeled to show degrees south and north or east and west. Pupils are presented the problem of locating an imaginary county in which they would like to live. Each child draws the outline of his country using grid squares to help him. The child is then asked to list the characteristics and properties of his country: for example, type of weather, terrain, soil conditions, kinds of food that could be grown, natural resources, and kinds of shelter needed for protection from weather. A discussion among the children is used to evaluate the information gathered about each imaginary country.

MAP STUDY. Maps should seldom be drawn free hand by teachers or pupils because an inaccurate representation gives a wrong impression of size, surface, location, and the like. It is important to make children aware of the fact that maps are accurate to the smallest detail. In reproducing maps, the accuracy must be maintained.

Maps can be made in any of these ways:

1. *Projecting technique:* This technique is used usually for making large wall maps for bulletin boards, murals, and group work.

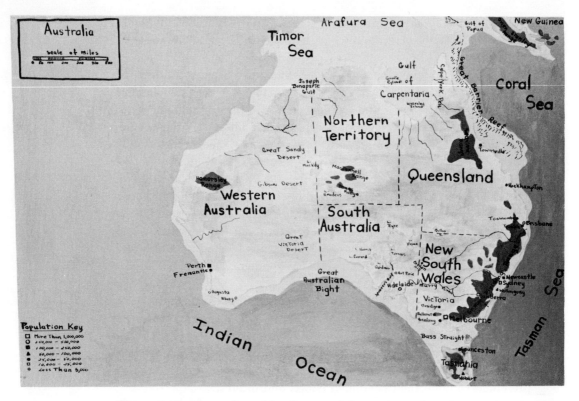

Figure 3–12. Map enlarged by the use of the pantograph and painted with water colors.

2. *Tracing:* With this technique maps will be the same size as the original, but information can be deleted or added.
3. *Squares:* These are used to add information or draw outlines but may not be as accurate as other methods.
4. *Pantograph:* This technique allows maps to be enlarged or reduced so that all of the features and characteristics are accurate and in proportion.

Maps should be suited to the age level of the group.

1. *Primary grades:*
    a. School grounds and buildings
    b. Residential areas (home and school community)
    c. Community and city (places of importance)
2. *Intermediate Level:*
    a. State: Location of state and its relationship to other parts of the country and world
    b. United States: Location of the United States and its relationship to other countries in the world

c. Countries of the world

d. Historical maps

Maps can depict many important facts such as:

1. Pictures of the community, state, or country (bridges, rivers, roads, lakes, and mountains)
2. The weather (rainfall, weather systems)
3. The products of a country (vegetation, minerals, and animals)
4. The airline, train, ship, and bus routes
5. The events in history (routes of exploration, birthplaces of great men, territories)
6. Time zones
7. Contour
8. Population
9. Hachure maps in which line symbols are used to show mountains or other raised surfaces

Other kinds of maps include

1. Natural wonders of the country, state, city, or region of the world
2. Man-made wonders of the country, state, city, or region of the world
3. Cross sections of an area showing the surface elevation

KINDERGARTEN. In the kindergarten and primary grades, social studies begins in the immediate environment. For example, the teacher in the kindergarten will want to acquaint her pupils with the school, its facilities, and their location and function. Pupils will probably tour grounds and school facilities. Graphic illustrations might help nonreaders seal this acquaintance and feel more comfortable with the new experiences presented to them. The teacher and/or pupils might want to prepare illustrations of the functions of the school nurse, bus driver, principal, custodian, and kitchen workers. These illustrations could easily be made by transferring them from a variety of sources by using one of the projection techniques. Primary grade children do not have the psychomotor skills necessary to use grid squares or pantograph; however, they do have enough skill to copy a projected image with a high degree of accuracy.

Language Arts

PICTURE CLUES. It is well-known that skill with and understanding of words are at least complemented and sometimes aided by skill with pictures. Beginning readers are limited in their reading vocabulary; yet, they can, and do, manage to gather some idea of plot sequence, cause and effect, and colorful detail. They do so partly from a study of accompanying pictures.

Many children come to school (kindergarten) with at least a little experience in picture reading. Although pupils will later progress to a use of pictures as supplements only, a teacher may at first wish to augment this experience in order to sharpen his pupils' senses of observation and increase their awareness of logical sequence. He might, thus, use the pantograph or grid-square technique to copy a series of illustrations from any children's book, putting each illustration on a separate piece of oak tag, and having the children arrange the pictures in logical sequence, answer questions about details, or recreate the story in words. He might use the projection technique to trace a background scene that forms the setting of a particular story; pupils could then answer questions and retell the story by illustrating on the background as they go along.

PHONICS. At the primary level, reading involves work with phonics. Much of this work depends on the pupil's ability to make discriminatory responses to visual as well as auditory cues. When teaching initial consonants and consonant blends, for example, a teacher might sharpen awareness of the sound in question with the aid of simplified and enlarged illustrations that he has transferred to oak tag or acetate by the pantograph or grid-square method. He might present illustrations, with accompanying labels, of a cap, a coat, a car, and a cup, for instance, teaching about the letter c. He might name one object and ask the pupils to name the rest, sounding and listening carefully to the first sound of the words. Although they might not yet know these words by sight, pupils would be more easily prompted by the illustration to pronounce aloud the word in question. Similarly, he could present a projection tracing of some scene and ask pupils to name all the objects beginning with c or to draw in some such objects. By using these, and borrowing illustrations from various sources, even a teacher who has little proficiency in drawing can build up a file of pictures to help stimulate this participation.

MEANING. Reading comprehension, of course, is the ultimate concern. Especially as he moves toward the intermediate grades, the pupil is expected to gather more and more implied, as well as stated, fact, meaning, and significance. This progress requires some specific practice guided by the teacher. He might, for example, read aloud to the class a story wherein some element such as hyperbole, vital to understanding and appreciation, is present but not outlined. As he did this, he might show the class pictures or transparencies that illustrate the story and make a graphic statement of fact, meaning, and significance. For instance, if the story says the fish on Johnny's line "must have been a mile long," a simple illustration of Johnny struggling with his fish would point out the humorous hyperbole involved. The pupils might thus realize that words can be used so that they intend something different or less extended than that which they state. The pictures or transparencies used could be transferred by any of the layout techniques from the original story; or they could be taken from diverse sources by the same technique.

1. Drawing figures used to illustrate a class-experience chart
2. Drawing figures to be placed on charts and bulletin boards about
   a. Letter and letter-combination sounds
   b. Syllabication
   c. Current story themes, such as seasons and holidays, perhaps in connection with other subject areas

MURALS AND SCENERY. Slides, filmstrips, transparencies, or pictures can be projected onto kraft or wrapping paper to help pupils make large murals or stage scenery. Selected material is projected onto the desired surface and the outlines are traced. When the outline is completed, the scene can be colored with paints or crayons. Scenes of practically any size can be created using the projection technique.

PUPIL-MADE MOVIES. Pupils develop a story that can be told by using a series of opaque or transparent pictures. Each child contributes one or more pictures to the story sequence. Care should be taken to insure that the pictures fit the maximum size of the projector. Opaque pictures drawn on paper can be arranged in sequence and taped together to form a continuous strip. The strip can be fed into the projector to give the effect of a movie sequence. Most opaque projectors have a crank and roller arrangement for feeding materials across the platen.

Transparent pictures can be arranged in sequence and taped together to form a continuous strip. However, some interesting effects can be obtained by using overlays or cutouts in connection with the movie strip. For example, as the movie strip with background scenery is moved across the projected surface, an overlay with an animal or person could be dropped on the movie strip to give the appearance of motion because the image on the overlay would remain projected while the background scenery changed. Additional overlays can be used to change the characters used in the movie.

Movies can be made on one continuous piece of paper or acetate. This technique requires drawing pictures so that the scenes blend logically from one to another. If the scenes blend correctly, no interruption will occur in the action or scenery being presented. For example, a panoramic view of Mystic Seaport could be made showing a series of homes, boats, stores, churches, and other buildings of this particular historical period.

PROPS FOR A PLAY. Statues of American heroes, cutouts of various types of transportation, and cutouts of various types of trees and plants can be enlarged for props to be used in a dramatic presentation. For example, small pictures of Washington, Lincoln, airplanes, trucks, boats, and other objects can be enlarged onto a piece of curved board or cardboard. These props can be made in a variety of sizes by using one of the projection techniques described in this chapter. Pupils can then hold and manipulate the cutout as they act out the planned dramatization. See Figure 3–13.

Layout,
A Basic
Technique
67

Figure 3–13. Props for a play enlarged by the use of an opaque projector.

Mathematics

NEW MATHEMATICS. One of the most popular expressions bandied about in discussions about American education today is the "new math." Contrary to popular opinion, what makes the new math new is not so much the content of the subject as the approach to the content. The goal today is an understanding of, and flexibility with, numbers. To attain this goal, the teacher must work with these two facts in mind: children must progress from the concrete to the abstract; children learn with most facility when they are relaxed and enjoying themselves. School activities according to Piaget should be designed to help children move from "sensorimotor" or "practical" intelligence to "representational" intelligence.[2] He suggests that as the child goes through this process of mental development the progress will vary from child to child. He also emphasizes the importance of defining the intellectual development for each activity. Piaget[3] devotes the last chapter of *The Origins of Intelligence in Children* to a discussion relating the six stages of

[2] Robert Sylwester, "His Ideas are Changing Our Schools," *The Instructor:* **78**:59, 156, 158 (February 1969).

[3] Jean Piaget, *The Origins of Intelligence in Children* (New York: Norton, 1963), pp. 357–419.

sensorimotor development to five given theories of intelligence. The teacher who understands these theories and incorporates them in his planning will find that some of his most important materials are visual aids (often used in game context). If real objects or large ready-made illustrations are not available, the teacher might want to use the grid-square technique and make large paper figures of various objects that the children can easily see and manipulate and divide. These will help them to understand parts of a number, commutativity, one-to-one correspondence between sets, and so on.

GAMES. Very often a teacher wants to create his own field of games, adapting each one to a different aim or aims. He might devise as a wall game a modified form of pin the tail on the donkey, for instance, to help the children gain facility with the parts of a number. If the tail spot were the bull's eye of a target and the rings around it were assigned an increasing number value as they approached the center, the pupils would get number practice in adding and checking their scores. The donkey (or any animal or storybook figure) could be transferred by the projection technique from any source to ordinary poster paper for the purpose. The teacher might devise as a floor game a combination of the preceding game and old-fashioned hopscotch. On the floor might be a sheet of paper presenting a clown's face with blank spots for eyes, nose, and mouth. The children would get one toss for each blank, to try to fill them in, using a disk such as a poker chip or a painted bottle cap. Their scores would then be three (or whatever the number under study) times the number of successful throws. Again, the face could be transferred from any source through the projection technique.

GEOMETRIC CONSTRUCTS. A pencil, compass, and a straightedge can be used by middle-grade children to make geometric constructs. A straightedge is a piece of material that can be used when drawing or checking straight lines. It is preferred that a piece of material without gradations be used in working with young children. A T square and a 30–60 triangle are examples of a straightedge. Children in the lower grades are ready to use these tools to make the following geometric constructs:

1. A 2-inch circle, a 3-inch circle, and a 4-inch circle
2. A 2½-inch circle with a line to represent the diameter
3. An arc from a 2-inch circle
4. A circle divided into four equal parts
5. A circle divided into six equal parts

Directions for geometric constructs can be presented children on Problem Cards as shown at the top of page 70.

The problem could be extended to dividing a line segment into four or more equal parts.

A plastic template with the correct solution could be used by the child to check his solution to the problem; the child could place the plastic template directly over his own response to see whether it corresponds to the

Problem: Bisect the following line segment.

$$\overline{A \qquad\qquad B}$$

A   B

To bisect line segment A B, place the point of the compass on point A and the pencil on point B. Draw an arc above and below line segment A B. Then place the needle point of the compass on point B and the pencil point on A and draw an arc above and below A B. The arcs must intersect. Label the intersection above the line segment C and the intersection below the line segment D. Draw a line from C to D. Where the line segments C D and A B intersect, mark the point E. Point E represents the point of bisection of A B.

correct solution, thus receiving immediate reinforcement of correct responses. Other values of preparing geometric constructs include practice in following directions, understanding the importance of accuracy (which should be learned at an early age), and satisfaction in achievement. Children can use their ability to represent geometric constructs to make interesting designs.

OTHER USES FOR THE GRID SQUARE METHOD IN MATHEMATICS

1. *Transparency overlays:*
   a. When teaching fractions
   b. When teaching discrimination in problem solving (successive elimination of unnecessary information when illustrating and solving a problem)
   c. When progressing from the concrete to the abstract by using pictures to which objects can be added or subtracted and in which objects can be regrouped
2. *Illustrations:*
   a. For bulletin board or chart on standard measures
   b. For background on some unit in problem solving (economics in a fishing community, how to shop wisely, and so on, can be done in connection with social studies)
   c. For calendars

Figure 3–14. Calendar enlarged through the use of grid squares.

Science

The scientific approach requires not merely a general and approximate idea of reality, but specific and accurate knowledge. Piaget, Montessori, and others in their writings support the statement that children from an early age should be encouraged to observe through all their senses and to make comparisons and contrasts. If actual objects and models are unavailable, the next best thing is a good graphic representation. Prepared graphic materials do not always meet specifications of size, simplicity, or specificity. In this case, the teacher (or the pupil) might want to make graphic materials to fit specific needs, while maintaining a substantial degree of accuracy.

INSECTS. In the primary grades pupils will study different insects and how they grow. They begin with insects such as the grasshopper, the young of which change only their size and their skins as they become adults. Here the teacher might want to show pupils not only life-sized representations of young and adult grasshoppers for direct contrast of size but also enlarged representations of the insect for comparison of intricate features. For the purposes of prolonged and facile study by the class, pupils and/or the teacher might make illustrations of the relevant materials to be hung in the classroom or incorporated into bulletin boards, displays, or murals.

Grid squares or the pantograph could be used to enlarge or decrease the size of illustrations for use in making transparencies and overlays (see Figure 3–15). Each overlay would present a few features at a time: antennae, eyes, mandibles, wings, air holes, ovipositors, legs, claws, sticky pads, and such. These same techniques could be used to make transparencies and overlays of individual parts that have structures of particular notability, such as the eye, with its many lenses.

Eventually, the same pupils will move on to insects of more complex growth patterns, such as the butterfly, which goes through at least four distinct stages, changing in other characteristics as well as size, during its life cycle.

For dramatic purposes, the teacher could make representations of this cycle, with a different overlay presenting each stage in sequence: egg, caterpillar, cocoon, butterfly. Pupils can use the materials or techniques described to compare a side-by-side view of two insects.

STRUCTURE OF LIVING THINGS. In the intermediate grades, pupils begin

Figure 3–15. Grasshopper enlarged by the use of grid squares.

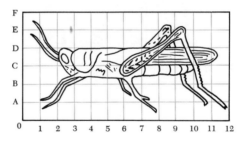

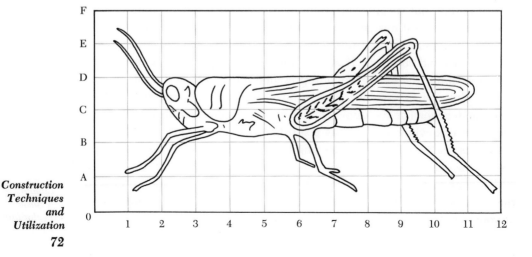

foundation studies of the structure of living things and the function of their various parts. The techniques described in this chapter could be helpful. For example, an investigation of the structures comprising the circulatory system might be undertaken by a class. The class might be divided into four groups: one to investigate and report on artery structure, another on vein structure, a third on capillary structure, and the fourth on heart structure. For an extended study of the subject, pupils might make projection tracings of the various structures and systems. An alternative would be for the pupils to agree on a uniform scale to be used by all groups and to employ the pantograph or grid-square technique. They could prepare cross-sectional transparencies of their respective structures, pointing out the special muscles and sections of the heart, the thin walls of the capillaries, and so on. By the same procedures, the groups might make transparencies of the entire artery, vein, and capillary systems and of the position of the heart. If the scale is followed closely by each group and if each group uses a different color for its particular structure, these four transparencies can be superimposed on one another to give a complete picture of the circulatory system.

If a similar study is conducted with transparencies of the respiratory system, pupils might eventually superimpose a transparency of the circulatory system upon one of the respiratory system. The same procedure could be followed with the bones and muscles, digestive and reproductive systems, nervous and muscular systems, and so on. As long as pupils use the pantograph or grid-square technique to help keep a uniform scale, they can build up a coordinated body of visual materials based on a variety of sources.

OTHER SUGGESTIONS FOR USE OF THE GRID-SQUARE TECHNIQUE IN SCIENCE

1. Representation of plant structure
2. Emphasis of distinguishing features of different plants
3. Representation of microscopic life: bacteria, protozoa, viruses, cellular structure in different tissues; microscopic processes in different stages, budding mytosis, leucocyte action
4. Diagrammatic outline of certain biochemical processes: photosynthesis, carbon dioxide-oxygen cycle, nitrogen cycle, the digestive process
5. Representation of molecular structure

CONCLUSION

It should be noted that the layout techniques mentioned in this section have in common the reproduction or juxtaposition of various representations with a high degree of accuracy. The different tools employed assure this accuracy of relationship. Reliance on the eye and free-hand drawing are not recommended when exactness of relationship is the most desired characteristic. A precision approaching machine standardization is striven for. A scientist, engineer, or designer is the type of worker who relies on these techniques. The more common skill of sketching used for diagrams and pictorial illustrations is discussed in Chapter 5.

LEARNING ACTIVITIES

1. With the pantograph, enlarge a map from a book so that it can be used on a 10- × 10-inch stage of an overhead projector.
2. If you are planning a large outline map for the background of a bulletin board, which of the techniques described in this chapter would be the quickest and most effective? List the advantages of the technique selected.
3. Use an opaque projector to copy a small map from a book onto a large piece of wrapping paper.
4. Describe how you would use the techniques listed subsequently with children. Remember that these techniques should not be considered art.
   a. Grid squares
   b. Templates
   c. Patterns
5. Select one or a combination of the techniques listed subsequently and develop instructional materials that would help a classroom teacher visualize a verbal presentation.
   a. Grid squares
   b. Patterns
   c. Pantograph
6. Plan a lesson in geometry for elementary school children that will utilize the drafting tools listed in this chapter. The lesson should be planned so that children can solve problems in a practical manner rather than with verbal answers.
7. If you were a first-grade teacher studying the local community, describe the procedures you would use with children in creating a map of their neighborhood.
8. Using a T square and triangles lay out the following angles:
   a. 75°
   b. 125°
   c. 15°
   Do you think it would be possible to teach children how to add and subtract angles using these tools? Plan a short lesson using these tools.
9. List some ways in which learning can be made more meaningful by the classroom teacher who has developed some understanding and skills in the following techniques:
   a. Grid squares
   b. Projection techniques
   c. Pantograph
   d. T square and triangles

10. Describe how layout techniques could be used in a learning situation to alter the learning styles of children.

REFERENCES

BROWN, LLOYD A. *Map-Making: The Art That Became a Science.* Boston: Little, 1960.

ERICKSON, CARLTON W. H. *Fundamentals of Teaching with Audiovisual Technology.* New York: Macmillan, 1965, pp. 301–316.

HACKLER, DAVID. *How Charts and Drawings Help Us.* Chicago: Benefic, 1965.

—. *How Maps and Globes Help Us.* Chicago: Benefic, 1963.

MORLAN, JOHN E. *Preparation of Inexpensive Teaching Materials.* San Francisco: Chandler, 1963, pp. 69–74.

PIAGET, JEAN. *The Origins of Intelligence in Children.* New York: Norton, 1963, pp. 357–419.

SYLWESTER, ROBERT. "His Ideas are Changing Our Schools." *The Instructor:* 78:59, 156, 158 (February 1969).

THOMAS, MURRAY R., and SWARTOUT, SHERWIN G. *Integrated Teaching Materials.* New York: Green, 1960, pp. 283–285, 409–410.

WITTICH, WALTER A., and SCHULLER, CHARLES F. *Audiovisual Materials: Their Nature and Use* (4th ed.). New York: Harper, 1967.

CHAPTER 4

Lettering *and* Manuscript Writing

One area of importance in connection with the construction of effective instructional materials is the selection and/or making of legible and attractive letters. Well-planned and colorful teaching materials can be made less effective by poor lettering. Lettering often makes the difference between dull instructional materials and those with a great deal of appeal. The need for careful lettering applies to posters, to displays, to exhibits of all types, to transparencies, to chalkboard work, to bulletin boards, and to other classroom experiences involved in a teaching-learning situation.

Lettering and manuscript are often referred to as printing. But printing is the making of marks on a surface by applying pressure to a stamp-like arrangement (block print, rubber stamp) that allows for duplicating many copies from one mold. Writing or lettering is the formation with instruments or by hand of characters and symbols representing ideas.

Lettering represents a means by which the teacher can communicate information and ideas to his students. Poorly formed, distorted letters make it difficult for children to translate these symbols into meaningful words and phrases. Simple and clear lettering avoids distraction and conveys information to students in an effective manner. Because lettering is used to transmit an idea, special techniques are needed to capture the concept that is being expressed. Lettering can be used to gain attention by the effective use of boldness or color. Size, form, color, spacing, and arrangement can be used to create an atmosphere or mood—for example, the spirit of a holiday on a poster or a display.

The following material is developed in a manner to familiarize teachers with lettering devices and techniques that will insure the effectiveness with which instructional materials convey ideas and concepts to the pupils.

Suggested Lettering for Elementary Grades

The single stroke Gothic letter is most commonly used in our elementary schools. This is the type referred to as manuscript writing. The letters in the manuscript alphabet are developed from circles, straight lines, or a combination of circles and straight lines. The characteristics of the letters make this type of lettering easy to read and write. Confusion is eliminated because each letter is distinctly different from every other letter. The letter *a* on the poster in Figure 4–1 illustrates the difficulty that can be encountered when the lettering utilized is not consistent with the letters found in the manuscript alphabet. These differences are expressed through the shapes and sizes of the spaces enclosed by the lines of each letter. For example, the dot does less to set off the *i* from the *e* than does the enclosed oval of the *e*. The letter *d* is distinguished from *cl* because of the spacing between the *c* and the *l*.

Figure 4–1. Faulty lettering: Two different a's are used, neither of which is standard manuscript lettering. Crowding can be seen in the lower caption.

78

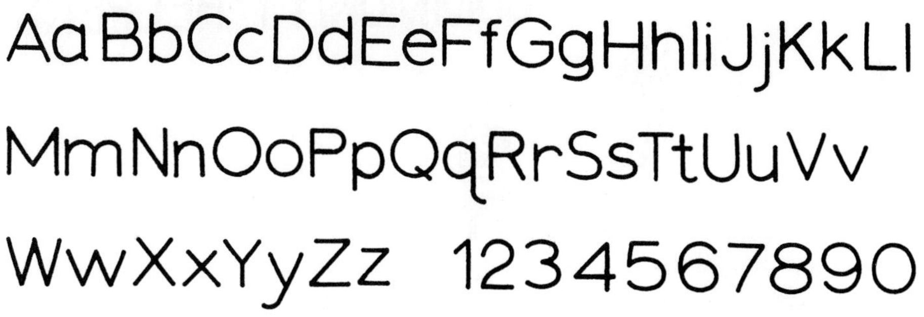

AaBbCcDdEeFfGgHhIiJjKkLl
MmNnOoPpQqRrSsTtUuVv
WwXxYyZz 1234567890

Figure 4–2. Manuscript alphabet.

Figure 4–2 illustrates the manuscript alphabet. It is notable for the ease with which the letters can be read. With a little practice and perseverance the teacher can develop skill in writing manuscript-style letters.

UPPER CASE AND LOWER CASE LETTERS. In cursive penmanship, the writer seldom confuses capital and lower case letters. However, in lettering, the distinction is not always so clear. Words lettered with a random mixture of upper and lower case forms are difficult for children to read and look silly and odd. DoN't YoU AgRee?

To avoid confusion and to distinguish between capital and small letters, these writers suggest that the terms *upper case letters* and *lower case letters* be used.

A common misconception about lettering is that capital letters are easier to form than lower case letters. The following illustration attempts to point out why this is a misconception. The lower case a, b, d, or p can all be formed from a circle and a straight line. The upper case letters require many combinations. The letter A is formed from straight lines only; the letter B

equals $\mathsf{F} + \mathsf{3}$; D equals $\mathsf{I} + \mathsf{)}$; and P is made from $\mathsf{F} + \mathsf{)}$.

The writers suggest that children use both upper and lower case letters when learning the manuscript alphabet.

When lettering instructional materials, the teacher should give careful consideration to the most effective use of upper and lower case letters. Upper case letters look more important and more forceful than lower case letters and therefore attract more attention. But they are more difficult to read, as may be seen by glancing at the posters in Figure 4–3.

The variation in the height of the lower case letters helps the eye catch the difference quickly and so speeds up the reading. Configuration clues are important aids in learning to read. Teachers can best make the shape of a word conform to the printed word by the use of lower case letters, except where capital letters are required. Figure 4–4 illustrates how configuration is utilized in teaching reading.

FORMATION OF LETTERS. It has already been pointed out that there is little difference in the skills required to make upper and lower case letters.

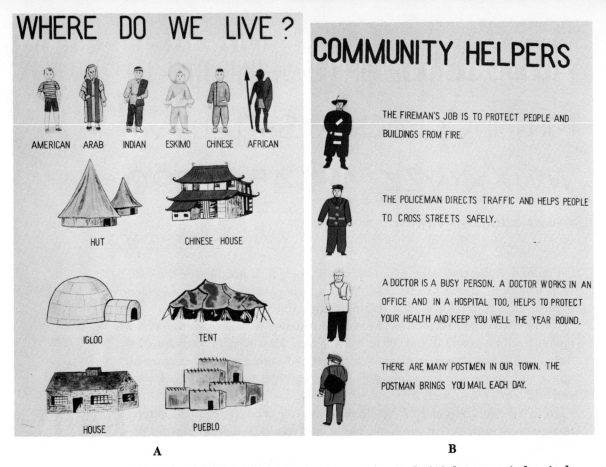

A   B

Figure 4–3. Posters (A) and (D) are easy to read, (A) because of the single words and (D) because of the proper use of lower case letters. (Broadside "October" by Rose Fyleman. © Punch. By permission of Ben Roth Agency, Inc.) (B) and (C) would be improved by the use of lower case letters.

Figure 4–4. Distinctive shapes give the child configuration clues in reading.

When learning to letter, or when teaching children to letter, it is best to develop dexterity in making circles and straight lines before forming the complete letters.

Shape and style are important factors to be considered in planning legible lettering. Heavy, even-stroke letters are easier to read than light-stroke letters. This **K** is easier to read than this K . Heavy, or bold, letters are

important for bulletin boards and displays because they are usually read from a distance. Along with boldness, size is an important factor in legibility or readability. The most effective test for size is to see the material as the

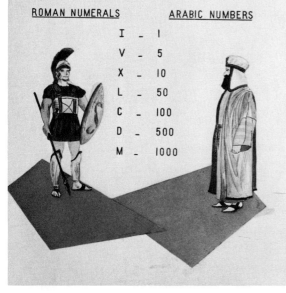

MORE THAN TWO THOUSAND YEARS AGO
THE ROMANS USED LETTERS TO STAND FOR NUMBERS.
ABOUT A THOUSAND YEARS LATER THE ARABS BEGAN
TO USE THE ARABIC NUMBERS WE USE TODAY.

THE FOLLOWING CHART SHOWS THE DIFFERENCE
BETWEEN ROMAN NUMERALS AND ARABIC NUMBERS.

ROMAN NUMERALS		ARABIC NUMBERS
I	_	1
V	_	5
X	_	10
L	_	50
C	_	100
D	_	500
M	_	1000

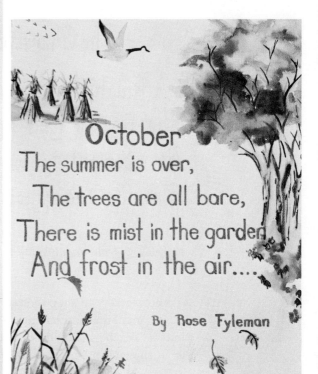

October
The summer is over,
The trees are all bare,
There is mist in the garden
And frost in the air....

By Rose Fyleman

C   D

viewer will see it. The person who is lettering should walk to the back of the room to check the letters for readability. The following chart can be used as a guide for nonprojected materials.

Minimum Letter Height for Lower Case Letters	Readability Distance for Size of Letters
¼″	8′
½″	16′
1″	32′
2″	64′

The style of the letter selected is very important. Some letters are very difficult to read. Figure 4–5 illustrates a passage by Chaucer written in Old English. The reader can easily realize the difficulty of reading the Old English. A lettering style that uses simple forms should always be selected for ease of reading.

The manuscript alphabet is commonly used in the lower grades. The two most important strokes are a straight | line and a circle O . Each letter is developed from a circle, parts of circles, straight lines, or combinations of circles and straight lines.

Lettering and Manuscript Writing

The Character of the Knight

A Knight ther was, and that a worthy man,
That fro the tyme that he first bigan
To ryden out he loved chivaleye,
Trouthe and honor freedom and curteisye.

Figure 4–5. Note the difficulty in reading this passage.

An easy way to shape letters is to think of them in families in relation to their common characteristics. Figure 4–6 illustrates some of the families of letters. Teachers should consider the letters in families in learning to letter or in showing others how to letter.

Note the relationship of vertical lines and diagonals in the letters **M** , **N** , and **W** . The particular arrangements suggested here are considered easier to read than **M** , **N** , and **W** . It is also important to notice that **W** is not **M** upside down; **M** has parallel sides; and **W** has slanted sides.

The most difficult letter for most people is **S** . The task of making the letter **S** can be simplified by using one of the following two techniques: The first requires the drawing of three straight lines to be connected with two curves **Ξ** + **ͻ** . The second requires drawing two curves to be connected with a straight line **S**

RULES OF COMPOSITION. Letters composed into words are not placed at a uniform distance apart, but are placed to give the appearance of being uniform. Figure 4–7 illustrates some of the factors that must be considered in spacing letters into words. The letters **I** and **i** require less space

Figure 4–6. Letters grouped according to families.

than any other in the alphabet, whereas W requires more than any other

letter. The round letters C , G , O , and Q require more space

than R , B , P , F , and E , the straight or combination

letters. The letter M takes more space than any of the round letters, but

less space than the letter W . The spacing between words should equal

the width of the lower case O , whereas the space between sentences

Hickory Dickory Dock

Hickory, dickory, dock;
The mouse ran up the clock;
The clock struck one,
The mouse ran down,
Hickory, dickory, dock.

Mother Goose

A

Figures 4–7. Poetry broadsides, one (A) with good lettering, the second (B) with poor spacing between letters and crowding of sentences.

B

DICKORY, DICKORY, DARE

Dickory, dickory, dare;
The pig flew up in the air;
The man in brown soon brought him down;
Dickory, dickory, dare.

Mother Goose

84

should equal the width of the lower case **W** . Skill and speed in coordina-

ting the hand and eye are important in forming and spacing letters.

LETTERING FOR SPECIAL EFFECTS. In the intermediate grades, teachers may be looking for different or unusual materials to make headlines for bulletin boards or displays. Certain readily available materials can greatly enhance the effectiveness of a display. Materials such as string, wool, yarn, light cotton rope, cord, colored tapes, paper straws, sand, and sawdust can be used to create exciting headlines for display materials. Yarn, string, or rope can be shaped into letters and pinned into place. Figure 4–8 illustrates how these materials are used to create textured lettering.

But in the attempt to attract attention, the teacher must not forget the rules of legibility. The three-dimensional effects of these letters will attract attention, and the texture of the cord will add interest; but if the lettering is difficult to read, the new dimension will have little value.

LETTERING AND BACKGROUND CONTRAST. Studies have shown that the greater the contrast between the lettering and its background, the easier the material is to read. (See Figure 4–9.) This contrast can be effected by using light letters on a dark background or dark letters on a light background. Contrast can also be achieved by using colors of high intensity with those of low intensity. For example, the bright values of red, yellow, orange, green, and blue contrast sharply with dull gray colors.

CUT-OUT ALPHABET SETS. Individual letters cut out from a variety of ma-

Figure 4–8. Examples of textured letters.

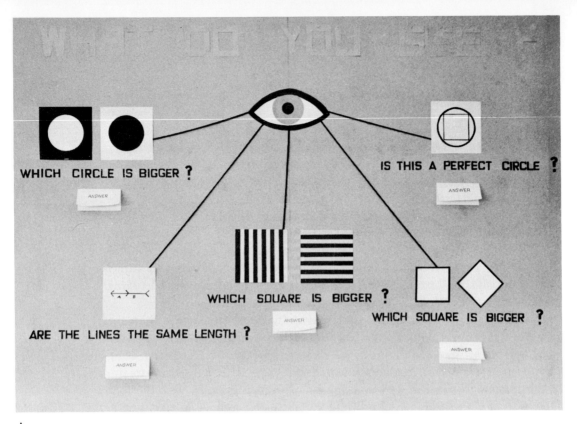

A

Figure 4–9. An excellent bulletin board (A) is less effective if the headline is blotted out because of poor contrast. Note the contrast between the letters and background in (B) the second bulletin board.

B

terials are very helpful to the classroom teacher. These letters can be pinned or tacked on bulletin boards or other display materials. Letters can be traced and cut from patterns, or they can be laid out directly on the original material. Letters can be cut out each time they are needed for a new display, or standard-size letters can be prepared for use again and again. A set of letters is usually referred to as a font of letters. A *font* requires several copies of each letter of the alphabet and six or seven copies of the commonly used vowels. Letters that are going to be used repeatedly should be constructed from substantial material. Balsa, ⅛-inch plywood, plastic, or Upson board are good materials for this purpose. In Figure 4–10, two techniques used in laying out letters are illustrated.

In the first technique, the graph paper is used as a guide for blocking out

Figure 4–10. Graph paper, a straightedge, and a compass were used as guides in making letters.

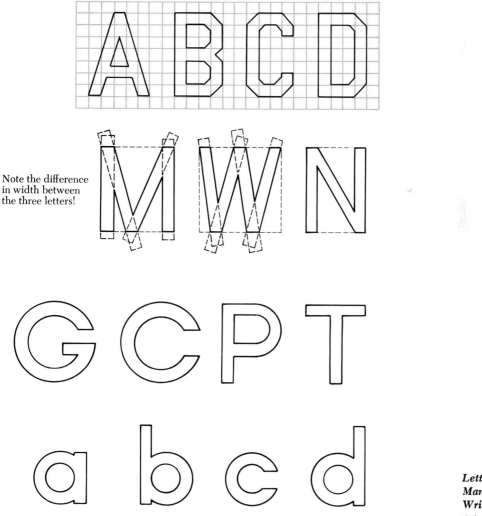

Note the difference in width between the three letters!

the letters. A straightedge can be used to guide the pencil along the desired lines. It is important to note how the blocks of the graph paper are utilized to form each letter.

A second technique requires cutting a square or rectangle to the desired size. The letter is laid out inside the selected shape, utilizing a straightedge made to the desired thickness from a piece of cardboard or oak tag. The straightedge can be manipulated to form the straight segments of the letters and can be used as a guide for drawing. A compass can be used for the round parts.

Wooden letters can be cut out of ⅛-inch or ¼-inch plywood with a jig saw or from balsa wood with a stencil knife. Plastic letters can be cut out with a stencil knife or scissors. Old plastic bottles or jugs can also be used for the letters.

FOLD-AND-CUT METHOD. Attractive block letters can be made using the fold-and-cut technique. Figure 4–11 shows how certain letters can be made by folding the paper vertically or horizontally.

Figure 4–11. Dotted lines indicate vertical or horizontal folds used to facilitate the cutting of letters.

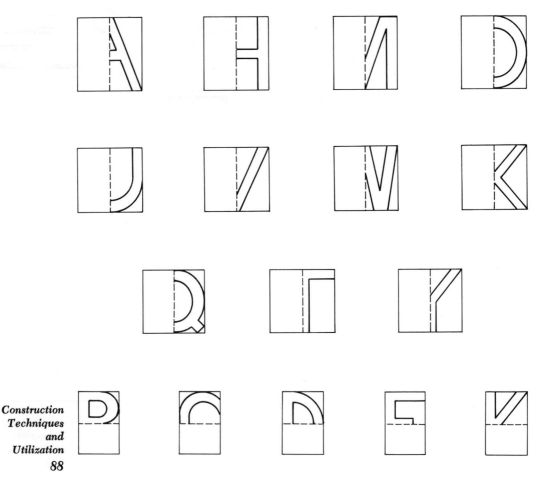

Figure 4–12. Letters that are cut out without folding the paper.

Commercially Prepared Lettering Materials

WRICO LETTERING MATERIALS. Wrico lettering guides and pens include a plastic guide (see Figure 4–13) and either a brush or a felt pen. The plastic guide is held straight up off the surface to be lettered by the use of the metal guide. The raising of the plastic guide minimizes smudging and smearing of the previously formed letters. Letters are formed by moving the pen through openings in the plastic guide. With a little practice, high-quality lettering can be accomplished.

Lettering guides can be purchased in upper and lower case manuscript alphabets. The guide sizes for the manuscript alphabet are illustrated in Figure 4–14.

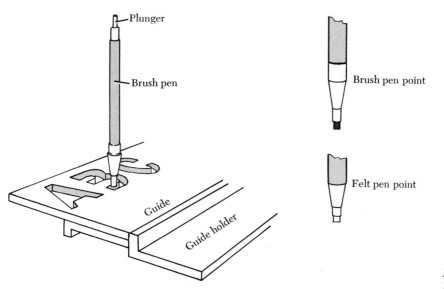

Figure 4–13. Wrico lettering guides and pens.

Aa Aa Aa

Figure 4–14. Actual sizes of Wrico letters.

Pens. Felt pens have less tendency to run or creep on a coated surface. The advantage of the felt pen is that once the cartridge is inserted into the pen, it can be used for an extended period without being refilled. The brush pen requires repeated refillings but works more efficiently on all types of surfaces. Both pens permit lettering in a variety of colors.

Stencils. Many inexpensive stencils are available for making attractive letters for charts, posters, and other instructional materials. Stencils for upper and lower case letters that range from ½-inch to 8 inches in size can be purchased. A pencil is used in tracing around the opening for each letter. Guide holes are used for the alignment of letters. (See Figure 4–15.)

Stenciled letters may be difficult for some children to read because of the spacing within the letters. The writers suggest that teachers close in stenciled letters. (See Figure 4–15.)

COMMERCIALLY PREPARED LETTERS. Today there is a variety of commercially prepared letters on the market to assist teachers in the development of effective and attractive instructional materials. Three-dimensional letters made from plastic, tile, or wood are available with pin or adhesive backing. Two-dimensional letters in plastic, felt, paper, and cardboard, with or without an adhesive backing, can be purchased. Both types of letters can be obtained in a variety of sizes, styles, and colors. Individual elementary

Figure 4–15. Stenciled letters before and after closing in for easy reading.

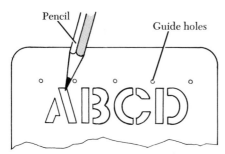

Pencil Guide holes

A

B

schools usually have only a limited number of commercially prepared letters because of the expense involved.

Materials and Tools for Lettering

Most commercial displays depend on the creative ability of the artist. He draws and paints the letters with his skilled hands. Although the reader may not be as skilled as an artist, with the right tools and materials and a little desire and practice, he can produce remarkable results.

Crayons. A large black crayon can be used to letter on manuscript paper. Children in grades K–3 can use crayons to letter without any difficulties. In fact they will enjoy using crayons because of their color variety and their effectiveness on cloth, paper, and other materials. Some of the newer types of crayons (multicolored) have increased the variety that can be obtained when lettering. Simple line letters like those in the manuscript alphabet can be drawn quickly with crayon.

Paint. Poster paints or tempera colors, which are opaque, are the best paints for lettering. Water colors are too transparent. The brush strokes made with tempera and poster paints blend in, whereas the brush strokes from the water paints can be very streaky.

If the display or object to be lettered requires a durable surface, a latex paint should be used instead of poster or tempera paints. Brushes used with latex paint can be cleaned with water and soap. Children should not use oil base paints because they are toxic if inhaled too much or put in the mouth.

Brushes. Lettering requires brushes that are flat across the tip. A professional look to the letters can only be achieved with brushes that are made for lettering. Brushes that are more than adequate for use by elementary children can be purchased inexpensively from supply houses.

Ink. Ink can be used for lettering to be read either at close range or from a distance. The latter also requires use of a brush. India ink should be used where uniform colors and value are important because it is opaque, thicker, and more viscous than other types of ink. However, only the black ink is completely opaque.

Pens. Special lettering pens are essential to good, fine lettering, and they come in a variety of sizes and shapes. The points of these pens are manufactured in various widths and designs to enable the user to make a variety of letters.

Felt Pens. Varieties of felt pens that can be used for lettering are manufactured today. The points of these pens vary in size and shape to enable the user to make many kinds of lines. Some pens are even made with exchangeable felt tips. For fine work, pens with nylon tips are available. It is important to remember that on absorbent paper or cloth the edges of the letters made with these pens are likely to be fuzzy, but they are excellent for flashy and fast work and for color. They are produced in a variety of colors.

APPLICATIONS

Reading

EXPERIENCE CHARTS, K–3. An experience chart is a large, lettered record of activities children have or will participate in as a group. Although the experience chart serves to strengthen reading skills and appreciations, its primary purpose is the development of language skills. It can be used to list plans, record the sequence of classroom events, and provide expression for creative thinking by the children. Even though some editing, done by the teacher and the children, may be needed in the composition, the expression of ideas is not restricted to words found in the basic sight vocabulary. In most instances, no restriction as to vocabulary should be exercised in the construction of charts for language purposes.

PREPARATION OF THE CHILDREN. Because the charts being developed are to be a record of experiences past, present, or future, the first step is to provide the children with some experiences from which to draw. These experiences may be either direct or vicarious. Direct experiences can be acquired through field trips, by construction activities, or by experimenting with science materials. Vicarious experiences can be obtained by viewing movies, filmstrips, listening to recorded stories, watching television, or role playing. Future experiences can be planned through the experience chart.

DISCUSSION PERIOD WITH CHILD PARTICIPATION. Teaching is more than providing children with meaningful experiences. During and after each experience, children should always be given sufficient opportunities to express themselves. New terms should be used and reinforced so that they become part of each child's vocabulary. Portions of the experience should be pointed out by the teacher and relationships suggested to past experiences. The child should thus be helped to form concepts with the ideas, vocabulary, and feelings gleaned from the experience synthesized in his mind. Discussion of various differences in concepts by the different children might lead to the formation of principles or of generalizations. During this discussion period, time should be spent on developing ideas and clarifying concepts in relation to the experience. Language development is a vital concomitant of children's discussions. All children grow in fluent and articulate speech as they discuss what they know through a direct or vicarious experience just completed. The immature, slow, or reluctant child should receive particular encouragement to take part. For he, too, has just had the experience under discussion and can meaningfully relate his reaction or summarization of it. Each successful contribution he makes strengthens his confidence in the all-important skill of oral communication.

USES OF EXPERIENCE CHARTS. When the discussion is ended, the children can summarize the experience and their reactions (concepts and principles) in lettering an experience chart. Usually the chart will be an informal culmination of the experience, but children may occasionally want to use an experience chart as a formal record. They may wish to present a work summary for a parent-teacher meeting, or apprise the principal of classroom activities, or just prepare various records for their own comparison throughout the year.

With their purpose firmly in mind, the children will decide on the best method of presentation. A narration, an outline, or a series of questions may be decided on. A graph or a cartoon might even be suitable.

PROCEDURE FOR CONSTRUCTING AN EXPERIENCE CHART. *Preliminary Draft.* The preliminary draft of an experience chart is usually made on the blackboard with the teacher playing an important part in guiding, evaluating, and revising. The children should agree on the main idea and dictate the title of the record, bringing out the fact that each chart should be built around one central thought. The teacher should develop and guide the discussion so that the contributions of the pupils are to the point, and suggestions are evaluated in terms of the ideas the children wish to express. The teacher writes on the board the ideas and expressions on which the group agrees, and helps the pupils see the relationships among their sentences. The composition should make clear the sequence of events and maintain unity.

Care should be taken that the language used be that dictated by the children with assistance from the teacher. Spontaneity of expression should be encouraged. As an experience chart is developed, it should be read and evaluated by the group.

Final Revision. Final revision should increase the pupils' appreciation for things well-said. The following ideas should be kept in mind to insure this end:

1. Unity, with reevaluation of the title and sentence sequence and their contribution to the central idea
2. Readability, with correct vocabulary and sentence and story length
3. Literary quality, with revision of sentences to insure interest

Revision of the chart provides another opportunity for reading.

Preparation of Illustration. Illustrations for experience charts are of two types: creative pictures drawn by the children; or pictures cut from magazines, newspapers, calendars, or the like. They should serve to make the chart more colorful and attractive and to provide instruction in the use of picture clues in reading. (See Figures 4–16 and 4–17.)

The illustrations should be the result of group planning, and the preparation can be by any individual or a group. The decoration is then used not only to increase the attractiveness of the chart, but also to develop skills and abilities in art.

VALUES GAINED FROM CHARTS DURING READING READINESS PERIOD

1. Children are helped to understand that reading involves interpreting a task that is written down.
2. Interest is stimulated because of the motivation of seeing ideas and names in print.

3. Left-to-right progression is demonstrated.

4. Words are learned readily because of the impact of meaning.

VALUES GAINED AS READING ABILITY IS DEVELOPED

1. Children learn that words help them to share experiences with others at another time and another place.
2. Children learn the concept that the written word is permanent, whereas the spoken word is transitory.
3. The teacher demonstrates that reading is related to many activities and can fit any activity in which the children engage.
4. Charts can provide excellent supplementary material in science and social studies. For example, reports written and illustrated by the children can be compiled and placed on a bulletin board.
5. The charts can function as a record of plans or a set of directions to be used in other content areas.
6. Charts can provide the pupils' first contact with capitalization and punctuation, and are an aid in teaching difficult vocabulary before it appears in books.
7. The child learns that charts are not always stories. They may contain a list of activities to choose from when one is finished with his work, or they may give study helps, such as how to skim or how to read for main ideas.
8. Charts can be especially helpful for children who need an extended readiness program in the area of language and concepts.

READING CHARTS. A reading chart is a chart containing a story developed by the teacher for the purpose of reinforcing some specific reading skill. The primary objective may be to bring in as naturally as possible the sight vocabulary of the basic reading books. The vocabulary of a reading chart in contrast to that of an experience chart is restricted by the reading vocabulary of the group.

Examples of Reading Charts. The illustrated charts indicate some ways in which reading charts can be used with children.

1. The teacher pastes a truck, a white building, and an airplane at the top of the chart to illustrate the story. (See Figure 4–17.)

2. Attention is called to the two-line length of sentences by asking the children not to stop until they reach a period. This is pointed out to students as the teacher moves her finger under the lines.

3. In place of a word not in the group's reading vocabulary, a sketch or a picture (called a rebus) can be used. For example, the word *butterfly* may not be a part of the sight vocabulary of the basic reading series. A picture is used in place of the word. (See Figure 4–18.) Sometimes the word appears under the rebus.

This is Fluffy.
Fluffy is white.
Fluffy can run.
We like Fluffy.

Figure 4–16. Reading chart without a picture. It can be placed in front of the classroom and children can be encouraged to draw a picture about the story.

The Construction of Reading and Experience Charts

READING TEXT

1. There should not be too much reading text on one chart. A few sentences will suffice. Sentences should be complete but simple and, at first, no longer than one line. They should be at the child's level to be appealing to the age group for which they are intended.

2. Phrases should not be broken at the end of a line. After children have acquired some reading skill, sentences of more than one line can be used. When sentences do run onto another line, they should be broken only at the

Mr. Jones is going away.

He will ride in the truck.

He will see

the big white building.

He will see airplanes.

The airplanes

will come down.

Zoom! Zoom! Zoom!

Figure 4–17. Reading chart that illustrates the use of two-line sentences.

Figure 4–18. A difficult word is avoided through the use of a rebus.

Here is Jerry.

He is on the grass.

Jerry has a 🦋.

The 🦋 is pretty.

Jerry likes the 🦋.

end of a thought unit, not in the middle of a phrase, and words should not be divided at the end of a line at this stage of a child's reading development.

SUBJECT

1. Charts should be meaningful by expressing accuracy and clarity of ideas. The subject matter should deal with children's recognized interests and needs with the concepts growing out of their experiences.

VOCABULARY CONSIDERATIONS

1. Experience charts need no vocabulary controls. However, children should not be required to master the vocabulary in the charts, except for certain words that appear in the basic reading series.

2. Reading charts should consist of vocabulary words that parallel as much as possible the vocabulary that the children will encounter in the basal reading series. The use of the rebus enables the teacher to extend the selection of topics.

ILLUSTRATIONS

1. Pictures should show some action instead of merely being illustrations of objects.

2. Children should be allowed to choose or draw their own pictures.

3. Placing the illustrations at the top of the chart and the sentences below adds to the attractiveness of the chart.

MECHANICS

1. *Reading Considerations:* Charts should facilitate the establishment of skills in reading by consistency in (a) thought phrases, (b) position of return eye sweep, (c) context and picture clues, (d) dynamic interest factors, and (e) repetition.

2. *Spacing:* Center the title about 3 inches from the bottom of the illustrations and place the first sentence 3 inches from the title. If no illustration is to be used, the title is 3 inches from the top of the paper. If the paper is unlined, draw light guidelines for each sentence with about 3 inches between sentences. The space between words and letters should follow the rules suggested in this chapter.

3. *Margins:* Charts should be attractive from the standpoint of neatness and balance. Keep the left margin about 1½ to 2 inches and the right margin approximately even and uncrowded.

4. *Writing form:* Charts should be written with manuscript letters, using a large, dark-colored crayon, Wrico lettering pens and guides, or a felt pen. The lower case letters should be one half to two thirds of the height of the capitals. The writing should be legible, uniform, and neat. Light, penciled guidelines can be used for each letter until proficiency is developed.

5. *Color:* All words should be lettered in the same color, preferably black, on white paper. When phonetic analysis is introduced, certain phonetic elements can be lettered in color to make them stand out, but only those combinations that the teacher wants to emphasize should be so colored.

6. *Capitalization and punctuation:* Only the first word in each sentence should be capitalized, with each word in the title capitalized. To lay the foundation for later written composition, the teacher should always use correct punctuation and capitalization.

7. *Paper:* Various types and kinds of paper can be used, including newsprint, wrapping paper, bogus and light-weight oak tag. In all cases, there should be a sharp contrast between the color of the letters and the paper used for the background.

Poetry Broadsides

In the days before our popular means of communication, poets and songwriters composed ballads that were printed on large sheets of paper and then sold. These broadsides became very popular. Today they are no longer sold in the streets, but an application of the idea is a splendid language arts tool. Broadsides can be prepared as art forms in the elementary grades and should follow some or all of these recommendations:

1. They should provide for the representation of an original poem or of a favorite short poem.
2. They should be lettered in an attractive way to fill the greatest portion of the space.
3. They should be illustrated with cut-outs, stick figures, line drawings, or the like.

The purpose of the broadside is to present in the most attractive way possible a literary work that the child wants to share with others. It combines the appreciation of art and poetry. Even music can be brought in if the poem is a song lyric or ballad.

The techniques of both lettering and sketching are needed in this activity. (See Figure 4–19.) For additional examples of poetry broadsides, see Figures 4–3D and 4–7.

Helping Slow Learners with Lettering and Writing

A guide or pattern can be constructed to help teach children to letter or write. Letters can be written on a base made from a piece of cardboard, which is then covered with a piece of clear plastic, X-ray film (reprocessed), or transparency film. Children can use a grease pencil or wax crayon to trace the letters from the base sheet onto the plastic sheet. If the child's tracing varies from the original shape, he has immediate knowledge of the variation in his response.

A Barnyard Tale

Once there was a rooster
As hungry as could be!
He hopped into the barnyard
To see what he could see.

He spied a wiggly worm
Beside a little gate —
So he pounced upon it quickly,
(He simply could not wait!)

He stopped with great alarm
When he heard a piggy wail —
"That's not a juicy worm —
It's my curly pink tail!"

Bonnie Jeffries

Figure 4–19. Student's original poem illustrated with felt. (By permission of Bonnie Jeffries).

Letters can also be cut out of sandpaper and wood for tracing purposes; however, this technique requires that the child feel his incorrect responses and does not allow him any opportunity to compare his response with the original form. The grease pencil has the advantage of allowing the child to compare his response and then remove it by rubbing the surface clean with a cloth.

Skinner [1] used a similar technique with a chemically treated paper that would turn a different color when the child's tracing varied. Fernald [2] used a tracing principle with children in a remedial program in reading. However, in this program children traced words in sand or in the air, which did not allow for the reinforcement of the response.

The plastic-overlay technique can be used with first-graders who are having problems with words like *come-came, there-three,* and *were-where.* This device allows a child to trace the words with the grease pencil onto

[1] Ellen P. Reese, *Behavior Theory and Practice.* Reel II (New York: Appleton, 1965), a film describing B. F. Skinner's "Write and See" handwriting program.

[2] Grace M. Fernald, *Remedial Techniques in Basic School Subjects* (New York: McGraw-Hill, 1943).

the plastic surface and then underline the difference with another color. He could even be asked to trace the letters that are different in another color.

Gotkin,[3] in a study conducted in New York City for the Institute for Developmental Studies, indicated that some of the difficulties in learning to name letters can be directly related to the child's inability to discriminate the shape of the letter as well as the sound that goes with it. The results emphasized the importance of using a variety of visual and auditory skills to help children learn the letters of the alphabet. Small,[4] in a study with children with dyslexia, also indicated the need for the learner to use both his visual and auditory senses. Both studies illustrate the importance of using cut-out letters in helping children solve their learning problems. These studies also indicate the importance of having children make their own letters from clay or substitute clay. Chapter 12 in this book gives directions for making four types of clay.

An alphabet board can be made out of heavy cardboard, and the letters can be made from plastic containers. Letter shapes are scooped out of the cardboard leaving a cavity for the plastic letters. Sandpaper can be added to the backs of the letter if necessary to help the child keep the letters in the

correct position; for example, the letter R should look like this R , not

Я . The following principles of learning should be kept in mind when

constructing instructional materials for slow learners: (1) immediate feedback, (2) proper size of the learning step, (3) adaptability to the individual's learning style, and (4) logical sequence.

CONCLUSION

There are several aspects that make lettering a skill of great importance for both pupil and teacher: (1) Through manuscript, it is the means by which pupils learn to write. (2) It is indispensable in the process of learning to read. It provides a consistent and immediate tool for representing the words and letters being learned on the blackboard, on charts, on cards, and at the pupil's desk. (3) Once mastered, the art of lettering provides a tool for communicating in a useful and attractive way. The many occasions for this communication were only lightly touched on in this chapter but can be expanded and extended by the reader.

[3] Lassar G. Gotkin, "The Alphabet As a Sensorimotor Experience," *The Instructor:* 77:82–83 (August-September 1967).

[4] Mary Walsh Small, "Just What Is Dyslexia?" *The Instructor:* 77:54–57 (August-September 1967).

LEARNING ACTIVITIES

1. Construct a broadside to announce an event that took place in colonial days, for example the Stamp Act.
2. Make a font of letters for your own use out of a material that will assure relative permanency.
3. Describe how you would utilize an experience chart in connection with a nature walk. If possible, take some children on a nature walk and after the walk develop with them an experience chart.
4. Select three poems and construct for each a broadside that would be appropriate for use with children. Explain how these broadsides could be used with children in a learning situation. What would be the advantages to children of making broadsides?
5. Make a set of labels that would be used to stimulate reading in a kindergarten or first grade. *Door, window,* and *desk* are examples.
6. Make a packet of flash cards to be used for practice on difficult words that cannot be illustrated, such as *was, there,* and *where.*
7. Prepare a minilesson involving the use of a reading chart to supplement a particular story in a first-grade reading book.
8. Evaluate the illustrations in Figures 4–7 and 4–9 for consistency with the principles on lettering described in this chapter. Select the best examples of lettering and criticize what you consider to be the poorest. It is important to note that the poster may be attractive, but the lettering may not be appropriate for use with children.

REFERENCES

EAST, MARJORIE, and DALE, EDGAR. *Display for Learning.* New York: Holt, 1952.

FERNALD, GRACE M. *Remedial Techniques in Basic School Subjects.* New York: McGraw-Hill, 1943.

GOTKIN, LASSAR G. "The Alphabet As a Sensorimotor Experience," *The Instructor,* 77:82–83 (August-September 1967).

JEFFERSON ELEMENTARY DISTRICT. *Art Appreciation and Experimentation.* Daly City, Calif., 1968, pp. 193–198. (mimeo).

KENDALL, L. "Better Lettering for Bulletin Boards," *Grade Teacher,* 84:97 (November 1966).

LEACH, MORTIMER. *Letter Design.* New York: Reinhold, 1960.

LIDSTONE, J. "Even Sign Making Can Be Creative," *Grade Teacher,* 84:90–91 (October 1966).

MINOR, ED. *Preparing Visual Instructional Materials.* New York: McGraw-Hill, 1962, pp. 27–51.

MORLAN, JOHN E. *Preparation of Inexpensive Teaching Materials.* San Francisco: Chandler, 1963, pp. 39–52.

REESE, ELLEN P. *Behavior Theory and Practice,* Film Reel III; New York: Appleton, 1965.

ROSS, GEORGE F. *Speedball Text Book.* (18th ed.). Camden, N.J.: Hunt Pen Co., 1956.

SMALL, MARY W. "Just What Is Dyslexia," *The Instructor,* 77:54–57 (August-September 1967).

WITTICH, WALTER A., and SCHULLER, CHARLES F. *Audiovisual Materials: Their Nature and Use* (4th ed). New York: Harper, 1967, pp. 82–90.

WYMAN, R. "Creating Readable Transparencies." *The Instructor,* 76:104 (May 1967).

CHAPTER 5

Sketching *for* *the* Classroom Teacher

The classroom teacher should understand the value of sketching as a visual language. The technique is most valuable when used as a means rather than as an end in itself. The teacher should not see sketching as art, but as an adjunct to the communication of education. It should be included with writing for verbal communication and arithmetic for numerical communication.

Man learned to sketch thousands of years before he learned to write. His first letters were simplified drawings. The hieroglyphics of the early Egyptians, the rock carvings in the caves of France, and the picture language of the American Indians indicate that even primitive and early man realized the need for a medium with which to supplement the spoken language. Picture writing later developed into the cuneiform writing common to the ancient Persians and Assyrians. In our modern society, sketching still ranks high for the purpose of conveying ideas.

The idea of sketching is not new to the reader. He has doubtless made hundreds of sketches in his lifetime. The ideas suggested in this chapter will assist in the making of better sketches. The worth or accuracy of the sketch can be tested by checking with others to see if they can recognize, understand, or interpret the message being considered without a number of questions.

Advantages

Immediacy, speed, vividness, and exactness are the principal advantages of sketching. There is no need for lengthy planning or preparation in order to use the technique. This advantage makes it particularly well suited to the language activities, where structuring can inhibit creativity and free expression. In the primary grades, the teacher can elicit stories or information from children by drawing simple outlines of objects, animals, or human figures, and letting the children describe a scene or provide information while the teacher completes the sketch. The children are using imagination and description in oral composition without the anxiety caused in making a report.

The same lack of self-consciousness can be fostered in a similar way to help children who come from different backgrounds talk about language and how it differs in groups of children. A quick sketch of a community or home scene drawn by the teacher could be described in different ways, and the accepted use of adjectives and other descriptive words can also be pointed out. Words such as *cool* or *neat,* to describe a favored situation, could be explained as slang and more acceptable terms substituted. By focusing attention on the drawing, rather than on the speaker, emotional overtones could be avoided.

This simple technique is useful in many other classroom situations where language is a prime concern. In teaching adults English or how to improve their communication skills, sketching can help the teacher in countless explanations. It can help the student, too, as he explores new facets of the English language.

A child who is mentally retarded is usually handicapped by an inability to verbalize. The teacher can utilize sketching in vocabulary lessons to give meaning quickly to words. This technique is helpful as a supplement to the use of pictures, because it is always available whereas a picture might not be, and because it can be immediately utilized. It can also be employed to show various forms or postures of objects or persons so that a child will not conceptualize erroneously (for example, A *ball* is always small and *red*).

American society depends greatly on graphic representation as a means of communication. Working drawings, assembly drawings, schemata, safety posters, and other techniques are used in the everyday world to communicate important messages to individuals in all walks of life. These drawings convey information using a limited number of words and a large number of shapes and forms. A highly industrialized nation makes demands on its citizens to interpret many kinds of visual representations of information and ideas. Therefore, it would seem feasible for classroom teachers to develop some degree of skill in using visual language as a means of expressing ideas to their students. The writers feel that skill in visualizing and interpreting these forms and shapes can be developed and enhanced at an early age. The school program should include provision for developing visual and perceptual skills when the child starts his formal education. In the classroom, these skills help the teacher clarify and simplify concept development, while preparing the child for the world of work in his later life.

Techniques

Sketching is in the realm of emotional and visual communication. Artistic talent cannot be taught, but the techniques needed to express feelings and ideas can be learned. Part of intelligence is the ability to perceive geometric forms and shapes in objects. In sketching, the ability to see relationships is called upon in almost every stroke. Many teachers say they lack artistic abilities or skills, when, in reality, they are deficient in the ability to perceive the basic elements of an object. The following pages will describe the information and techniques needed by the classroom teacher to improve his competency in sketching. It must be remembered that it is not the purpose of these directions to make artists of teachers but to provide them with skills to help them give concepts form, shape, and meaning.

The techniques described in this section illustrate how objects, or segments of one object, can be isolated in relationship to one of six basic shapes. An understanding of these and of the rhythms of line and points; the massing of forms; space, light, and shade; color and texture, and their dynamic interaction into balance; and of proportion, motion, pattern, scale, composition, and unity of design constitutes a grasp of the fine points of attractive and realistic drawing. The technique of cartoon drawing is also described, and the use of stick figures for rapid sketching is explained.

Drawing Objects

BASIC SHAPES. Sketching techniques can be simplified through the use of the following six basic shapes, or a modification of them, as illustrated in Figure 5–1. The basic forms in drawing are the rectangular prism, the cube, the cone, the pyramid, the cylinder, and the sphere. The most important of these is the rectangular prism.

Rectangular prisms are drawn in two ways. In the first method (see Figure 5–2), the prism is started with a rectangle, the lines of which are parallel and perpendicular to a base line. A second, parallel rectangle is drawn slightly to one side and slightly above the first. Then lines are made to connect the two.

In the second method (see Figure 5–3), the two rectangles are drawn with the lower lines at a 30° angle to the base line and are connected as shown.

It is important to realize that in both methods all lines running in the same direction must be parallel. When this rule of parallel lines is not followed, distortion results.

Figure 5–1 demonstrates how the basic rectangular prism can be utilized in developing other basic shapes. Figure 5–4 illustrates the steps involved in drawing the base circle of a cone or cylinder.

Draw a rectangle F, B, E, and J, as shown in Figure 5–4 top left. Locate center lines XY and WZ, as shown in Figure 5–4 top right. Draw two arcs, one between points XZ and the second between points WY, as illustrated in Figure 5–4 bottom left. Complete the circle by drawing the end arcs between XW and ZY, as shown in Figure 5–4 bottom right.

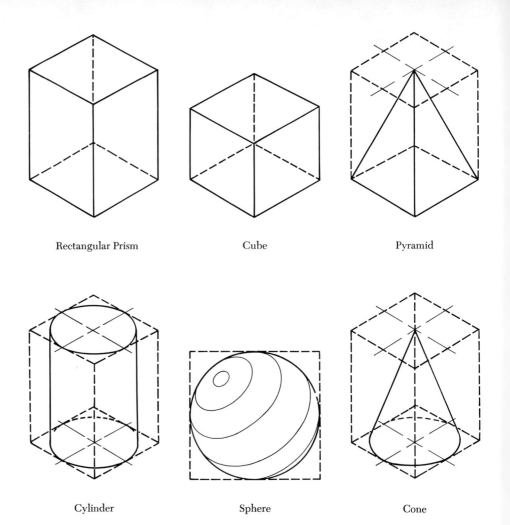

Rectangular Prism   Cube   Pyramid

Cylinder   Sphere   Cone

Figure 5–1. Basic shapes and their relationship to the rectangular prism.

Figure 5–2. Rectangular prism drawn by making a rectangle as the face surface and extending lines in either direction.

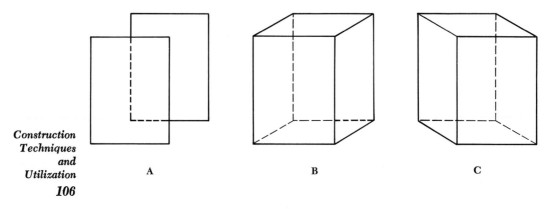

A   B   C

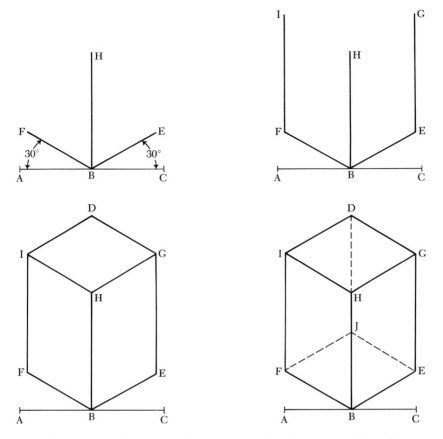

Figure 5–3. Rectangular prism showing two sides drawn at 30° angles from a vertical corner line.

Figure 5–4. Steps in drawing an elipse, the base for the cone and the cylinder.

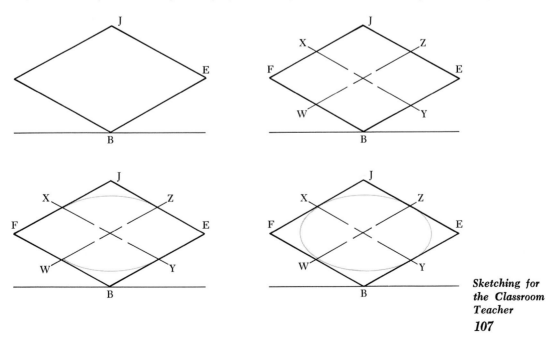

1. A single line represents only one dimension, that of length. With a line, an individual can express vertical, horizontal, diagonal, curved, and spiral movement. The first step necessary in drawing any object is being able to draw a line correctly. Figure 5–5(A) illustrates examples of the various expressions that can be achieved through line utilization.

2. Shape is represented by more than a single line and is two-dimensional in nature. A two-dimensional object has length and width; therefore, is absolutely flat with no dimension of depth, as illustrated in Figure 5–5(B). Note that when the area is completely surrounded by lines it is called shape.

3. Form is three-dimensional in nature and represented by length, width, and depth. Depth gives an object thickness, as illustrated in Figure 5–5(C). Form also changes the name of what is being drawn. The square and the triangle become a cube and a cone.

4. Figure 5–5(D) illustrates the utilization of the element of tone. Tone, or value, is represented by the lightness or darkness of the form. Tone is the over-all color of an object and it can be light, medium, or dark in value.

5. Figure 5–5(E) illustrates how the element of shading is utilized in basic sketching. This technique gives the object three-dimensional qualities be-

Figure 5–5. One-, two-, and three-dimensional shapes and their relationship to object drawing.

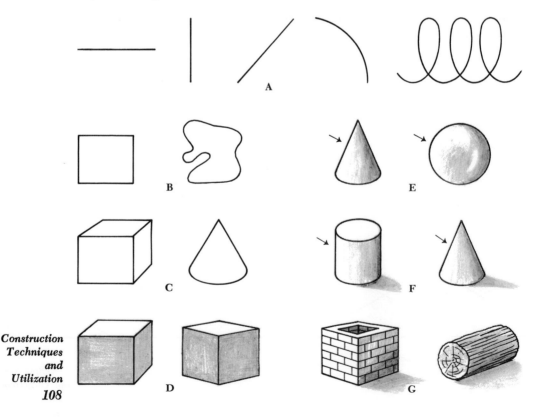

cause it suggests thickness. In any illustration or picture with several objects, the shading should be on the same side of all the forms.

6. Figure 5–5(F) illustrates how the element of shadow is utilized in basic sketching. A shadow shows the patch of darkness that is caused by the object blocking light. The size and shape of this shadow vary with the shape and with the size of the object and the distance of the light source. The shadow is on the same side of each object in the same picture.

7. Figure 5–5(G) illustrates how the element of texture can be utilized in basic sketching. Texture can be the most important element in object drawing. Texture changes the simple forms into things or objects that are recognizable. It indicates the roughness, smoothness, or design on a surface. Texture brings out the characteristics of the surface.

Familiar objects are the results of applying the previously stated simple sketching techniques to a desired object. When the anatomy of treatment is applied to the basic forms, the object becomes recognizable to the viewer. Figure 5–6 represents some of these basic shapes composed into familiar objects.

Sketching an object often requires the use of variations and combinations of the basic shapes. The illustrated barn is drawn from rectangular prisms and half prisms, whereas the silo is drawn from a combination of a cylinder and a cone. (See Figure 5–7.) Variations of the basic shapes are important when sketching objects from nature. Figure 5–8 shows the utilization of simple geometric shapes, combining or connecting these shapes into familiar objects.

Figure 5–6. Objects become familiar as a result of the anatomy of treatment.

Figure 5–7. A combination of basic shapes.

A cone becomes a tree or bundle of cornstalks.

Two circles and two curved lines form a pear.

Circles, ovals, and straight lines become simple animals.

Texture and shade make simple shapes and lines more realistic.

Figure 5–8. Steps in converting basic shapes into objects and animals.

111

PROCEDURE FOR GIVING VALUE TO YOUR ILLUSTRATION. Object drawing can be incorporated into a perspective drawing of a whole picture. Such an illustration will require the utilization of the basic elements employed in object drawing plus a few additional elements. The following material will present these additional elements:

1. Figure 5–9(A) represents the element of position. Position can create perspective because objects or parts of objects drawn nearer the bottom of the page appear closer.

2. Figure 5–9(B) illustrates the elements of size. Large objects or parts of objects also appear nearer than smaller objects. Figure 5–9(A) and (B) show both position and size. Objects that are near the observer are those that appear to be larger.

3. Figure 5–9(C) illustrates surface lines or texture. Surface lines give form to an object. The lines in the figure distinguish between closeness and distance. For example, if the curved line is drawn up, as in the left section of Figure 5–9(C), the surface appears closer to the observer. When the curved lines are drawn in a down position (right section), the surface will appear away from the observer.

4. Figure 5–9(D) illustrates the element of overlapping. Overlapping is similar to position in that it gives the illusion of distance. Lines hidden or cut off from view by other lines appear farther away.

5. The elements of shading and shadow in perspective drawing are similar to the technique used in object drawing. Shading and shadow are important in making the objects look realistic.

6. Figure 5–9(E) illustrates the element of density. Density is similar to shading, but it must be remembered that the darker values or tones appear nearer than the lighter values or tones. Those objects nearer the viewer should be drawn darker and with more detail than those objects farther from the viewer.

7. Figure 5–9(E) illustrates the element of foreshortening. Foreshortening is distorting slightly the shape of the object by placing horizontal lines closer together than would be normal. Notice in the illustration how lines x and y are foreshortened to give the appearance of distance. Does 1 or 2 look more like a lake?

PERSPECTIVE. Perspective gives shape and solidity to our visual world. It enables an individual to draw an object that appears to be three-dimensional. Perspective is an illusion that causes objects in the distance to appear to be smaller than objects nearby. For example, although we know that a chair 10 feet away is the same size as the one 2 feet away, the one closer appears larger. When you stand behind a row of buildings of exactly the same size, the buildings appear to get smaller and smaller in the distance.

Establishing Eye Level. The horizon is where the land or water and the sky meet. The eye level and horizon line are the same thing. Eye level depends on an individual's height above the ground. When starting to draw a picture, it is important to decide where the eye level is for a particular scene. A good way to establish eye level is to hold one hand, with fingers

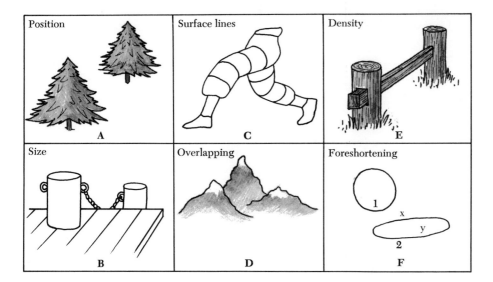

Figure 5–9. Pictures treated for value.

straight and together, directly below the eyes. By looking straight ahead, it is possible to see where the line falls on the object to be drawn. When planning a poster, picture, or a mural, establish an arbitrary horizontal line and a visual point before drawing any objects. Figure 5–10 illustrates how objects are drawn in a picture at different positions from a visual point.

One-Point Perspective. Perspective drawing is based on the principle of converging lines. Parallel lines go on forever and never meet, but the railroad tracks appear to converge at the horizon. The road appears to get narrower and narrower in the distance until its edges finally come together. The point where the lines appear to meet is called the vanishing point, no matter how many lines there are. Objects or scenes that are viewed head-on illustrate one-point perspective, as in the case of the block, Figure 5–11(B), and the highway, Figure 5–11(A). Only one set of parallel lines is involved, so only one vanishing point is needed.

Two-Point Perspective. Turning the block so it is viewed from a corner instead of head-on (see Figure 5–12), results in two sets of parallel lines, each leading away into the distance. Like the parallel lines in the one-point perspective, each set of parallel lines will have its own vanishing point; thus, the name, two-point perspective. The location of the vanishing points changes as the angle of the block is changed.

Determining the Proper Angle. When locating the vanishing points in two-point perspective (see Figure 5–12), be careful not to space the points too close together, as this will produce an exaggerated and unrealistic shape. Spacing vanishing points widely apart results in the most pleasant and natural view.

Three-Point Perspective. A tall building, when viewed from below, ap-

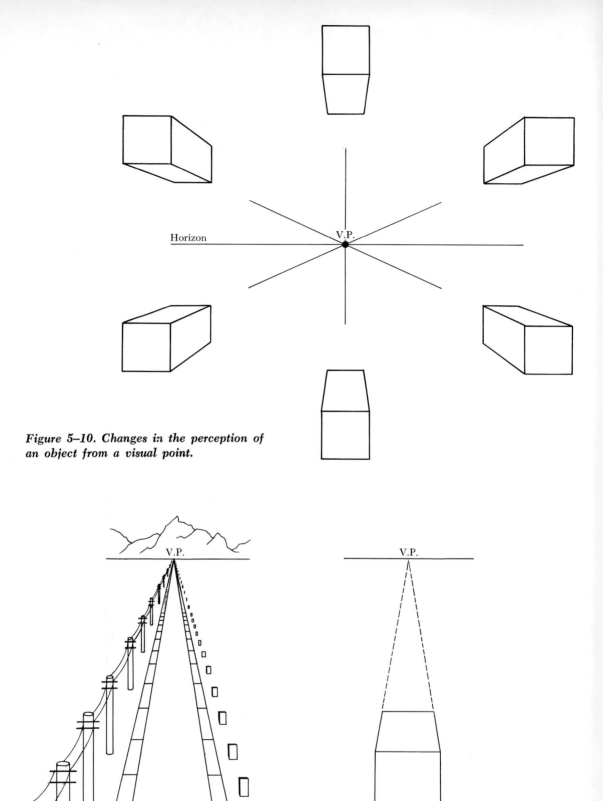

Figure 5–10. Changes in the perception of an object from a visual point.

Horizon

V.P.

V.P.

V.P.

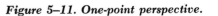

B

Figure 5–11. One-point perspective.

A

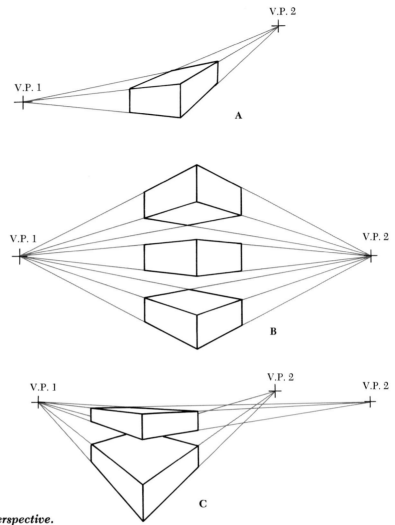

Figure 5–12. Two-point perspective.

pears to get smaller at the top. This establishes a third series of parallel lines converging on a vanishing point well above the horizon line. This is referred to as three-point perspective. (See Figure 5–13.)

COMPOSITION. Composition is an important element in planning any picture. The objects should be arranged to lead the eyes around the picture and not out of the picture. Figures 5–14(A) and (B) can result in a dull composition because the pictures are divided in half. Eye movement is important to interesting and exciting composition. A road can be used to lead eyes around the picture to other objects. [See Figure 5–14(C) and (D).] The road moves the eyes to the tree, and the tree leads the eyes into the sky. Other objects could be used to lead the eyes across the sky. The tree also blocks the eye movement from going off the edge of the paper.

Certain undesirable elements should be avoided. Objects drawn to the same size tend to divide the attention of the observer. Too many straight

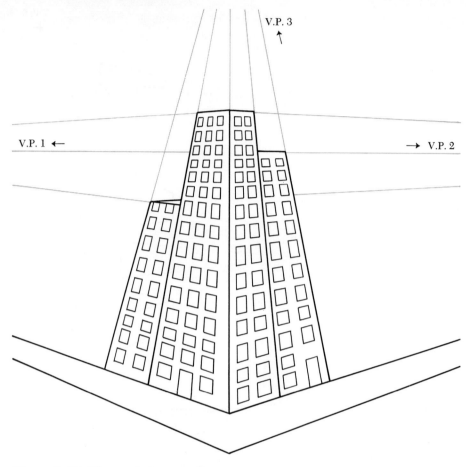

V.P. 3

V.P. 1 ←

→ V.P. 2

Figure 5–13. Three-point perspective.

Figure 5–14. Consideration must be given to eye movement. (A) and (B) are static; (C) and (D) are dynamic.

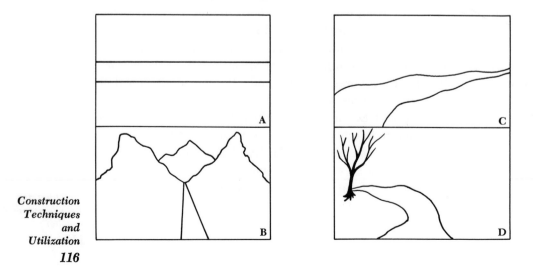

A

B

C

D

lines or a lack of tone value makes poor composition. Failure to observe the principles of perspective distorts the picture.

These, then, are the elements of clear, accurate, and interesting pictures: line, shape, space, tone, shading, texture, and perspective. Practice in blending them in compositions that also provide for movement and balance is the way to master sketching.

Short-cut methods are often applied through the use of cartoons or stick figures. These variations are discussed next.

Cartoons

It has been proved that at all age levels cartoons attract attention and arouse interest. Cartoons selected for a specific purpose and appropriate level of sophistication can provide the teacher with a tool that can be used to stimulate learning and change the instructional pace. They also provide the teacher with an excellent motivating device, and if used appropriately can open up a whole range of worthwhile learning activities.

The techniques described in this chapter for learning to draw cartoon people and simple animals have been used with success by the writers with undergraduate students and young children. The procedure for learning the technique can be compared with the teaching of writing or lettering where the formation of letters comes after the ability to make various strokes. For example, in manuscript writing it is important to learn how to make circles and straight lines before making letters.

CARTOON PEOPLE. Illustrations of people arouse interest, direct attention, and create empathy when used on bulletin boards, murals, reading charts, or other types of instructional materials. With a little ingenuity, many types of people can be drawn by teachers and pupils. People will add feeling, life, fun, and personality to materials as nothing else can. (See Figure 5–15.)

How to Draw Cartoon People

1. Draw an oval or a circle with a crayon or felt pen.
2. Draw a smaller circle or two dots for a nose in the center of the larger circle or oval.
3. Locate the eyes and draw two small dots to represent them.
4. Locate the mouth and draw a curved line to represent it.
5. Does the face look like one of those in Figure 5–16? Practice making different faces. Remember that a face can start with an oval or circle and facial expressions can be added by straight lines, circles, crescent shapes, and curved lines.
6. Make some changes in the characteristics of the faces. (See Figure 5–16.)
7. Eyebrows can be added by drawing loops over the eyes. (See Figure 5–17.)

A

B

118

C

D

Figure 5–15. Stimulating verbal learning with cartoons. Oral or written stories or lively social discussions can be motivated with such simple cartoons.

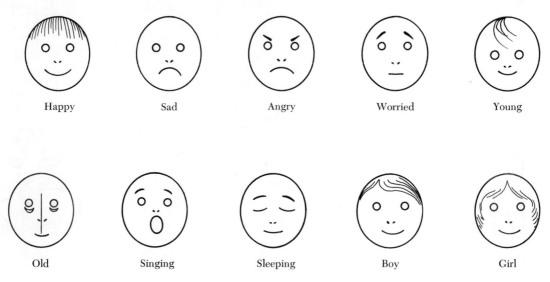

Happy   Sad   Angry   Worried   Young

Old   Singing   Sleeping   Boy   Girl

Figure 5–16. Simple lines create facial expressions.

Figure 5–17. Treatments that can be used to make the cartoon people look different.

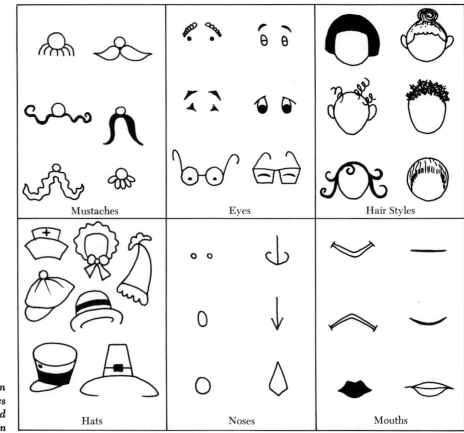

Mustaches   Eyes   Hair Styles

Hats   Noses   Mouths

8. A mustache can be added by using one of the examples shown in Figure 5–17. The reader can imagine other possibilities.

9. Add two circles to the sides of the head for ears, as in Figure 5–18(A).

10. Start again with a happy face. Add some long curved lines on the side of the face for hair, as in Figure 5–18(B). Also add small curved lines on the forehead for bangs.

11. Put a bow on top of the head by making a larger circle on either side of a smaller circle. Color can be added to the bow, the cheeks, the nose, and the hair.

12. The characteristics can be altered by using the suggestions for hair styles, eyes, noses, mustaches, hats, and mouths in Figure 5–17. For example, eyeglasses and loops for curls will make the face like a grandmother's as in Figure 5–18(C).

13. Make the neck of a man by adding two lines under the face. Draw a large circle for the body that will connect to the neck. Add legs and feet, arms and hands. (See Figure 5–19.) Arms and hands may be placed in various positions.

A   B   C

Figure 5–18. Treatments that can be used to make the face of a man, girl, or grandmother.

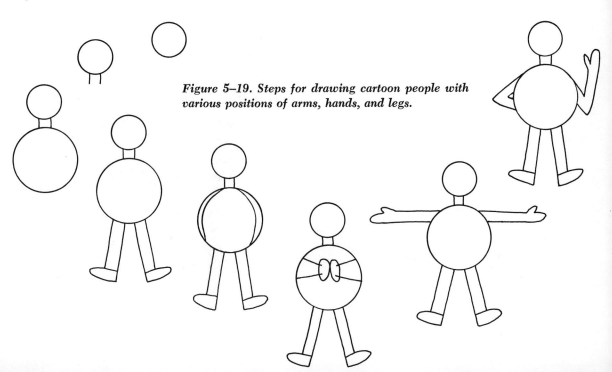

Figure 5–19. Steps for drawing cartoon people with various positions of arms, hands, and legs.

14. Decorate the cartoon man with clothing. Figure 5–20 illustrates some examples of the different types of clothing that can be used. Remember, color can make the clothing more attractive.

15. Make a cartoon girl. Make the neck of a girl by adding two lines under the face. Instead of drawing a circle for the body, draw a triangle for a dress. Use a short triangle for a small girl and a long triangle for a woman. (See Figure 5–21.)

16. Add arms, hands, legs, and shoes to the body.

17. Decorate the cartoon girl or woman with clothing. Figure 5–21 illustrates some examples of the different types of clothing that can be used. Use color if possible.

18. Figure 5–22 illustrates how these simple cartoon people can be uti-

Figure 5–20. Examples of clothing for male cartoon people.

Figure 5–21. Examples of clothing for female cartoon people.

lized by teachers and children to develop interesting and exciting instructional materials.

19. A variety of people can be made from geometric shapes. (See Figure 5–23.) Rectangles, triangles, and circles can be arranged and rearranged. Geometric shapes in a variety of sizes can be cut from construction paper by young children and then manipulated so that they form people. These same shapes can be used with the printing techniques to be described in Chapter 7 to create interesting greeting cards.

ANIMALS. Simple animals can be made with straight lines, curved lines, and circles. The simple forms can be used by the classroom teacher to communicate ideas to children. They help the teacher interpret and stimulate verbal information. This technique is also very effective when used by children to make posters, murals, and other instructional materials.

How to Draw Simple Animals

1. Select a pencil (soft lead), crayon, or felt pen that will work easily on drawing paper.
2. On a piece of scrap paper, practice drawing loops, straight lines, and curved lines, as in Figure 5–24(A).
3. Combine some of these loops and curved lines into some basic body shapes, of animals or insects as in Figure 5–24(B). Remember, these shapes are to be made into cartoon-type figures and not realistic-looking

Figure 5–22. *Cartoon people featured in instructional materials can be utilized to stimulate learning.*

What would Jean wear in the rain?...in the snow?

A

B

Can You Draw Your Father Doing His Job?

C

Figure 5–23. Geometric shapes can be used to draw cartoon people.

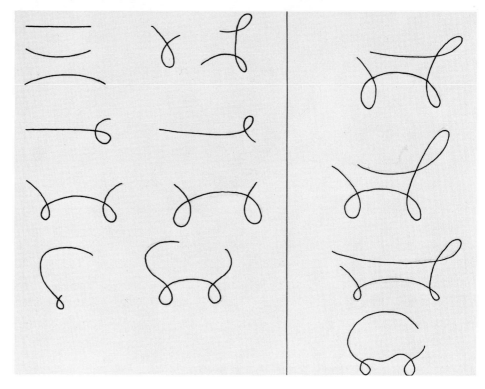

A

B

C

Figure 5–24. Steps in making cartoon animals.

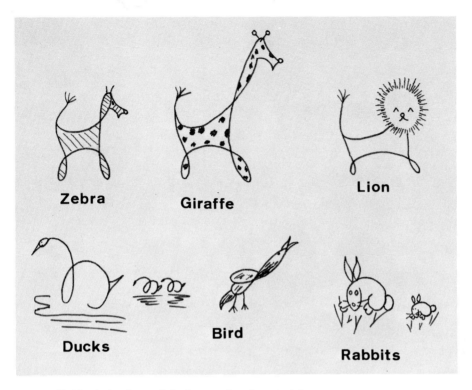

Figure 5–25. Animals used in instructional materials.

figures. The simple figure may be a butterfly, pig, giraffe, turtle, or dog. Think of such questions as the following when drawing the body:

a. Does it have a long body?
b. Does it have a long neck?
c. Is it fat like a pig?
d. Is it small like an ant?

4. Finish the body of the animal or insect by adding a head, tail, or other characteristics, as in Figure 5–24(C).
5. Figure 5–25 illustrates how these simple animals or insects can be utilized by teachers and children to develop exciting instructional materials.

Stick Figures

Stick figures are easy to draw and can function as satisfactory bodies without further adornment. They can show action and attitude with surprising effect, despite their simplicity. A little practice in drawing straight lines and circles will assist the beginner in learning to draw stick figures. This technique will enable anyone to draw an endless variety of human beings or animals performing various activities. A boy swimming or kicking a ball is an example. The stick figures can consist of single lines or they can include a few simple garments or features to give them additional character.

A

B

Figure 5–26. Animals used to stimulate oral or written expression.

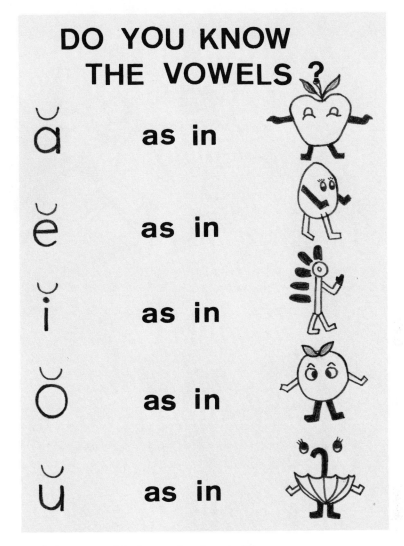

Figure 5–27. Stick figures used in instructional materials.

These simple stick figures can be used to add another dimension to verbal instruction. (See Figure 5–27.)

How to Draw Stick Figures

1. Draw the head and spine first in whatever position the situation calls for.
2. Add arms and legs to the body. These usually fall naturally into position.
3. Add those characteristics or features that help the stick figure convey a message. (See Figure 5–28.) For example, a skirt and long hair help distinguish female from male; size, clothing, and hair style help distinguish the child from the adult.

A

B

Figure 5–28. Simple additions to the stick figures bring out various characteristics.

130

APPLICATIONS

Language Arts

STORYTELLING. Storytelling can be developed through a simple sketching technique. The teacher sketches an outline shape, such as the body of a dog, fish, cat, or the like. He begins to question children about what the shape reminds them of. It is important that the teacher ask leading questions that bring out statements rather than single-word answers. From a simple shape or form, the teacher can develop a picture and the children can make up an imaginative story. Children thus have an opportunity to improve oral language skills by means of an imaginative method rather than one structured with predetermined answers.

PICTURE STORIES. Illustrations can be drawn and labeled to prepare kindergarten children to make the transition from reading pictures to reading words.

Teachers can sketch characters of a story as the plot begins to unfold. These illustrated characters help children understand and interpret the meaning of a story.

VOCABULARY DEVELOPMENT. Sketching is a way of telling and showing by the use of illustrations in place of words or actual objects. The teacher, instead of trying to define or clarify the meaning of a new word with hand movements and added verbal explanations, can draw an illustration to help explain the meaning. Figures 5–29 and 5–30 indicate how illustrations can convey an idea.

Many word meanings can be quickly brought out with sketching. An example would be the learning of the terms *homonyms, homographs,* and *homophones.* Children are often confused by the fact that some words of the same sound have different meanings and spellings. Visual representation can be used to make the meaning clear. (See Figure 5–30.) Heteronyms, words of the same spelling, but different in meaning and pronunciation, can also be clarified.

Science

RECORDING OBSERVATIONS. Insects, plants, and animals can be sketched as children study them in their natural environment. The sketch enables the child to record in visual as well as verbal language the reactions of insects, plants, and animals for later inquiry.

A sketched plan can be developed showing the results of experiments conducted on simple machines. Motion, space, and energy can be similarly diagramed. Words, then, are not the only tool used by scientists to record scientific information.

After a nature walk, children might use sketching as a summarizing activity. Certain items of nature could be sketched to illustrate the season of the year. When the children compare the sketches, they can explain what was happening in nature and why.

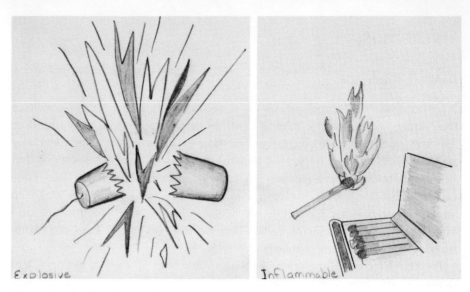

Explosive Inflammable

Figure 5–29. Sketching helps illustrate meaning.

Figure 5–30. Applications of simple sketching techniques to vocabulary development.

mail

male

nail

nail

flower

flour

pitcher

pitcher

132

Plants raised from seed in a primary classroom could be observed at regular intervals, and the changes recorded with sketches. Explanations of the changes could be developed along with the sketches.

Mathematics

SETS. Teachers may well use sketching in teaching lessons on sets, the union of sets, or the intersection of sets. Often, using simple sketches of familiar objects as the elements of the sets makes the concepts easier for the primary children to learn.

GEOMETRY. Geometry taught in the early elementary grades can be greatly facilitated by the quick sketching of basic shapes. Children's concepts of geometric shapes can be sketched for easy checking by the teacher. They can readily learn to draw geometric solids in perspective at the primary level.

Applications to Other Media

Simple sketching techniques can assist teachers in the development of attractive and stimulating instructional materials. Educational media should be used in the learning process to clarify or enrich instruction. Such use requires that the teacher identify a problem and then develop instructional materials that will clarify, simplify, and assist in the solution of it. Ideas for instruction cannot be limited to ready-made illustrations and materials. Meaningful instructional materials are likely to be generated if a teacher can develop imaginative and creative illustrations. Teachers with sketching ability do not need to limit their ideas to what is already on the market, but can create instructional materials unique to the solution of problems in their teaching situations.

TRANSPARENCIES. Transparencies provide the teacher with a medium for countless illustrations in all curriculum areas. When he is skillful in the sketching technique, he is not limited to prepared illustrations; thus, he gets far greater service from this useful electronic device. The children too can learn to prepare their own transparencies to illustrate their reports.

BULLETIN BOARDS AND DISPLAYS. The realization that the bulletin board display is a medium for involving pupil participation is important. By doing the planning and work under the guidance of the teacher, the children come to realize how much the schoolroom and learning are really their responsibilities.

Among the variations children may wish to use in creating their displays are drawings, stick figures, and cartoons. Sketching provides an effective method for illustrating the facts of science (insects, plants, or animals), periods of history on a time line, or geometric shapes and forms for developing mathematical concepts. Cartoons are real attention-getters and are excellent for explaining abstract concepts. They are especially useful in portraying the issues of politics.

MURALS. Murals represent a technique in which visual communications can be used to tell a story. Children can use cartoons, stick figures, and realistic shapes to develop some interesting concepts in social studies, history, science, geography, and health.

DIORAMAS. Dioramas are visual communications that combine three-dimensional objects with a background to make an event in history more meaningful to the child. Sketching is a useful means of preparing the background.

CONCLUSION

Sketching is easily mastered by acquiring facility with a few basic shapes and a few principles of composition and design. Representation through cartoons and stick figures makes it even easier.

The chief values of sketching are availability, immediacy, versatility, and adaptability. The teacher who has mastered the technique has visual resources always available. The blackboard, ever at hand, can be used at any time for a quick sketch to illustrate any concept. The overhead projector can be employed frequently and appropriately because the teacher has been able to prepare slides or transparencies quickly. The bulletin board can be filled with sketches or cartoons in short order. Murals, charts, or dioramas can be easily prepared. All of these actions can be performed by the children, too, after they have learned facility in drawing or cartooning. A learning aid full of quick meaning and fun as well, sketching is well worth developing.

LEARNING ACTIVITIES

1. Using the techniques for sketching objects, draw the six basic shapes.
   a. Combine any three basic shapes into a familiar object.
   b. Draw a house with a garage.
2. Draw examples of objects that will illustrate the following sketching elements:
   a. Size
   b. Position
   c. Surface lines
   d. Overlapping
   e. Shading
   f. Shadow
   g. Foreshortening
   h. Converging lines
3. Draw an object that will illustrate
   a. One-point perspective
   b. Two-point perspective
   c. Three-point perspective

4. Draw a dynamic composition utilizing the sketching techniques described in this chapter.

5. Using cartoon people, develop instructional materials that could be used in a learning situation to convey an idea or develop a concept in one of the following curriculum areas:
   a. Art
   b. Language Arts
   c. Reading
   d. Physical Education
   e. Mathematics
   f. Music
   g. Social Studies
   h. Science

6. Create some simple animals or insects that are different from those illustrated in this chapter. Combine these animals or insects into a composition or develop some teaching materials with them.

7. Stick figures can be used to add another dimension to instructional materials. Select a concept, and with stick figures develop instructional materials that will help simplify the teaching-learning process.

8. Develop a simple teaching plan of how these sketching techniques could be used with children in a learning situation:
   a. Cartoon people
   b. Simple animals or insects
   c. Stick figures

9. Try the following sketching techniques with children. Let the children practice the simple strokes before making any picture, poster, or mural.
   a. Cartoon people
   b. Simple animals or insects
   c. Stick figures

REFERENCES

BRACKMAN, WALTER. "Cartoons in the English Class," *Clearing House,* 30:268–270 (January 1956).

BROWN, J. W., LEWIS, R. B., AND HARCLEROAD, F. F. *Audiovisual Instruction.* (3rd ed.). New York: McGraw-Hill, 1969, pp. 424–427.

CUSTIS, L. "I Can't Draw People," *Arts & Activities,* 60:14–16 (January 1967).

ENTIN, J. W. "Using Cartoons in the Classroom," *Social Education,* 27:109 (May 1958).

GNAGY, JON. *New Art Book.* New York: Arthur Brown, 1950.

KNISLEY, WILLIAM H. "Let's Use Presty-Cartoons More," *Ohio Schools,* 40:23 (December 1962).

LAW, A. "How to Help Them Put Perspective in Their Pictures," *Grade Teacher,* 84:100–103 (October 1966).

LOWENFELD, VICTOR, AND BRITTAIN, LAMBERT. *Creative and Mental Growth,* 5th ed. New York: Macmillan, 1970.

NELSON, LESLIE W. *Instructional Aids.* Dubuque, Iowa: William C. Brown, 1958, pp. 123–140.

SINNEMA, J. R. "Cartoons in Conversation Classes," *Modern Language Journal,* 41:124–125 (March 1957).

SMITH, HAYDEN R., AND LEPTICH, DEAN A. "Effective Use of Cartoons in the Classroom," *Clearing House,* 38:38–41 (September 1963).

WEISS, HARVEY. *Pencil, Pen and Brush.* New York: William R. Scott, 1961.

WITTICH, WALTER A., AND SCHULLER, CHARLES F. *Audiovisual Materials: Their Nature and Use* (4th ed.). New York: Harper, 1967, pp. 153–168.

CHAPTER 6

Bulletin Boards *and* Displays As Stimulation *to* Learning

A conspicuous and vital part of any classroom is the bulletin board and the displays it contains. Careful planning is required to present pleasing, attractive, colorful displays, capable of communicating information. Pupils learn through their involvement in the planning and preparation of these exhibits as well as from viewing the completed project.

Bulletin boards have long been used in education. Many teachers, however, do not effectively utilize this important educational space in their classrooms. The mere posting of announcements or displays of outstanding work is not necessarily making the best use of the area. The promotion of competition among teachers for startling effects, a practice spurred by administrative evaluation of the teachers' output, might even be termed a misuse of the space. This practice is usually fostered when teachers are assigned the responsibility for decorating corridor display areas.

Effective and well-planned bulletin boards involving the cooperation of pupils and teachers can greatly contribute to the learning process. Careful planning within the classroom enables the display to fully communicate and stimulate the student's learning process. Pupil involvement in the complete process of bulletin board displays or in exhibit construction is necessary to derive the maximum advantage from display areas. The value in permitting the child to do research, planning, and designing lies in the stimulation it provides in his quest for knowledge.

The purposes of bulletin boards can be summarized as follows:

1. They promote learning of a concept by providing a clear-cut summary or explanation.
2. They guide and direct learning by a display of principles or directions.
3. They provide a creative learning experience in the planning and execution of the display.
4. They promote research in the gathering of information.

The teacher must decide how the display area is to be used to assist him in the teaching process. Is it going to be used as an instructional technique planned and executed by the teacher, or as a learning activity planned and executed by the child? If the former is indicated, the teacher must decide on the learning stage of the pupil and how the display area can be used to facilitate discrimination learning, concept formation, or problem solving, as indicated by the learning stages. The teacher must remember that active participation by the learner is more effective than the passive reception that usually accompanies the learner's observation of many displayed materials.

Educational psychologists emphasize the importance of active learning and the need for reinforced practice. Both of these learning principles can be satisfied in teacher-planned display areas if the materials can be manipulated and if devices are provided with which the child can check his response with the correct one. Figure 6–1 illustrates bulletin boards that involve the learner actively to different degrees. Figure 6–1(A) illustrates the principle of reinforced practice.

The second technique might be used to allow the child to develop a display as a final report for a research project or special assignment. This practice would bring into play the learning-style aspects of the decision-making model. The place of this assignment can be illustrated by the following activity:

The children have been exploring an aspect of Colonial life according to their interests. Each child is expected to prepare a report to give the class the highlights of his discoveries. The teacher considers the learning style of each child and the level of his performance and, following the decision-making model in Chapter 2, decides with the child on the mode of presentation. Some children will make oral reports, some will prepare dramas, some will bring in experts to make explanations, and some will utilize display areas for a visual report. The assignments have similar elements, no matter what the mode of presentation is. Each child must collect and read information related to his area of study, make decisions on which information or material best describes the topic, and make or collect materials. There may be some differences in the type of material collected, but all could use some verbal and some visual materials, even collecting or making three-dimensional materials. The major difference would be that the child using the display for his final report would not need to struggle at this point with the task of writing. For this child, writing can be developed at a different stage in the learning process and with a different emphasis. He may, however, be helped to utilize oral expression by explaining portions of his exhibit or by answering questions from the other children. Such oral activity would focus the child's attention on his work and do much to prevent nervousness and self-consciousness. The finished products of all the children can be evaluated by the class according to standards of presentation, appropriateness, and impact. For the child who is preparing the bulletin board, the teacher must affirm that the activity meets a sound educational goal that will be reinforced in the preparation of the bulletin board. He must be sure the child understands and agrees with the purpose of the display and be ready to assist with suggestions and sources of material. He must be convinced that the child's ability is equal to the task and that the child understands the procedures. He must then allow him to derive maximum benefit from the planning, preparation, and execution of the task by letting him work out the project for himself, stepping in only in response to a request or to evidence of frustration.

Figure 6–2 illustrates bulletin boards that might be final reports.

These two illustrations indicate alternative approaches that can be used in the teaching-learning process. They also illustrate how display areas can be used to facilitate learning. They require no expensive equipment or materials, only those found in most classrooms.

Principles of Bulletin Board or Display Preparation

1. *Define the purpose:* The teacher's educational objectives should be furthered through the use of the display. To simplify a complex idea or to explain an abstract idea might be the purpose.
2. *Create a dynamic headline:* The purpose of the headline is two-fold: to attract attention and to involve the reader. The impact of the display or bulletin board will be strengthened if the observer can identify himself with the material or situation in the display. A technique often used to involve the reader is to pose a question. For example, "How tall are you?" lets the reader involve himself to the point of answering the question and wondering why it was asked.

    Materials displayed without a dynamic headline lose effectiveness in their impact. The observer must try to figure out for himself the central idea, and thus his attention is not immediately focused on the objective of the display. It is therefore important that teachers and pupils work out imaginative, attention-getting headlines together.

    The following are examples of dynamic headlines suitable for use in the elementary grades:

Which One Are You?	Leap to Safety
Are Clouds Made of Cotton?	Are You a Fire Hazard?
Invisible World	Fight Fires with Care
Charge the Atmosphere	Stop! For Safety
Sleep all Winter!	What Shall I Wear Today?
Headed for Adventure	Mother Nature Welcomes Spring
Look! It's Easy	Swing into Reading

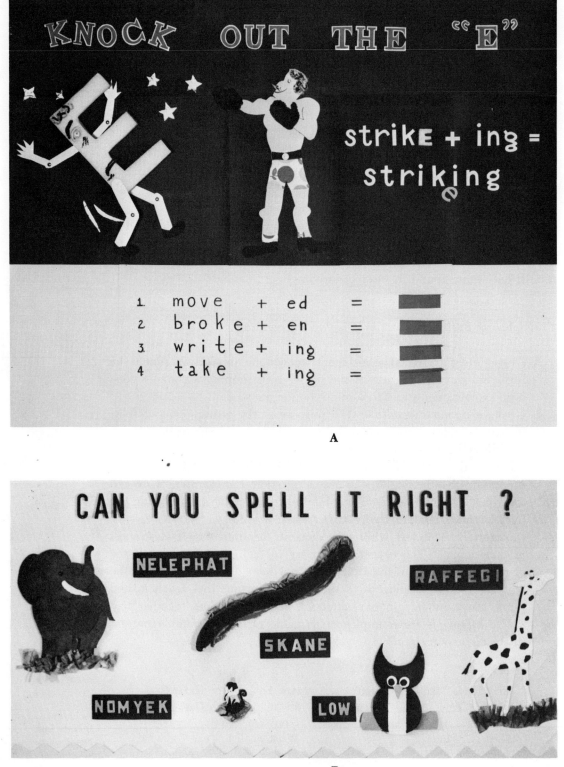

A

B

C

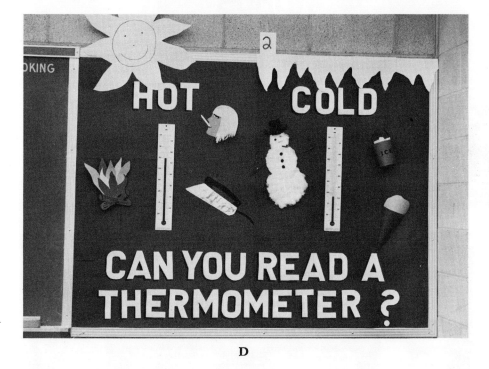

D

Figure 6–1. Bulletin boards that involve the viewer. (A) provides for immediate knowledge of response. (B) gives directions for construction. (C) provides an activity, the answers for which can be provided immediately for reinforcement. (D) asks a question but does not provide for reinforcement.

A

Figure 6–2. Examples of summarizing reports using varying degrees of verbalization.

B

142

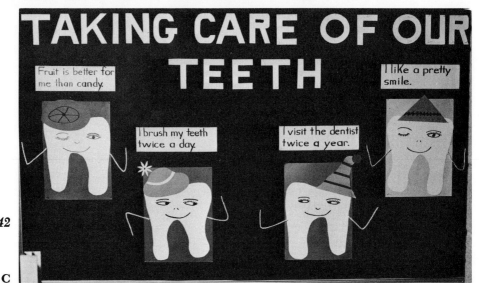

C

The use of image words in these headlines is particularly good for attention-getting. "Swing into Reading" brings up more dynamic mental pictures than "Going into Reading." The likeness of fluffy clouds to cotton wool is something young children have all observed. The headline, "Are Clouds Made of Cotton?" immediately brings up a familiar thought to wonder about. An imaginative and unusual use of telling words makes very effective headlines.

It is important to remember the ages of the children and their reading levels. The most startling headline would have little effect if children could not read it. To enlarge the scope of ideas for young children, illustrations can be used in place of words, like the rebus in the reading charts.

3. *Select the material and techniques needed to illustrate the headline:* Timely pictures, interesting stories, diagrams, small objects, cartoons, silhouettes, books, and pamphlets can be utilized to extend the interest established by the headline. Teachers should think of the following techniques when collecting materials:

   a. Puzzles will catch the thinking attention of the viewer.
   b. Interest is obtained when the display or bulletin board offers active participation by the viewer. For example, if a button can be pushed or a string pulled, children will be fascinated.
   c. Motion attracts attention. Simple electric display motors can be used to provide movement.
   d. Pockets that hold materials to be manipulated help involve the viewer in the display.

   It is important that the material used to illustrate the headline accomplish the second job; that is, keep the viewer interested in the material until the whole story of the display or bulletin board is told.

4. *Arrange the illustrative material effectively:* The arrangement of the material in the display should be in accordance with principles concerned with effects that are static or dynamic (that is, feelings of stillness or of movement) and effects of unity or of disunity and clutter. An effect of unity is a result of the careful selection of detail to bring out one concept. An effect of clutter is a result of too much detail or a lack of planned eye direction. It results in disunity and loss of impact. These principles will help to provide a unified and dynamic display:

   a. Establish a center of interest. An eye-catching center of interest is one of the most effective ways of attracting attention. Unusual shapes, contrasting colors, moving parts, and three-dimensional materials make important highlights. A careful arrangement of materials around the highlight will draw attention to the center of interest.
   b. Use white space for emphasis. It is important to break up solid blocks of materials because they are monotonous. A well-planned display or bulletin board has an equal amount of white space and display material. The designed area should be clear and simple with

a minimum of detail. Figures 6–3, 6–4, 6–5, and 6–6 illustrate some of the factors that should be considered in the planning of white spaces. Simplicity is important to good arrangement. Materials should be analyzed and evaluated for their effectiveness and appropriateness to the idea or concept being conveyed. An interesting topic is sometimes weakened because too many illustrations and written materials are used to explain a concept, creating a clutter that lacks direction for the viewer.

c. Provide balance. It might be imaginative to suppose that there is a strong human need for balance, because man moves about precariously on two legs, constantly making fine adjustments to keep his balance. Actually it is more realistic to assume that man has learned to appreciate balance by the many examples that he encounters through life. At any rate, he seems to feel comfortable with balanced arrangements in his environment. There are two kinds of balance: formal and informal. People prefer one over the other as a matter of taste. Informal balance lends itself more readily to a dynamic effect. Symmetrical or formal balance can be achieved by mentally drawing a vertical line in the middle of the display area. The objects presented on one side of the line are of the same size and shape as those presented on the other. One side is referred to as a mirror image of the other. Whenever anything is removed from one side, the design is no longer in balance. When something is added, rearranged, or deleted to give equal (imaginative) weight on both sides but no longer a mirror image, the display is then in informal balance.

These factors should be considered in providing for balance:

(1) Symmetrical or formal balance lends itself to a narrow display area, a formal subject area, or a permanent information area. It is suitable for presenting a difficult and complicated idea or concept because of its simplicity. Figure 6–3(A) and (B) illustrate materials arranged in formal balance.

(2) Informal balance attracts more attention and interest, and gives an imaginary feeling of movement or action. It is effective with simple ideas and concepts and lends itself to display areas that are wider than they are long. (See Figure 6–3(C) and (D).)

(3) A large object can be balanced by a smaller, shiny object.

(4) Large shapes can be balanced on the opposite side with many small shapes.

(5) Three-dimensional forms require concentrated areas of materials to offset their prominence.

d. Show similarity through unity: A good display needs unity to convey its meaning. Therefore, the importance of unity cannot be overemphasized in planning effective bulletin boards and displays. Teachers often have a natural feeling for unity. They are apt to put like with like, to group materials to illustrate a concept, and to line up pictures in a straight, orderly manner. But paradoxically the factors that create unity tend to destroy the eye-catching features of an attractive display. The individual constructing a bulletin board or display should make a judicious use of unusual shapes, colors, and textures, but prime importance should be placed on the unity of the display.

The achievement of unity can be effected by applying these directions:

(1) Emphasize one important item more than any other. Color, size, subject matter, or shape can be used to make one object or illustration more prominent than the other components of the display.

(2) Tie the objects together; yarn, rope, string, or paper strips can be placed around, under, and over illustrations to tie them literally. But the eye must be able to do it figuratively.

(3) Prepare an unusual background.

Figure 6–4(A) illustrates material used in an arrangement that makes the display monotonous to look at. Figure 6–4(B) shows the same shapes arranged in a sequence that is of interest because it has high contrast.

Figure 6–5(A) shows a display that attracts little attention because the materials are scattered and lack form or unity. The material in Figure 6–5(B) illustrates how the material can be tied together into a display that has unity. Unity is obtained in Figure 6–5(B) by using a tight corner-to-corner arrangement. The white space around the edges serves to frame the display and give it unity.

Figure 6–6 illustrates a display that is cluttered. It is important to evaluate materials, and select only the most appropriate. Figures 6–3(B), 6–4(B), and 6–5(B) show examples of material arranged in a clear and simple manner.

e. Plan for eye movement: The arrangement of display materials should add to and clarify the headline. Materials should be arranged so that they guide the viewer's eye movements around the display in an orderly and logical sequence. The well-planned layout or design should be arranged in such a manner that the materials will be viewed in a predetermined sequence to tell a complete story. Figure 6–7 illustrates some of the important factors to be considered in arranging materials for a bulletin board or display. It is of value to remember that balance and unity cannot be forsaken for eye movement.

In Figure 6–7(A), the eyes are directed to the center of the display. The arrangement lacks a sequence to guide the viewer around the display. Something needs to be added to give the eye a sequence to follow.

In Figure 6–7(B), the eyes move from the lower left-hand corner to the lower right-hand corner. However, the movement requires the eye to jump from the heading without direction to the starting point of the sequence. A little more attention to eye movement would have made the story more easily understood.

The shapes in Figure 6–8 tend to give direction to the display. The eye is attracted by the unsual shapes, but the line assists in

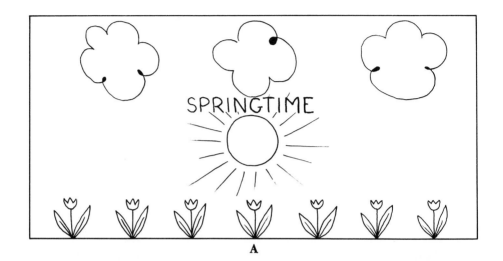

A

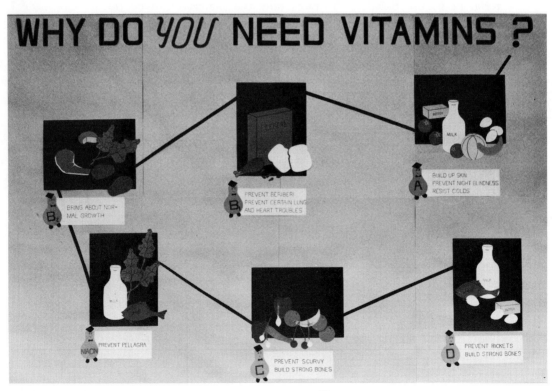

B

guiding the viewer around the material in logical sequence. Many variations of the path of eye movement such as an L, an O, or an inverted Z pattern, can be used to plan a layout. However, the design must be quite simple. These common shapes should be used as beginning ideas only, and the pattern should be considered imaginary. It is only an aid to the planner in arranging the material.

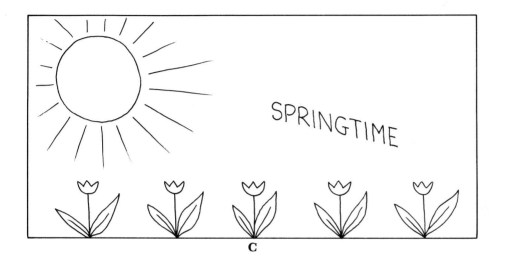

C

D

Figure 6–3. Diagrams and applications of formal and informal balance.

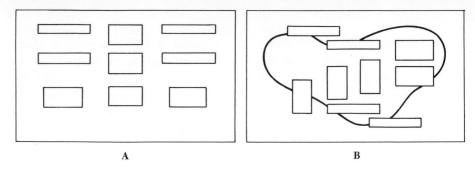

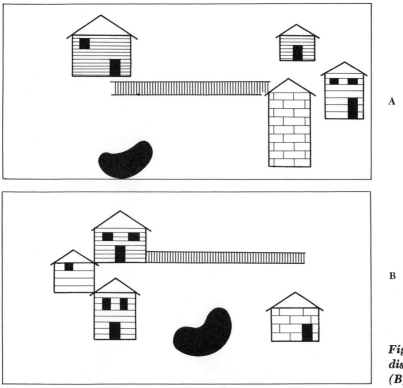

Figure 6–4. Diagrams of static (A) and dynamic (B) arrangements.

Figure 6–5. Diagrams of disunified (A) and unified (B) arrangements.

Figure 6–6. Too much material destroys the purpose.

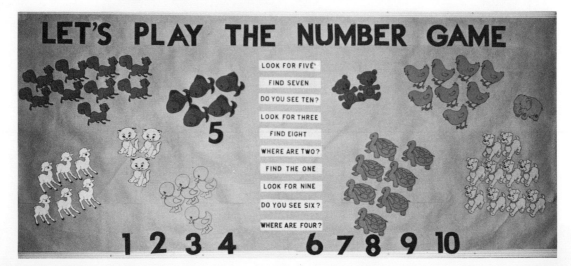

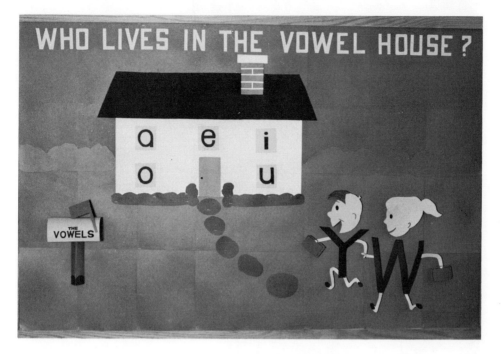

A

B

Figure 6–7. Bulletin boards with less than adequate provision for eye movement.

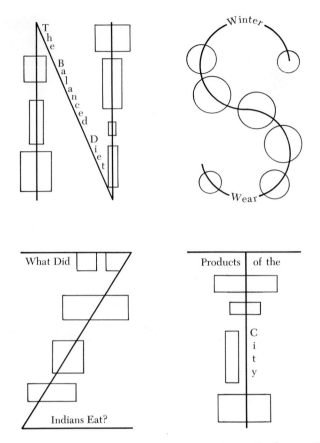

Figure 6–8. Diagramatic representations of schemes for eye movement.

In planning the path for the viewer's eye, it should be remembered that, from habit, individuals read from left to right. Copy may be used to explain material, but it can also be used to guide the viewer around the display in logical sequence. The copy can be placed on a curve, on a slant, or on a horizontal plane, but these patterns should not interfere with the readability of the copy.

f. Give special attention to the position of forms and figures: The direction in which the animals or figures are facing tends to guide the eye from one object to the next. Figure 6–9 illustrates the use of an animal to guide the viewer's eye.

5. *Utilize color:* Young children seem to like bright colors; therefore, a judicious use of color can be employed to attract attention and interest. Strong colors seem to flicker when in combinations. For example, bright red letters used on a blue-purple background would result in a flickering effect. This technique can be used as an eye-catcher, but if overdone, it will result in a display that is difficult to view. It is usually recommended that soft or dull colors be combined with bright colors in planning a display.

Figure 6–9. The animals' positions guide the viewers' eye direction.

Colors can be used to direct the eyes to various parts of a display. For example, a brilliant color used only twice on one display will tie these points together. A bright color next to a slightly dull surface that is next to a duller surface will direct the eyes in an orderly sequence around the board. The same color sequence can also be used to illustrate the relationship between ideas.

6. *Add texture to make the display interesting:* Texture can be used to give displayed materials a feeling of three dimensions or reality. Variations in texture cause individuals to get involved in the display. Many techniques can be used to give the display material an interesting texture. Sandpaper for the roof of a building or flocking for the fur of an animal will help make the displayed material interesting.

APPLICATIONS

The learning experience is the *raison d'être* for the bulletin board, and pupil participation is the key to the learning experience. The most efficient use of bulletin board space entails making the display an integral part of the classroom learning activities and giving the pupils an active role in creating and using the display. The ways of achieving this end are numerous.

Language Arts

In beginning reading, pupils often have difficulty distinguishing between b and d and require much practice in auditory and visual discrimination between them. The teacher might prepare a bulletin board to help provide this practice. "Can You Tell Us Apart?" (b and d can narrate for themselves, with the teacher reading their lines.) The material would include illustrations of upper and lower case forms ("Hi! I'm the letter b. I usually

look like this: **b** . Sometimes I dress up and look like this: **B** ") It would also show objects the names of which include the sound of the letter

("You can hear me in the beginning of: ball   bat   bell

book.   You can hear me in the middle of: bubble
    table   stable   rubbers.   You can hear me at the end
of: tub   doorknob   curb.")

Once this had been done for both letters, the pupils would be challenged to look over first a series of illustrations and then a series of words and to put a red star under the pictures or words with the b sounds in them and a blue star under those with d in them. After this lesson had been completed, the pictures and words in the exercise might be altered to give additional practice. In any case, the display would be a convenient reminder of the differences between the two letters.

Mathematics in the Primary Grades

A bulletin board display might be helpful in the pupils' discovery of classes of plane figures and their characteristics. Before an appropriate geometry lesson, the teacher might set up a display ("Shape Up! Know the Shapes Around You!") grouping the ellipses, the triangles, and the quadrilaterals into families. During succeeding geometry lessons, the pupils would be invited to add descriptions of each family to the bulletin board; they would do so by working with plane figures to discover what makes a triangle a triangle, and so on. Similarly, they would be encouraged to describe different members of the families and to discover what makes an isosceles triangle isosceles ("I'm a special △ called an isosceles △; do you know what makes me special?"), an equilateral triangle equilateral, and so on. Here, challenge to complete the display helps motivate the pupils, while the figures and classifications given provide background information.

Science

If the class is studying metamorphosis in the lower forms of life, the teacher might combine a variety of media in the introduction of the topic. He might write and read aloud to the class a story about an unknowing little boy who brings home a tadpole for a pet and soon discovers that his tadpole looks different every day. The story would leave unanswered the questions about this change; pupils might discuss possible answers themselves. Then the teacher would present his bulletin board in answer to the question: "What happened to Jimmy's tadpole?" The display would illustrate the successive stages of metamorphosis from tadpole to frog. If, at this point, the class were fortunate enough to see a live tadpole, the display would include a progress chart on which the development of the tadpole ("What's Happening to Our Tadpole?") would be recorded.

Social Studies

In a primary-grade social studies class, discussion stimulates interest in exploring the neighborhood. A group decides to make a display of the community in which they live. They want their display to be in bulletin board form. They decide to do a physical representation of the neighborhood. Perhaps their first step is to procure a map of the area from their town hall. Considering that such maps are infrequently updated, additions may have to be made. The group can examine the area by checking the accuracy of the map in naming streets, in adding new highways, and so on. Stores, recreation areas, and housing sites would augment the map. The actual physical representation of the community will be preceded by making an outline map of the area. The information gathered will then be evaluated and analyzed for value in conveying concepts about the community and its functions. The final result is the prideful product of the group in their display, an increased knowledge of the community, whetted interest in map making, and experience in gathering information and in the skill of selectivity.

In a middle-grade classroom, the pupils themselves might set up and alter appropriately a continuous display that varies with the area under study. After studying a country, for example, they would decide on several categories under which they could class their knowledge of its governmental system, its economic system, its technical resources, its history, and its aesthetic values and way of life. They could then choose and classify the vital information to be used in the display. With the teacher guiding them in the principles of layout, lettering, and the like, the pupils would then set up the display themselves. They might want to use a very general theme-title that could be retained for succeeding displays, for example, "Ready, Set, Go . . . to (Sweden, Japan, Egypt, and so on)," illustrated appropriately. Therefore, they would follow the pattern of procedure, simply reevaluating and, perhaps, altering their categories and layouts as necessary.

The same ideas might be adapted to a current events bulletin board. With a general theme-title such as, "Here's the Scoop!" a news bulletin board could be assigned to two groups who would alternate jobs: one group would bring in news articles, either actual or written up from radio or TV, and the other would screen the articles for importance and accuracy. The first group would bring in its contributions, the class would discuss their implications, and the second group would make the decision on the display materials. The entire class would decide which of the previous day's articles should be kept on file for further reference. Such articles might be retained as part of the display if they were placed in a pocket representing the brief-case of a reporter in one of the lower corners of the board. These articles would be brought into succeeding discussions. In this way, the pupils would better learn to perceive the continuities, the causes, and effects in world events.

Music

Even in the fine arts, the bulletin board can be an integral part of the learning experience. In music, a teacher might set up a display that would include a large staff, a toy xylophone, and a piano. On the staff might be placed "notes" (made of rubber, cork, styrofoam, or the like), painted different colors, that the pupils would be challenged to play with the instruments. The notes might be movable so that viewers would be invited to compose their own songs. (See Figure 6–10.)

CONCLUSION

The bulletin board is not merely an item of decoration or of challenge to other teachers. It is a learning aid that is unique in its ability to focus on one aspect of any subject and strike home with a telling point. Its usefulness as a synthesizing or summarizing aid is important. It relies on impact and involvement to emphasize and clarify its challenging headlines. Careful planning and work should go into its preparation, but it should never be an end in itself; furthermore, the time spent on it should be commensurate with the learning values it provides.

In bulletin board preparation, techniques of layout, lettering, and sketching are utilized. Therefore as a technique itself, it combines nicely all the principles discussed thus far in this section.

Figure 6–10. Bulletin boards can involve the viewer in many curriculum areas.

LEARNING ACTIVITIES

1. Diagram a bulletin board in formal balance and one in informal balance. Give a headline for each.
2. Evaluate any of the bulletin boards pictured in this section utilizing the purpose of bulletin boards and the principles of layout and lettering.
3. Describe a class activity that might culminate in a bulletin board display.
   a. Tell how the display would be planned and executed.
   b. Justify the use of the bulletin board by giving the values to be derived.
4. List five headlines that might be used in connection with any particular social studies or science unit or topic—for example, clean air or magnetism.

REFERENCES

BURGERT, ROBERT H., AND MEADOWS, ELINOR S. *Bulletin Board Ideas.* Dansville, N.Y.: F. A. Owen, 1960.

EAST, MARJORIE, AND DALE, EDGAR. *Display for Learning.* New York: Holt, 1952.

HORN, G. *Bulletin Boards*. New York: Reinhold, 1962.

JOHNSON, DONOVAN A., AND LUND, CHARLES H. *Bulletin Board Displays for Mathematics*. Belmont, Calif.: Dickenson, 1967.

KOSKEY, THOMAS A. *Baited-Bulletin Boards*. San Francisco: Fearon, 1954.

—. *Bulletin Boards for Holidays*. San Francisco: Fearon, 1958.

MATHRE, T. *Creative Bulletin Boards*. Minneapolis: Denison, 1962.

PETRONIA, SISTER MARY. *Bulletin Boards for the New Math*. Dansville, N.Y.: F. A. Owen, 1965.

RANDALL, R. *Bulletin Boards and Displays*. Philadelphia: F. A. Davis, 1962.

WESELOH, A. E. Z. *Bulletin Boards*. San Francisco: Fearon, 1959.

WITTICH, WALTER A., AND SCHULLER, CHARLES F. *Audiovisual Materials: Their Nature and Use* (4th ed.). New York: Harper, 1967, pp. 195–222.

CHAPTER 7

Printing, A Valuable Learning Tool

Printing is a process of prime importance in education. The invention of the printing press and movable type were the first great breakthroughs in the communication field. These developments led to a completely new technique of recording history and passing information on to the subsequent generations. In addition to the impact of printed material on education, a vast influence beyond the scope of this book, there is a phase of printing that enables teachers and pupils to make learning devices and to understand in an elementary way what printing is. This phase is concerned with carving a design on various everyday articles and, through a medium such as ink or paint, transferring the design and replicating it on such materials as paper or cloth.

The writers have seen teachers construct perception cards for mathematics by cutting out circles from construction paper and pasting them on a sheet of paper. The circles were uneven and time-consuming to cut out. The process can be hastened by using one of the printing techniques explained in the following pages. For example, a 1-inch dowel with tempera paint could be used to print several circles on a sheet of paper. This process, stick printing, can even be handled by children in the first grade. It is important to remember that printing allows the reproduction of shapes, designs, and figures with accuracy and speed.

Linoleum, cardboard, vegetable, stick, leaf, and sponge printing can be utilized in the production of interesting materials for communication. Greeting cards, flash cards, graphs, maps, and charts can be constructed using these suggested printing techniques. The thing that must be remembered about printing is that it means reproducing more than one copy from the original form. The writers have seen children spend hours making a linoleum block and then print one card for a grade. This procedure gives the child little insight into the printing process. In fact, it can be considered a misuse of linoleum printing and may be one reason why teachers have not made greater use of printing techniques in developing communicative materials. This most important of the printing methods is considered first. The tools and materials needed and the process are described in detail. It is hoped that mastery of this technique and the others described will open the way to the easy production of materials that, when integrated with the learning experience, will provide new ways for children to express themselves and that will become useful learning devices. Suggested ways of applying the various printing techniques are explained too.

PRINTING TECHNIQUES

Linoleum Block Printing

1. *Tools and Materials for Printing*
   a. *Linoleum Cutters:* The cutters are used for gouging away surface areas that are not to be printed. A set of linoleum cutters usually consists of a handle and five cutters.
   (1) *Handle:* The handle holds the various blades and helps to control the force and direction of the cutter. It is flattened on the underside to prevent the tool from rolling off the bench, thus protecting the cutting edges of the blades and keeping the tool in the proper position for grasping at all times.
   (2) *Blades:* The blades have various shapes and names and fit into the handle for use as needed:

   No. 1   Liner for small work and detail
   No. 2   V-shaped gouge for sharp detail and outline
   No. 3   Large liner for large work and bold outline
   No. 4   U-shaped gouge for flat gouging and lettering (not found in all sets)
   No. 5   Large gouge for routing or removing the large open areas or the background down to the burlap
   No. 6   Knife for straight cutting

   b. *Bench hook:* The bench hook (see Figure 7–1) is a device for holding the linoleum block secure while cutting a design. It should be used so that the idle hand can be kept away from the cutting edge, thus reducing the danger of serious injury.
   c. *Brayer or roller:* The brayer is used for applying ink to the surface being printed.
   d. *Printing inks:* The two basic types of inks used in schools for print-

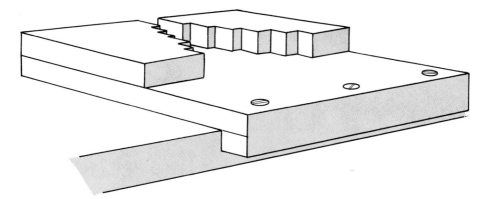

Figure 7–1. Bench hook made in a classroom.

ing are water-based and oil-based inks. Because water-based inks make the cleaning of tools and hands easier, they are more appropriate for young children to use. However, water-based inks should not be used on surfaces exposed to water, because they wash off. Water-based inks do not penetrate oil, a factor that makes them difficult to apply to a surface that has been handled, because of the oil from the operator's hand.

Type of Ink	Type of Container	Solvent	Printing Surface Recommended
Water-based inks:	Tube	Water	Paper, Cork
Oil-based inks: Block Printing Ink	Tube	Turpentine	Paper or Cloth
Printer's Ink	Tube Cans (Fraction of a pound)	Turpentine	Paper or Cloth

For vegetable, string, and stick printing, tempera paints should be used instead of inks. For devices made with the use of the brayer, ink is the medium usually applied.

e. *Materials to be imprinted:*
   (1) Paper
       Newsprint
       Drawing paper
       Construction paper
       Wrapping paper
       Japanese rice paper
       Special block printing paper

(2) Cloth
>Linens
>Cotton
>>Sail cloth
>>Indian head
>>Unbleached muslin
>Burlap

f. *Printing pad:* An inexpensive printing pad can be constructed using the following materials and procedures:

(1) *Base:* A piece of ½-inch plywood can be used. The length and width are related to the size and nature of the material to be imprinted.

(2) *Padding material for base:* Felt, a woolen block, or foam rubber can be used. The padding material should be about ¼-inch in thickness and the same length and width as the plywood base.

(3) *Cover:* A cover is made from a piece of unbleached muslin that should be 1 inch longer and wider than the plywood.

(4) *Assembly:* Apply glue to the top of the plywood base.

Place the padding material on the glued surface and apply pressure, making sure that the material is smooth and flat.

Place the unbleached muslin on top of the pad and fold it over the sides of the base to form a cover. (See Figure 7–2.) Thumbtacks can be used to secure the cover to the sides of the base. Tacking enables the cover to be changed when it becomes dirty.

g. *Inking surface:* A flat nonporous surface on which ink can be rolled to obtain an even coat of ink on the roller of the brayer is often advisable. The inking surface can be metal, hardboard, cardboard (shellac coated), or plastic.

h. *Battleship linoleum:* Battleship linoleum comes in white, tan, and green. It is a fine-textured and resilient substance possessing these qualities for printing:

Figure 7–2. A homemade printing pad.

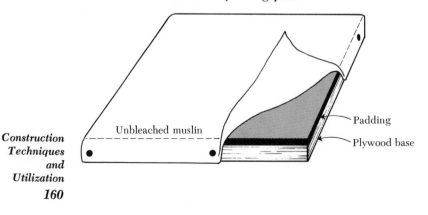

Unbleached muslin
Padding
Plywood base

(1) It does not chip or split easily.

(2) It does not dry out after long periods of time.

(3) It can be glued to wood.

(4) It can withstand rough treatment.

Battleship linoleum can be purchased in these ways:

(1) Mounted on wooden blocks in a variety of sizes

(2) Sheet form (unmounted), usually sold by the square yard

(3) Scrap pieces, secured from a local floor-covering outlet

2. *Safety considerations:* Teachers should consider the pupil's psychomotor behavior before allowing the use of any pointed or sharp tools. Children within a given grade or age group may vary greatly because of their previous experience with tools and equipment either in school or at home. With today's emphasis on the individual, the authors feel that the teacher should decide upon the readiness level of each child.

3. *Directions for preparation of copy to be printed:*

a. The copy for a linoleum block should be simple and consist of heavy lines and solid areas. Fine lines are difficult to carve and will break down under the heavy pressure of printing. Figure 7–3 illustrates good and poor examples of copy for a block print.

Solid Areas

Figure 7–3. Good and poor copy for a block print contrasted.

Fine Lines

b. The design can be an original, or it can be copied from a picture.

c. There are three basic techniques for preparing copy:

(1) *Silhouette:* A silhouette is a design in which all parts are printed in solid masses or profiles, with no attempt to show detail. Figure 7–4(A) is an example of a silhouette in linoleum block printing.

(2) *Intaglio:* Intaglio is just the reverse of silhouette; the design is cut away leaving the background to print. Figure 7–4(B) is an example of an intaglio print.

(3) *Outline:* In the outline technique, the design is represented by a single line, the shape of the design. Figure 7–4(C) illustrates how the surface is removed from both sides of the desired line. Care should be taken not to carve the lines too finely because they will break down.

d. Linoleum blocks must be carved in the negative (that is, in reverse) in order to produce a positive impression. Hence, the original copy from which the block will be made must be transferred into the negative before the carving is undertaken.

e. To make the negative print, a sheet of carbon paper is placed face up under the copy or design. With the corners fastened with masking tape, all the lines are traced. The carbon impression on the back of the sheet will be in the negative, as shown in Figure 7–5(A). The design will face in an opposite direction as the sheet is turned over. If the copy is made on transparent paper, it will need only to be turned over to be in the negative, as shown in Figure 7–5(B). Figure 7–5(C) illustrates a piece of transparent paper in the reverse. If the original is not to be destroyed, a copy can be made on opaque paper by tracing the original design on a piece of transparent paper and turning it over.

f. The design is transferred to the linoleum block for carving by plac-

Figure 7–4. Examples of the three techniques used in carving blocks.

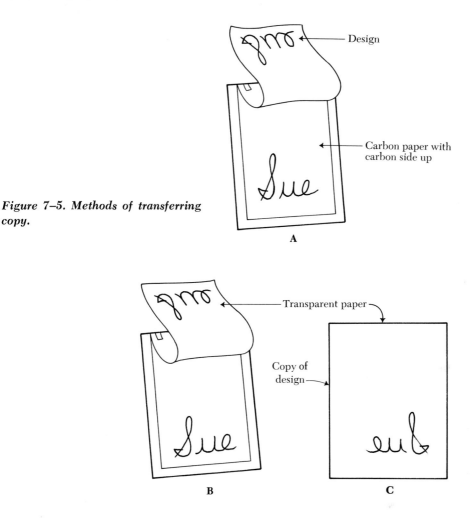

Figure 7–5. Methods of transferring copy.

ing a carbon sheet, face down, over the block and placing the copy, negative side up, over the carbon sheet. By placing the negative side up, the block will be carved in the negative, as shown in Figure 7–6(A); hence, it will print in the positive.

g. Secure the corners of both the carbon paper and the copy to the block with masking tape to prevent movement while tracing the design. If the design should be moved while being traced, the design will not be accurate or one part will not line up with another part.

h. Proceed to trace the design on the block, leaving ample margins. Then remove the copy and the carbon paper. The traced design should be identical with the original copy, and the lines should be dark and clear.

4. *Procedure for Carving a Linoleum Block:*

a. Place the block on the bench hook, as shown in Figure 7–7. This precaution will enable the block to be turned in any position so that the operator can always push the linoleum cutter away from himself.

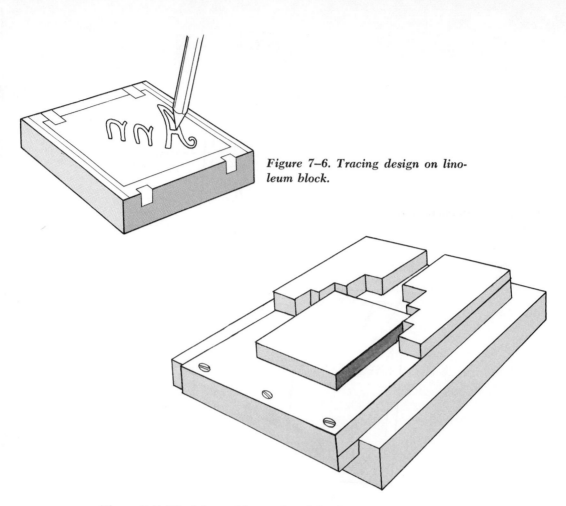

*Figure 7–6. Tracing design on lino-
leum block.*

Figure 7–7. Block in position on bench hook.

b. The first operation in the actual carving of the block is making a shallow cut around the entire design with the smallest V-shaped cutting tool, which is called a veiner. Grasp the block cutter firmly in the right hand. With the forefinger extended over the blade, push the blade forward. The outsides of the lines are followed with a smooth even pressure, making an even trough. This outlining operation is done to make the design stand out from the background or to separate the design from the background before the carbon lines wear off.

c. When the outlining has been completed, take a gouge, a large U-shaped tool used for taking large cuts and routing, and remove the large open spaces or the background down to the burlap, as shown in Figure 7–8. If the design is not cut down to the burlap, parts of the background will print. Great care must be taken to follow the outline made with the veiner and not to cut into any part of the design.

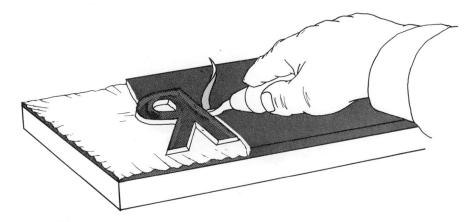

Figure 7–8. Gouging out the design.

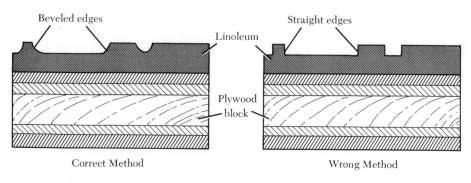

Beveled edges   Straight edges

Linoleum

Plywood block

Correct Method   Wrong Method

Figure 7–9. Cross section of cut block.

d. The design should be beveled away from the surface to give added strength and stability to the printing surface. Lines that are carved straight up and down are weak and will soon break down under the heavy pressure of printing. Note the illustration showing beveled and straight edges. (See Figure 7–9.)

e. When carving into the corners of the design, the tool should be driven carefully toward the corner from each direction so that the cuts will meet exactly at the point of intersection of the lines. This will make a clean sharp cut at the corners.

f. The block should be cut down to the burlap in large open spaces and at the edges, as shown in Figure 7–10. This process is called routing. The farther from a printing surface, the deeper the cut should be to prevent the background from picking up ink when the block is printed.

g. The block may need additional trimming and routing after the first impression is taken to eliminate any rough edges.

Printing,
A Valuable
Learning Tool

165

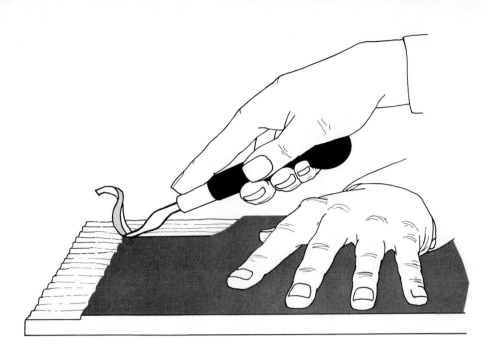

Figure 7–10. The routing process.

h. Neatness, patience, and care should be exercised while cutting. A careless stroke or slip of a tool can ruin a block. It is far easier to cut the lines right in the first outlining of the design than it is to correct carelessly made, uneven lines after they are once cut into the linoleum. Always keep your free hand away from the knife so it will not be hit if the knife should slip.

5. *Procedure for Printing:*

   a. Select ink in the desired color and apply a small amount (about the size of three peas) to a sheet of hardboard or metal. Remember that light colors do not print well over dark-colored materials.

   b. Roll the ink out into a thin film on the hardboard or metal surface, using the brayer.

   c. Place the material (paper, cloth, cardboard, or the like) to be imprinted on the pad, as shown in Figure 7–11(A). The material being imprinted should be of a single thickness.

   d. Run the brayer across the ink several times and then carefully run it across the surface of the design several times or until the deposit of ink is even, as illustrated in Figure 7–11(B).

   e. With a piece of clean cloth wrapped around the tip of the finger, wipe away any excess ink that may have been picked up on areas other than the design.

   f. Carefully place the block, inked surface down, against the article to be imprinted. Be sure it is placed precisely, as it cannot be moved without damaging the print once it has touched the surface.

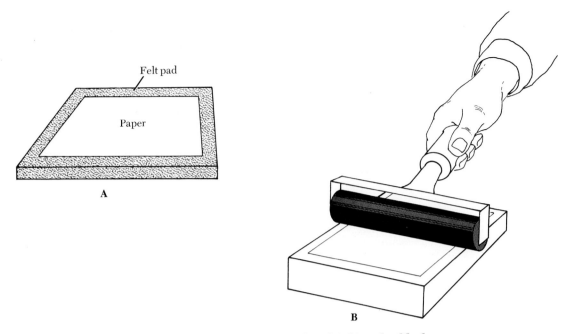

Figure 7–11. Preparation of surface to be imprinted and inking the block.

Figure 7–12. Applying pressure for the actual printing.

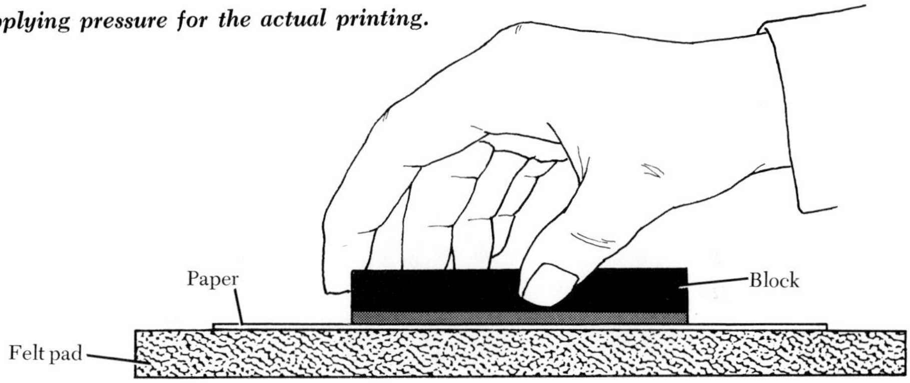

g. Holding the block steady, place an even amount of pressure on the block, as shown in Figure 7–12.

h. Lift the block away and allow print to air dry.

Cardboard Printing

1. *Materials:*
   Heavy cardboard
   Pencil
   Stencil knife
   Pine board (size determined by need)

2. *Procedure:*

   a. Select a piece of heavy cardboard, the size determined by the design. The thickness of cardboard should be $\frac{1}{16}$-inch or more.

   b. With a pencil, lay out the desired design on the piece of cardboard. The design can be drawn freehand, copied, or traced on the cardboard surface.

   c. Cut around the outline of the design.

   d. With a stencil knife, remove the interior sections from the design. That is, remove the sections that are not to be printed. Large areas should be cut completely through the surface; smaller areas are cut only partially away. (See Figure 7–13.) Cardboard is usually manufactured from layers of paper, and texture can be obtained when the lines are cut through one or two layers of cardboard as in the examples of the fins and tail.

   e. Mount the cardboard on a wooden block to make it easier to handle. Apply quick-drying glue to the cardboard and place it on the block. Allow it to dry under a weighted surface.

   f. Directions for printing are the same as those given for block printing.

Figure 7–13. Cutting a design in cardboard. The eye should be cut completely through the surface, whereas other lines should be cut only partly through.

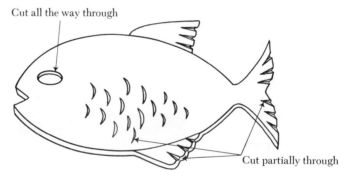

Cut all the way through

Cut partially through

Figure 7–14. A vegetable prepared for printing.

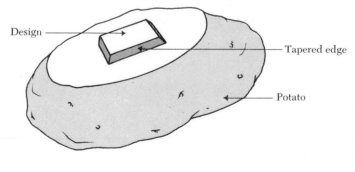

Design

Tapered edge

Potato

Vegetable Printing

1. *Materials:*
   Vegetable (potato, carrot)
   Paring knife
   Paints (tempera, water color, or powdered)
   Surface to be imprinted (tissue, wrapping paper, or construction paper)
   Container for paint
2. *Procedure:*
   a. Select the vegetable and cut it into two pieces of approximately equal length.
   b. Allow the cut vegetable to stand until the surface is dry. Freshly cut vegetables "bleed" and are very difficult to work with.
   c. Select a pencil with soft lead and trace or draw a design on the cut surface.
   d. With a paring knife, cut around the design. The edges of the design should taper out as shown in Figure 7–14.
   e. Each half of the potato or carrot will make one design.
   f. The design can be printed in one or more colors. Select the desired colors and mix the paint to the consistency of cream.
   g. With a small paint brush, cover the raised surface of the design with paint. If more than one color is desired, the added colors are painted on the raised surfaces of the design.
   h. Carefully place the paint-covered design down on the surface on which the print is to be applied. Apply even pressure to print. Lift it away carefully to prevent smudging.
   i. Make two or three prints from one application of paint; then repaint the vegetable for additional prints.

Stick Printing

1. *Materials:*
   Surface to be imprinted (paper, cardboard, cloth)
   Soft pine board (size depends on design)
   Tempera paint
   Wood file
   Paintbrush
   Sponge
   Container for paint
2. *Procedure:*
   a. Select a piece of wood, the end of which is the desired size and shape. If the shape to be printed is round, use a piece of wooden dowel stock or an old broom handle. Molding, in a variety of shapes, can be purchased from any lumberyard. These can be used to produce unusual shapes. Figures 7–15 illustrates some of the shapes.

Printing,
A Valuable
Learning Tool

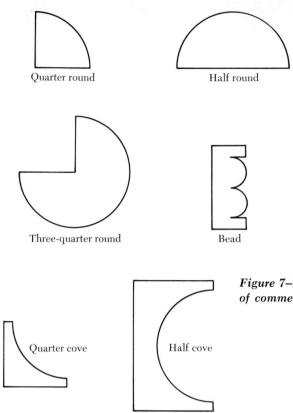

Quarter round

Half round

Three-quarter round

Bead

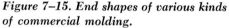

Quarter cove

Half cove

Figure 7–15. End shapes of various kinds of commercial molding.

b. Cut the piece of material to about 2 inches in length. It should be long enough to enable the individual to handle the piece of material like a rubber stamp.

c. If molding or stock with the desired end shape cannot be found or purchased, the design can be traced or drawn with a pencil with soft lead onto the end grain of a piece of wood. It can then be shaped with a knife, wood file, and 2/0 sandpaper.

d. Because the end grain of wood is rough, the printing surface of the stick should be sanded smooth before printing is attempted.

e. Select the surface to be imprinted. Paper, cardboard, cloth, or cork are examples of materials that can be used for a printing surface.

f. Select the desired color, tempera paint, and small paintbrush. Apply paint to the design.

g. Press the surface to be printed against the surface to be imprinted and apply pressure. Separate the two surfaces, being careful not to smudge the printed surface.

h. Two or three impressions can be made before the surface is re-painted.

i. A sponge can be placed in a container of paint to act as a stamp pad, eliminating the need for painting the surface with a brush.

Leaf Printing

1. *Materials:*

   Leaves
   Surface to be imprinted
   Printing inks (water soluble)
   Brayer
   Inking surface

2. *Procedure:*

   a. Select the leaves to be printed.

   b. Apply the printing ink to the working surface of the leaf. The working surface is the bottom side of the leaf. Inking the surface is the same as for block printing.

   c. Select the surface to be imprinted (paper, cloth, cardboard, or cork).

   d. Place the inked surface of the leaf face down on the material to be imprinted. On top of the leaf place a sheet of paper larger than the leaf area. With the back of the hand, apply pressure to the surface. For best results the hand should move across the surface.

   e. Separate the two surfaces; care should be taken not to smudge the printed material.

   f. The procedure can be repeated to secure the desired number of prints.

   g. An interesting effect can be achieved by using more than one leaf and color. Ink is applied to each leaf, blade of grass, or the like. The inked surfaces are then placed on the surface to be imprinted and steps (d) and (e) are repeated.

Sponge Printing

1. *Materials:*

   Sponges
   Newsprint
   Newspapers
   Surface to be imprinted (construction paper, oak tag, or cardboard)
   Paints (powdered tempera or water colors)
   Containers to hold paints (coffee cans)

2. *Procedure:*

   a. Select a sponge or a number of sponges that can be cut into several different shapes such as triangles, squares, rectangles, and circles. It is important to keep all pieces small enough to be handled by the fingers.

   b. Wet the sponge thoroughly. Then squeeze out water so that the sponge is completely damp but not wet.

   c. Mix the desired colored paints to the consistency of very thin cream.

d. Dip the sponge into the paint. Squeeze out some of the paint so that there is no dripping.

e. Holding the sponge between the fingers, dab onto the surface to be imprinted. Be careful not to rub or scrub the paint onto the surfaces.

f. The texture of the sponge and the different shapes can be manipulated to increase the variety of designs obtained with this printing technique. The background is printed first and the details last.

String Printing

1. *Materials:*

Tempera paint
White or manila drawing paper
Wide-mouth container
String
Scrap paper

Figure 7–16. Making a string print. The string is positioned in the folded paper and removed with pressure.

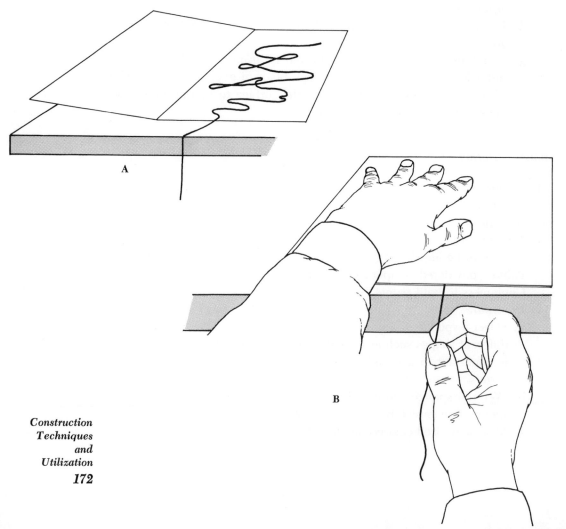

A

B

2. *Procedure:*

    a. Select a piece of 9- $\times$ 11-inch white or manilla drawing paper. Fold the paper in half the short way.

    b. Cut a piece of thin string the length of your arm.

    c. Mix the desired colored tempera paints in a small container. The container should have a wide opening to enable the string to be placed in and withdrawn with ease.

    d. Place the string in the container. Be sure the string is covered with paint except for about 4 inches of one end, reserved for handling.

    e. Remove the string from the paint and wipe the excess paint from the string with a scrap of paper.

    f. Open the piece of folded paper, as shown in Figure 7–16(A), and drop the string on one half of the paper. The placement is accomplished without any consideration of pattern or design.

    g. Fold the piece of paper together forming a sandwich, with the string as the filler.

    h. Place one hand on top of the paper as shown in Figure 7–16(B). With the second hand, pull the string from between the two pieces of paper. A design will be formed on both halves of the paper.

    i. Without dipping the string into the paint, the printing process can be repeated. The second print may be of a higher quality than the first print because there is less tendency for the paint to smudge.

    j. A second color can be added to the design by applying a small amount of paint to the string with the fingers and then repeating steps (f), (g), and (h).

APPLICATIONS

Language Arts

LANGUAGE FACILITY. Imaginative thoughts and stories can be the subject of oral or written composition at any grade level. These can often be inspired by the use of printing to create unusual shapes or designs that suggest ideas. String printing can be used in this way. Pupils can be asked to write a short story about their string print. Figure 7–17 illustrates an example of a string print and story written by a fourth-grader.

String prints can be of particular use in teaching the disadvantaged child. Lack of communication skills is usually one of his greatest problems. To help him overcome shyness and develop verbal facility, any exercise that challenges his imagination and intellect and distracts his attention from an awareness of his conversational shortcomings can be fruitful. String prints, because they rely on an appeal to inventiveness, can stimulate pupils to create stories of make-believe people, animals, and situations, suggested by the free form of the string print. The suggested figures can stimulate oral and written expression in story or cartoon form.

Make-believe people, animals, and other creations can also be developed

Figure 7–17. " 'Pulling Strings.' My pitcher ended up like a propeller. It had three blades and a tip on the side. It would probably make an airplane go awful." A fourth-grader's composition stimulated by a string print.

by pupils' using combinations of the printing techniques suggested in this chapter. These suggested figures and cartoons can be used to stimulate oral or written expression on the part of the pupils.

READING. Reading readiness cards can easily be made with vegetable, cardboard, leaf, or stick printing. Even one shape, a leaf print for example, could be used for a visual discrimination exercise, as seen in Figure 7–18. The leaf printed upright three times and upside down once on a card could be used to strengthen the child's ability to pick out what is different. This is a good example of discrimination learning. It is a necessary step that must precede concept formation and generalization. It extends the detail or the number of referents in the environment and helps the child to conceptualize by becoming aware of differences. If used in a small-group situation, differential reinforcement can be used immediately. The child must learn both to discriminate and to generalize in order to form concepts, principles, and problem-solving techniques.

Mathematics

SHAPES. Many shapes—geometric, pictorial, and fanciful—can be made and set aside for mathematics exercises. These can be used in various ways: to teach numbers, to make sets, to identify geometric shapes, to make graphs. Flash cards and games can be assembled to provide variety in drill. The teacher can capitalize on the many situations involving grouping that arise in the classroom. When grouping children for games, discussions, and projects, attention can be called to the numbers in the groups and the number of different groups. Other natural groupings, such as pairs, fives, and tens can be used to help children think in terms of more than a single item at a time. The concept of grouping can thus develop from the many natural examples. Stick printing can be utilized in number problems. It is of particular value in the primary grades to show number groupings and to understand how processes change the grouping.

CHARTS. In primary arithmetic, children must do a great deal of work with

Figure 7–18. A visual discrimination exercise that can be made with leaf prints.

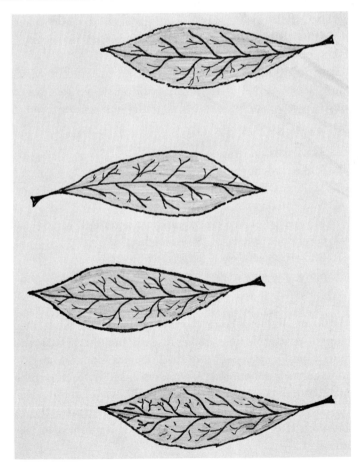

concrete objects. But they must also prepare to transfer number concepts from the concrete to the abstract. An intermediary step can be taken using a wide variety of picture charts. The pictures and shapes used on these charts can be prepared by using vegetable, stick, sponge, leaf, or linoleum prints. Large charts can be constructed for classroom use and small cards for use in pocket charts. The print provides a quick way to make groupings to show the meaning of numbers (see Figure 7–19) and to show the commutative, associate, and distributive principles of the fundamental processes.

For example, to teach the meanings of the numbers from one to ten, a pocket chart could be made with ten pockets. With a stick print of a shape such as a triangle, a number of cards could be made for each pocket showing the appropriate number of triangles grouped in various ways. The children can test their knowledge of the numbers by placing the cards in the correct pockets.

Charts showing the meanings of larger numbers and how the place of the numeral determines its value can be readily constructed. Many such devices are needed to bring home to children the concept of number as an idea.

NUMBER COMBINATIONS. Youngsters who have trouble with numbers might work with printing techniques to fabricate their own mathematics materials.

Using stick or vegetable printing, a child could make a set of number cards that would show the combinations that make ten (see Figure 7–20), or any other number.

SETS. Printing techniques can be used to find out whether a child understands sets. Instead of requiring children to write answers to the following questions, the teacher can ask that the answers be printed.

1. Make a *set* of *three* objects.
2. Make a *set* of *four* different objects.
3. Make *two* equivalent *sets*.
4. Make *two* nonequivalent *sets*.
5. Make a *set* of *two* circles and *two* squares.
6. Circle *one subset* of the preceding *set*.
7. Make *two sets,* each with *two* objects.
8. Show *one–one* matching.

Utilizing linoleum block printing, many teaching materials can be developed. A sample one makes use of the three basic shapes: a square, a triangle, and a circle, cut into the linoleum blocks. Many prints of each in different colors are mounted. A booklet is used by each pupil in conjunction with the mounted pieces. The booklet contains matching shapes. Oral instructions by the teacher or by audio tape accompany the use of the booklet. The work is divided into learning tasks. Examples of the learning task are described here:

A

Figure 7–19. Printing utilized in number charts.

B

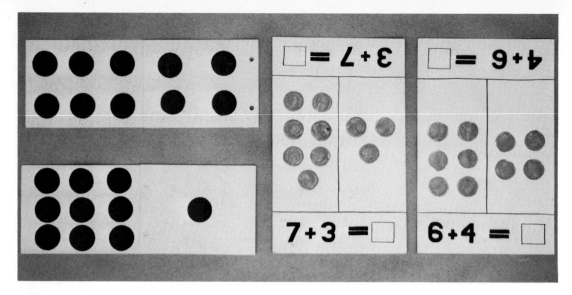

Figure 7–20. Number cards utilizing stick printing.

A

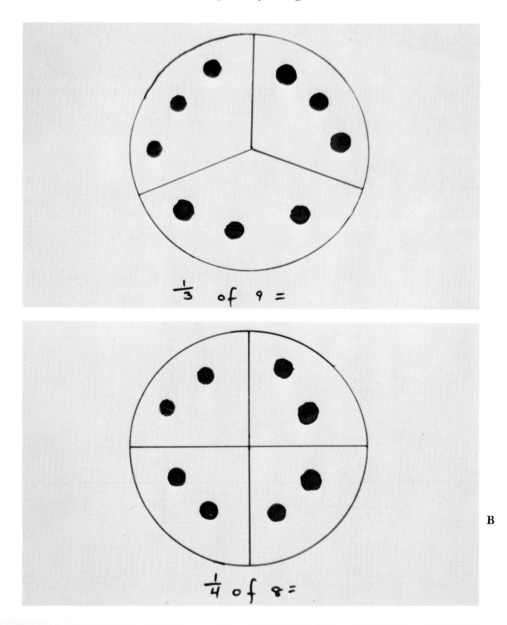

B

1. *Shape matching:*

   Task A: Place different shapes of the *same color* as shown in the booklet in front of the child. It may be a good idea to start with only two shapes, one of which matches the shape in the booklet, and later increase the number of shapes.

   Task B: After the child has mastered Task A present him with different shapes of *varying colors.* This task should help the child think in terms of shape and not color.

2. *Color matching:*

   Task A: The child is presented the same shapes in varying colors to see if he can match colors.

   Task B: This task requires introducing to the child various shapes in different colors. The child must disregard shape variations and focus only on color.

3. *Fractions:*

   Task A: The child can be asked to make one quarter of the circle yellow, using the illustration in the booklet on which to place the mounted sections.

   Task B: Remove the booklet and see if the child can answer the question by manipulating the mounted pieces.

4. *Shape combinations:*

   Task A: Shapes can be combined to make new shapes. Two triangles go together to make a diamond shape.

5. *Pattern reproduction:*

   Task A: The child is asked to reproduce the patterns in the booklets using a combination of shapes and colors.

   Task B: The child can use the shapes to create his own designs.

6. *Free forms:*

   Task A: Children are asked to produce free forms utilizing the basic shapes.

The materials described in this section were printed by the teacher for children to use, but the same material could be printed by the learner so the teacher would have a visual record of the learner's response.

Science

LEAF STUDY. Leaf printing suggests itself immediately as a science tool. Indeed, in learning about the leaves themselves, it can be very useful. Many charts and diagrams can be made with leaf, cardboard, stick, and sponge printing.

LEAF LOTTO. A lotto game (see Figure 7–21), can be made from leaf prints to help teach children the different types of leaves found in their native locality and in others. The following instructions describe how to make leaf lotto:

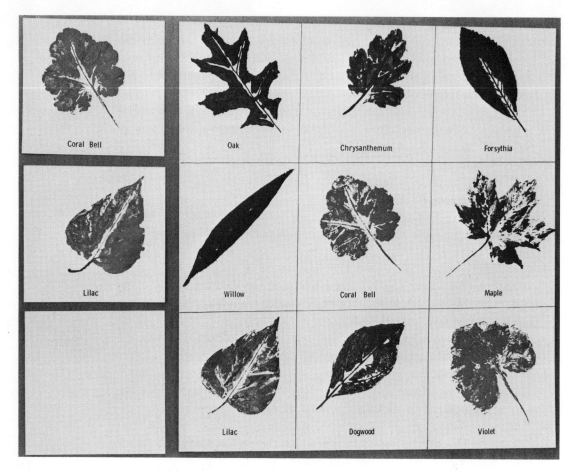

Figure 7–21. Lotto game made with leaf printing.

1. Cut pieces of oak tag into six, 12-inch squares.
2. Cut pieces of oak tag into nine, 4-inch squares.
3. Cut construction paper into forty-eight, 4-inch squares.
4. Select nine different leaves.
5. Lay out each 12-inch square card into nine 4-inch squares. On each card print the nine different leaves being sure that no two leaves are printed in the same position on different cards. These cards are called lotto cards. On each 4-inch square card print one of the nine leaves. These cards are called name cards.

Give each player eight blank paper squares. These are to cover the leaf print on the lotto card as the name is called.

RULES FOR THE GAME

1. The first person to have two straight rows (any direction) of leaves covered on the lotto cards is the winner.

2. Players can take turns calling the names of the leaves from the 4-inch name cards.

Variations of this game can be used in other subject areas. It is adaptable to many reading recognition problems, for example.

Social Studies

MAPS AND CHARTS. Printing has great value in the visual representation of social studies concepts. Figure 7–22 suggests how maps, charts, and graphs can make use of all types of printing for impactful visual presentation of facts.

MASS PRODUCTION. With printing, an activity can be developed to open up to pupils in the primary grades one economic concept, that of mass production of goods. An activity, such as the making of greeting cards, could be set up on an assembly-line basis. The children could work out the production system as the management in a factory would. Then they can become the workers, each performing an assigned task on the "assembly line." One child could gather stock, another could stamp the design, a group could apply color, and another group could do the appropriate lettering. "Inspectors" could oversee the work. This process would not only provide useful gifts, but would also give children a first-hand idea of the principles of mass production. Some economic and social problems might be suggested and could be discussed in their larger context by the pupils.

Art

DECORATING. Printing can be used to achieve design in creative art. All the printing techniques can be used to create patterns for over-all designs, border designs, or centers of attention in many kinds of decorations. Attractive room decorations, interesting in themselves, can be made. Many types of useful objects can be decorated with printing: wastebaskets, tissue holders, pencil boxes, desk calendars, and various kinds of containers, to mention a few.

COLOR. The printing techniques described in this text can also be used to illustrate color combinations and the importance of color to any art activity.

PRODUCTIVE THINKING TASK. Productive thinking [1] is thinking that manifests verbal or nonverbal responses from given or known information and can be classified as follows:

1. *Convergent thinking* deals with the production of conclusions or responses that are fairly circumscribed or even uniquely determined by the given information. The child is given certain shapes to print and

[1] J. P. Guilford, "Traits of Creativity." In H. H. Anderson (ed.), *Creativity and Its Cultivation.* (New York: Harper, 1959), pp. 142–61.

AGRICULTURAL RESOURCES OF THE UNITED STATES

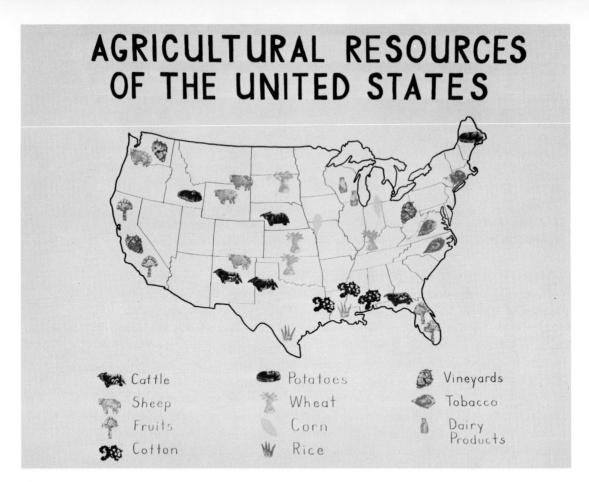

Cattle
Sheep
Fruits
Cotton

Potatoes
Wheat
Corn
Rice

Vineyards
Tobacco
Dairy Products

A

Figure 7–22. Sponge and vegetable printing add color and interest to maps and charts.

B # HELP PREVENT FOREST FIRES

Timberland Destroyed by Fire in the United States

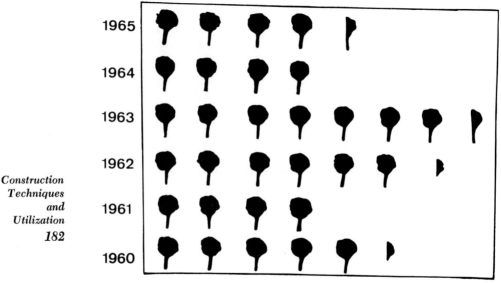

1965
1964
1963
1962
1961
1960

Each Symbol Represents 100,000 Acres

uses them to print the same design as the teacher's, while another child may only make minor changes in the original design.

2. *Divergent thinking* deals with the individual's ability to vary his thinking in many different directions. This type of thinking requires flexibility, originality, and elaboration factors to operate. It usually requires a variety of responses. This technique could be illustrated by the child who takes the shapes for printing and creates some completely new designs or objects.

The printing techniques described in this chapter can be used by children in many interesting ways. Printing can help the child overcome difficulties he may have in expressing an idea through the use of a drawing or verbal explanation. Figure 7–23 is an example of this technique in use.

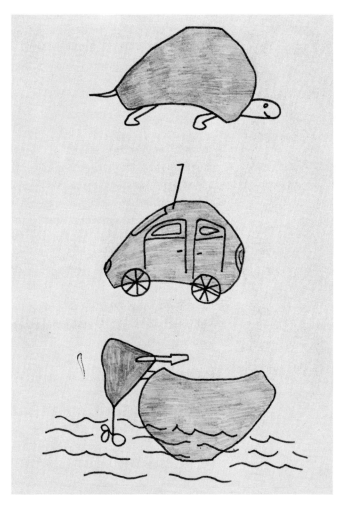

Figure 7–23. Examples of expressions of productive thinking through the use of a printing technique.

CONCLUSION

Printing techniques are a great boon to the teacher. They enable him to make a vast number of teaching devices so necessary to an individualized program. The devices can be assembled together with teaching tasks that can be used by groups of children with limited supervision or by individuals. The various printing techniques can be used in advance by the teacher to provide charts, booklets, counters, games, pictures, and shapes that will be ready for use at the proper time. The techniques can also be employed by the teacher and the pupil in classroom activities to facilitate learning.

The most important value in the classroom of these techniques is their ability to reproduce identical shapes and design in any desired quantity with speed and accuracy. Once a linoleum, a cardboard, vegetable, stick, or leaf print is prepared, it should be used many times to insure that the preparation time was well spent on a useful device. Once the teacher has grasped the printing technique and understood its value, it will become a ready tool to add interest and clarity to the learning process.

LEARNING ACTIVITIES

1. Using vegetable, stick, or cardboard printing, develop some basic geometric shapes that could be used to print interesting designs. With these shapes develop several designs.
2. Print a picture using sponge printing.
3. Plan a lesson showing how one of the printing techniques could be used to simplify a concept in the following curriculum areas:
   a. Science
   b. Social Studies
   c. Mathematics
4. With a group of four or five fellow students, plan a series of cards for all occasions. Have each member of the group design and print a card for a particular occasion. These cards will then be exchanged between group members.
5. With a group of fourth- or fifth-grade children, try doing some string prints.
   a. Have children write stories about their prints.
   b. Have children make some prints with more than one color. Use prints to develop with children some concepts about color.
   c. Discuss with children other ways in which these prints could be used.
6. Make a deck of number cards (1–10) using a printing technique. With the cards, devise a game for a small group. List the educational purposes of the game.

7. Prepare a set of flash cards for one of the following curriculum areas that could be used to develop the concept of readiness.
   a. Reading
   b. Mathematics
   c. Language Arts
8. Develop a lesson using vegetable, sponge, stock, or cardboard printing that could be used with children to develop divergent thinking.
9. Describe how the printing technique explained in this chapter could be used by children to enhance their classroom paper.

REFERENCES

ADAMS, VERDIE F., JR. "Sponge Fun." *The Instructor,* **78**:82 (January 1969).

AHLBERG, G. AND JANERYD, O. *Block, Silk, and Screen Printing.* New York: Sterling, 1961.

AMON, MARTHA R., AND RAWSON, RUTH H. *Handcrafts Simplified.* Bloomington, Ill.: McKnight and McKnight, 1961, pp. 44–52.

ANDERSON H. H. *Creativity and Its Cultivation.* New York: Harper, 1959, pp. 142–162.

DAVID, S. M. "Printmaking." *School Arts,* **67**:30–31 (January 1968).

FONVILLE, J. L. "Put the Grain to Work: Woodblock Printing." *School Arts,* **67**:16–17 (October 1967).

FOSTER, M. "Roller Prints." *School Arts,* **68**:10–13 (September 1968).

HALL, J. C. "Art Becomes a Happening: String Prints." *Arts & Activities,* **62**:26–28 (September 1967).

HART, TONY. *The Young Designer.* New York & London: Frederick Warne, 1968.

LAW, A. "All About Block Printing." *Grade Teacher,* **84**:103–5 (November 1966).

—. "Many Methods of Making Block Prints." *Grade Teacher,* **84**:78–80 (December 1966).

McCLURE, C. "African Potato Printing." *School Arts,* **66**:32–33 (April 1967).

STURTZ, S. "Block to Block." *School Arts,* **67**:18–21 (October 1967).

WARWICK, J. F. "Scrap-block Printing." *School Arts,* **67**:14–15 (October 1967).

WASSERMAN, B. "Linoleum Printing and the Art Experience." *Arts & Activities,* **64**:38–41 (September 1968).

—. "Printmaking Today." *Art Education,* **21**:21–23 (June 1968).

WEISS, HARVEY. *Paper, Ink, and Roller.* New York: William R. Scott, 1958.

CHAPTER 8

Papier Mâché *and* Its Uses *in the* Classroom

Papier mâché is a versatile medium that can be used for three-dimensional learning materials in every area of the curriculum. Its importance as a tactile and visual adjunct to learning constructs is sufficient motivation for the teacher to plan its use in the classroom. Piaget and Montessori in their writings have repeatedly emphasized the great importance of sensorimotor activity, particularly of visual and tactile exploratory movement. They also emphasize the importance of these experiences in providing the foundation to cognitive development.

Unfortunately, papier mâché has gained a reputation similar to that of other craft activities, in that many teachers consider it a dirty, messy, and time-consuming experience. However, teachers who are accustomed to directing children in the use of papier mâché and who understand the importance of organizing the procedures have found it to be one of the most versatile media for enriching classroom learning experiences.

Many teachers are of the opinion that objects constructed from papier mâché are crudely made. Contrary to this view, papier mâché objects constructed with care can be refined products of self-expression. The only limitations that seem to be placed on papier mâché are those of the individual to conceive new and different uses for it. Animals, puppet heads, and masks can be constructed from papier mâché to portray characters being studied by youngsters. In social studies and science, globes, planets, cutaways, and contour maps can be constructed in connection with the various units being studied. Making these three-dimensional models enables children to have experiences in research, planning, and constructing with materials. The results are rewarding explorations into the creation of artistic forms and an improved understanding of concepts.

Papier mâché greatly extends the range of stimulus situations that can be brought into the classroom. Verbal communication, although of indisputable value in the classroom, is not the only way to present information. Many subjects are illuminated and extended through models and actual objects. The three-dimensional illustrations, when used as an integral part of the learning experience and not as treasures taken from the shelf and dusted off on special occasions, provide a stimulus and a way of involvement in the learning process that promote intrinsic reinforcement for pupils.

For example, the teacher could tell the children about the characteristics of old and young river beds, or the children could read about these formations. This verbal learning would not be in accordance with the learning style of every child. Instead those who experience verbal difficulties might construct a model illustrating these two land formations and their characteristics. But learning should not end with the finished project. These objects should be used to stimulate verbal learning by a follow-up verbal explanation and discussion of the models. A child in a program that was concentrating on language development constructed a papier mâché model of a human ear with movable parts. (See Figure 8–1.) The child became so excited about his finished project that he wanted to tell everyone about it. Mindful of his language problem, the teacher encouraged him to prepare a report for presentation in the classroom. The child learned the names and pronunciations of all the parts of the inner and outer ear and their functions and made an effective oral report. The culmination of the experience was a presentation to children in other classrooms. Quite a feat for a child whose customary responses were monosyllabic!

Papier mâché objects can be used to provide the stimulus that is required in all types of learning. These objects can provide the cues in chain learning or the variety of stimuli in multiple-discrimination learning. At the principle level, they can be used as a series to initiate generalization, as an example of a principle, or as detail to support a large concept. Their construction allows the child to utilize the processes of observing, hypothesizing, testing, comparing, and generalizing. The teacher can help the child achieve maximum benefit from the learning experience by asking him questions that will promote his reflection and reasoning as he works with the sculpturing and the resultant objects. Various summaries of the construction experience in such forms as questions to be answered by using the device, evaluation of effects created, sets of directions, imaginative stories and plays utilizing constructed animals or persons are examples of verbal activities stimulated by papier mâché. Explanations and generalizations of concepts illustrated in three-dimensional scenes bring the learning experience from concrete manipulation to abstract reasoning.

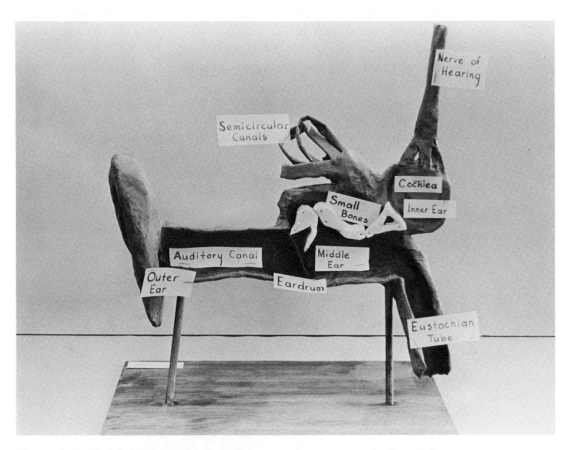

Figure 8–1. Model that stimulated verbal expression of scientific knowledge.

Construction

For successful experiences in papier mâché, the teacher requires only the minimum of equipment and supplies. Quantities of discarded newspapers, wheat paste, and some bits of string or wire are all that are needed. Many finished papier mâché projects are painted with ordinary water-based paint (tempera), and very effective finishes can be obtained by covering the papier mâché with colored paper, cotton, shredded burlap, or other scrap material.

Papier mâché objects can be constructed by two general methods: the pulp method and the layer-on-layer method. In both methods, a base must be used to provide a form on which to apply the papier mâché. The selection of a proper base will save much time and effort in the construction of any object. Four types of bases can be used: an actual object, chicken wire, rolled or crushed paper, or an armature. The form can be removed or it can be a permanent core.

ACTUAL OBJECT. In this technique, a removable base that is the actual shape and size of the desired finished product is used. In order to insure removal of the papier mâché covering without damaging the base object, the object is coated with oil, or covered with a piece of dry newspaper before the papier mâché is applied. One of the following four methods should be considered when making any item from the actual object:

1. Objects to be covered with papier mâché on only one surface: A bowl or tray that has a wider top than bottom can be used as a base. When the papier mâché is dry, it can be slipped off the base object.
2. Objects used as a removable core: Such a core—a candle holder, for example, can be covered with papier mâché. When the substance is dry, the core can be removed by cutting the paper covering in half with a knife or razor blade. The two halves can be placed back together

Figure 8–2. Partially finished model showing paper interwoven in chicken wire.

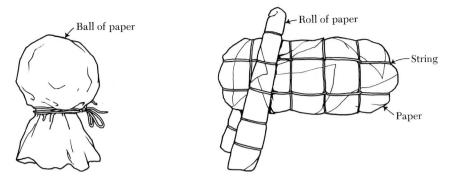

Figure 8–3. Crushed newspaper rolled and tied to form bases for papier mâché objects.

using strips of papier mâché. Many actual objects can be used without being harmed with this method.

3. Objects that can be deflated: A balloon or a beach ball can be used as a base while inflated. When applying the papier mâché, a small hole can be left around the air-intake valve of the balloon or ball. When the papier mâché is dry, the balloon or ball can be deflated and pulled through the hole, or it can be left in the center as a permanent core.

4. Objects that need not be removed: Plastic containers, light bulbs, and plastic clay make good object cores. For example, a vase could be constructed using a plastic soap container as a core. The plastic container becomes an important part of the finished product, because it makes the inside of the vase waterproof.

CHICKEN WIRE. Chicken wire can be used effectively for a base because it possesses the property of being easy to bend and press into shape. After the desired shape is obtained, strips of dry newspaper are woven into the chicken wire, as shown in Figure 8–2. These strips increase the holding power of the papier mâché to the base.

ROLLED OR CRUSHED PAPER. Newspaper can be rolled or crushed into various shapes and tied with string. The various shapes are fastened together to form bases for animals or people. (See Figure 8–3.)

ARMATURE BASE. Pieces of wood, cardboard, or wire can be used to form the desired base. These materials are placed together to form stick-like figures, as shown in Figure 8–4. The figures are then covered with wire or paper to build up the base.

Procedure

THE LAYER-ON-LAYER METHOD. The layer-on-layer method is especially effective for large, regular shapes.

1. Tear newspaper into 1-inch strips. If the paper is torn with the grain, it will tear evenly.

Upson Board Outline

Frame Construction

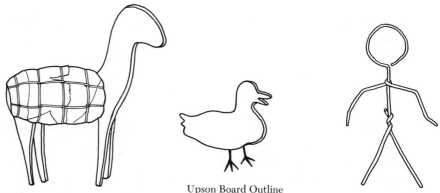

Rolled Paper and Upson Board

Upson Board Outline
and Coat Hanger Wire

Coat Hanger Wire

Figure 8–4. Armatures made from a variety of materials.

2. Mix wallpaper paste and water together in a container until it has the consistency of heavy cream. A wide-mouth container (dish pan) is preferred for use by young children.

3. Dip the strip of paper into the paste and wipe off the excess by running the pasted strip between the fingers.

4. If the base is to be removed, remember to plan for this operation. The base is removed after applying three or four layers of paper.

5. Paper towels torn in strips should be used as the last layer for best results. These are applied dry over a wet surface.

6. Allow the papier mâché to dry.

THE PAPIER PULP METHOD. The papier pulp method differs from the layer-on-layer method in that it is not generally used over an armature or a base. Very soft paper is torn into small bits and saturated with a water-paste mixture until it is of such consistency that it is readily molded into a shape as clay is modeled. This method is excellent for modeling small animals, birds, people, plants, trees, and the like. (See Figure 8–5.)

1. Tear small pieces of soft paper (paper towels, facial tissues) into small bits.
2. Place the small pieces of cut-up paper into a jar filled with water and wallpaper paste. Use one-third cup of paste to a quart of water. Allow the paper to soak overnight.
3. Pour off the excess water and squeeze the paper pulp so that it is semimoist.
4. The paper pulp can then be shaped or modeled in the hands.

FINISHING PAPIER MÂCHÉ

1. After the papier mâché has completely dried, select appropriate finishing materials according to the desired texture and appearance of the final object.
2. Vary the texture and appearance of the surface:
   a. Tempera paints are appropriate for most types of papier mâché. They have good covering qualities and are easy for children to work with.
   b. Suede-Tex (a commercial product) is appropriate where a durable suede finish is desired.
   c. Enamels are suitable for a glossy, colored finish.
   d. Shellac or varnish can be used as a protective coating over the tempera paints.
3. Give objects a realistic appearance:
   a. Marbles for the eyes
   b. Shirt stays for teeth or fangs
   c. Felt for the tongues of the animals
   d. Yarn and rope for the hair of puppets and animals

USING A STRING OR YARN TECHNIQUE

1. Select the desired base, a balloon, beach ball, or the like.
2. Select the appropriate material, yarn or string. Color and diameter should be considered in selecting the material to be used.
3. Mix wallpaper paste and water together.
4. Dip the string or yarn into the paste and wipe off the excess paste by running the strips between the fingers.
5. Apply the string to the object, as shown in Figure 8–6, and allow it to dry.
6. Remove the balloon or beach ball by deflating, leaving a cage-like sphere. This technique can be used to construct a sphere that will show the equator and lines for latitude and longitude. Figure 8–6 illustrates this technique.

Figure 8–5. Examples of figures molded with paper pulp.

A

B

C

D

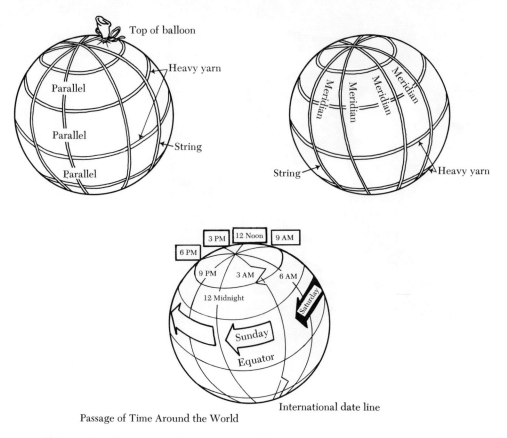

Passage of Time Around the World

Figure 8–6. Steps in making a string globe.

APPLICATIONS

Science

SCIENCE OF LIVING THINGS. The world of living things fascinates children today as it always has. At one time, much stress was placed on the knowledge and identification of plants and animals. Today this has been subordinated to other considerations. Most important of these is the concept of interrelationships in nature: of animals with animals, of animals with plants, of plants and animals with their physical environment. Children have a deep curiosity about living things, and their education should both satisfy and increase this curiosity.

The growing urbanization of our country makes it more difficult in some ways to open up the world of living things to children. Teachers are challenged to use every opportunity and every possible resource. The models illustrated are examples of how interaction in nature can be made more interesting and meaningful for children. It must be kept in mind that the making of such models results in more learning than just the viewing of the completed models because of the research done in the preparation and construction.

A papier mâché model of life in the spring might show some of the events that occur above and below the soil: robins nesting in the tree; a rabbit on the ground partly camouflaged by its color, which blends in with the background. The soil is penetrated with tunnels made by worms and other small animals. These animal-made holes illustrate how the ground is kept porous to allow rain water to find its way into the ground and thus provide moisture for trees and other plants.

Underground would be a nest of yellow jackets (wasps). A chipmunk family could be shown with a supply of food obtained from the plants in the surrounding countryside.

A papier mâché model of life in the winter (see Figure 8–7) might show how that environment differs from that of spring. The ground, covered with snow, and trees, barren of foliage, present a somber scene. In contrast, under the frozen soil and within the bark of trees, there is life. The model might consist of hidden dens, crevices, and chambers where one could find living seeds, eggs, and sleeping animals. In addition, the hibernation of the cold-blooded animals and the winter dens of nonhibernating animals such as rabbits and raccoons could be portrayed.

A papier mâché model of a tree stump (see Figure 8–8) helps tell an in-

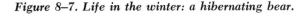

Figure 8–7. Life in the winter: a hibernating bear.

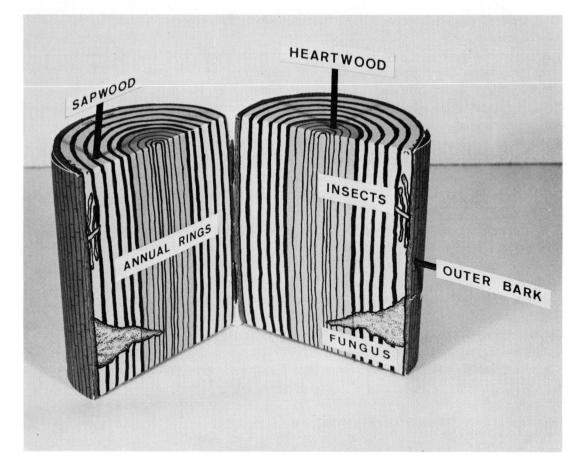

Figure 8–8. Story of tree growth.

teresting story about the growth of a tree. Its annual rings reveal the number of years of growth, while the width of the annual rings indicates the variation in growing conditions from year to year. For example, the rings are usually narrower on the north side of the tree because of less sunlight. The damage caused by enemies of a tree can be illustrated on the model: wood-chewing larvae of insects channeling their way through the tree, or a parasitic fungus penetrating the tree's living tissue.

The world of flowers and their environment might be introduced to the children through a project involving the construction of a papier mâché blossom and papier mâché bees. (See Figures 8–9 and 8–10.) The flower could be developed in two stages: one to show the complete plant, and one to reveal the parts as the petals are removed. In addition, the construction of the bee would introduce a knowledge of the bee and its role in nature's society. The result would be a unified knowledge of flowers, their functions in life, and the effect of environment on the process. It should be noted, however, that papier mâché models should not replace the actual growing of flowers by the children.

Figure 8–9. Cutaway model of a flower.

Figure 8–10. Models of bees.

LAND FORMATIONS. Papier mâché mountains can be constructed by the children, using chicken wire and a plywood base, to create a series of plateaus representing various altitudes. Figure 8–11 simulates a Mexican mountain. Note that at each plateau, products are illustrated that would grow at a given altitude. The tip of the mountain is completely free of vegetation. Children can thus learn the effect of altitude on growth. This

Figure 8–11. Display of crops grown at various altitudes of Mexican terrain.

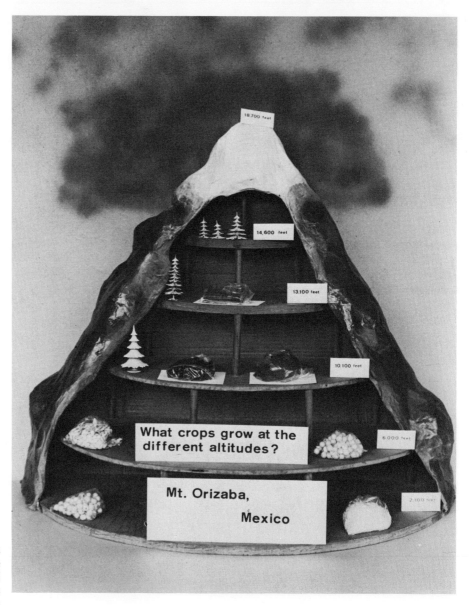

Figure 8–12. Stages of a river bed formation. A. Youth: *In the upland area where the slopes are steep, the river is fast flowing and its erosion is downward and rapid. It cannot be used for transportation but is an excellent source of power. B.* Maturity: *At this stage, the river begins to flow more slowly and develops lateral erosion. Many large tributaries enter the main river and land drainage is well organized. C.* Old age: *Finally comes the plain course with the river widening slowly over flat country in which it is often depositing rather than eroding. The river covers only a small portion of the valley floor.*

same mountain could be used in teaching the concepts related to atmospheric pressure, interest in which is often stimulated by newspaper reports of athletes' reactions to performing in high places.

Figures 8–12 and 8–13 illustrate the various kinds of land formation that can be constructed from papier mâché. Note that Figure 8–14 has moving parts to help clarify the concept of a fault block mountain.

GLOBES. Globes of papier mâché and yarn can be constructed by children. (See Figure 8–15.) Sections of the globe can be cut away to show how the center of the earth may look. This type of globe enables the children to actually locate and lay out the continents, oceans, North and South Poles, equator, and the lines of longitude and latitude. Figure 8–6 shows how yarn, wallpaper, and paste are used to construct a globe that explains the international date line, time around the world, meridians, and parallel lines.

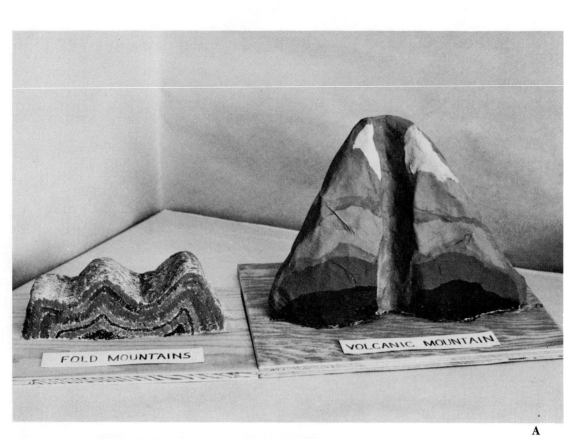

Figure 8-13. Types of mountain formations.

A

B

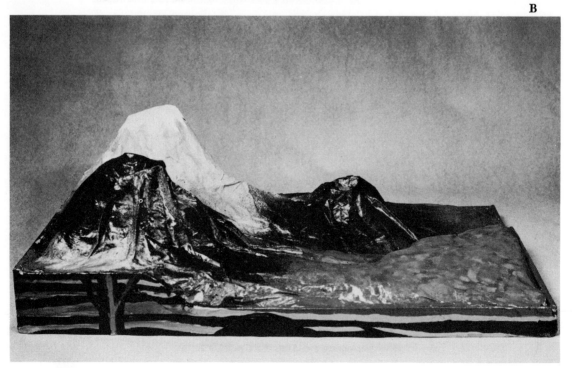

Figure 8–14. A movable part helps in the explanation of land formation.

Figure 8–15. Child reading directions for making a globe.

PEOPLE AND ANIMALS. Papier mâché can be used by children to create people, animals, and creatures of an earlier civilization. (See Figure 8–16.) It also can be used with children to show their conception of life on another planet or at the bottom of the ocean.

TRANSPORTATION. Interesting models of different kinds of transportation can be constructed out of papier mâché. (See Figure 8–17.) These models can show the different forms of transportation from past, to present, to future. Models also can be made of the different types of transportation found throughout the world.

Figure 8–16. Triceratops.

Figure 8–17. A typical two-boom, single-outrigger canoe used by Island people of the Far East.

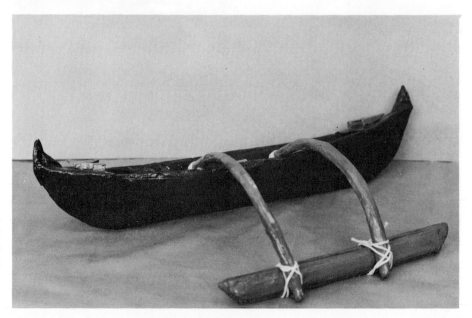

ARTS AND CRAFTS. Many and varied types of art work can be constructed with papier mâché. (See Figure 8–18.) The plasticity of the medium makes it ideal for shaping into conventional or free forms. A great variety of form, texture, and color combinations makes this material ideal for creative expression. Objects for the home, the classroom, or the stage can be created as gifts or props. Jewelry in odd shapes and combinations of form and color, an important part of the contemporary fashion in dress, is ideally created from papier mâché.

Simulated crafts of the various ethnic groups of the world can give insights into the habits of people responding to environment.

Many articles created for their artistic value alone can be fashioned with this medium. Vases, bowls, animal forms, sculptured portraits, masks, and free form sculptures are only a few of the possibilities for which this simply prepared and easily manipulated material can be used.

Mathematics

GEOMETRIC SHAPES. All of the various geometric shapes can be created in papier mâché. Miniature objects or shapes can be made to be used as counters or as the components of sets.

Language Arts

LANGUAGE DEVELOPMENT. Puppets (see Figure 8–19) can be used to provide experiences in drama for pupils at all grade levels. They encourage self-expression through dialogue and can encompass several curriculum areas in one activity. A puppet show can encourage the production of spontaneous dialogue in imaginative stories created by the pupils. By assuming the personalities of the puppet characters they have created, pupils are no longer inhibited by their own limitations.

READING. The kangaroo shown in Figure 8–20 is used to hold flash cards for reinforcing reading skills. Reading might be encouraged and more highly developed by the use of scripts of prewritten dramas to supplement the stories fabricated by pupils.

SOCIAL STUDIES. Language arts can be combined with social studies by staging a puppet show about different countries. Pupils can increase their knowledge of the customs, native dress, and life of countries around the world.

Papier mâché masks can also be used in dramatization. They provide children with an imaginative way to suggest characterization. They can also be made to illustrate the art and customs of other cultures.

A

Figure 8–18. Examples of jewelry and other crafts.

B

206

A

Figure 8–19. Puppets used to stimulate dramatization. In B, marbles have
been used for eyes, shirt stays for
fangs, felt for the tongue, and flocking
for texture.

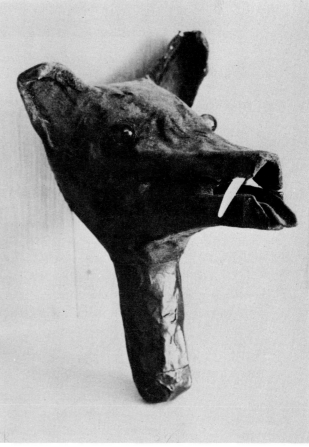

B

207

Figure 8–20. Finished model of Figure 8–2 now being used to stimulate reading activity.

CONCLUSION

Once the techniques of papier mâché are mastered, the teacher and pupils have a ready tool for three-dimensional expression. The third dimension is a difficult concept for many pupils. The creation by them of actual or simulated objects gives them this understanding readily.

A great variety of useful and attractive objects can fill the room through the medium of papier mâché. Learning devices, puppets, props, models, and many kinds of gifts can be easily and beautifully created.

Children's interest will be sustained, and the skills of research, reading, language facility, and construction will be developed. Learning concepts will be grasped in many unforgettable ways.

LEARNING ACTIVITIES

1. Justify the making of a papier mâché model as an integral part of a learning task. Be sure to include all the factors that would contribute or that would assist the learner in obtaining the stated objective for this task.

2. Evaluate the classroom applications for papier mâché suggested in this section in terms of how they could enhance learning.
3. Write a script for a puppet show and make a puppet for each character in the play out of papier mâché. Put on your puppet show for a group of children.
4. Construct a model from papier mâché that will help simplify a concept in the following curriculum area:
   a. Science
   b. Social Studies
   c. Mathematics
5. With a group of children write a script for a puppet show and then have each youngster select a character to make. When all the puppets are finished, have the children present the puppet show.
6. Select a period in history and with some fellow students, construct the people, animals, and creatures that would be found during that time.
7. Papier mâché can be used to construct some interesting craft items. Make one of the following items out of papier mâché:
   a. Vase
   b. Candle holder
   c. Plant holder
   d. Easter basket
8. Design and make some jewelry out of papier mâché. Remember to select finishing materials that are appropriate for this type of activity.
9. What psychological processes would be called upon in the fabrication of the following papier mâché models?
   a. Life in the spring
   b. Land formations
   c. Globe
   d. Forms of transportation
10. Select a concept that could be taught to a group of fourth-grade children. Considering that children learn in different ways, plan a lesson that would enable individuals to gain an understanding of the selected concept by using at least three learning styles.

REFERENCES

ADAIR, MARGARET WEEKS. *Do-It-In-A-Day Puppets for Beginners.* New York: Day, 1964.

AMON, MARTHA R., AND RAWSON, RUTH H. *Handcrafts Simplified.* Bloomington, McKnight and McKnight, 1961, pp. 123–127.

GORDON, E. "Toys in Motion: Papier Mâché Folk Toys," *Arts & Activities,* **59**:12–15 (June 1966).

HOWELL, R. J. "Milk Carton Mini-Mansions," *Arts & Activities,* **62**:20 (December 1967).

JEFFERSON ELEMENTARY SCHOOL DISTRICT. *Art Appreciation and Experimentation.* Daly City, Calif., 1968, pp. 244–247. (Mimeo.)

LYON, M. T. "Papier Mâché: The Art of Personal Adornment," *School Arts,* **68**:22–24 (September 1968).

MATTHEWS, B. "Papier Mâché Puppets," *School Arts,* **68**:27 (October 1968).

SPAR, F. M. "Self Portraits in Papier Mâché," *Arts and Activities,* **61**:11–13 (March 1967).

WADE, B. A. "Do-It-Yourself Zoo," *Arts & Activities,* **63**:24–25 (April 1968).

CHAPTER 9

Frame Construction *and* Its Value *in* Enriching *the* Environment

Frame construction is the term applied to the building of hollow structures such as puppet stages, store fronts, barns, post offices, tables, dioramas, and animal cages. The materials used are inexpensive and a limited number of tools is required. Therefore, making structures with this technique requires little skill and their preparation is safe and economical.

The school curriculum can be enhanced through the use of various kinds of structures that will make the learning environment more realistic. Frame structures are often desirable in connection with studies of the farm, grocery store, post office, and bank. These structures enable children to enact selected segments of a unit in purposeful and imaginative ways, to experience role playing, to plan and present dramatizations, and to care for plants and animals.

Frame construction involves children and teachers in activities that require the use of simple tools and materials to make a variety of things. Toys, mobiles, models, classroom equipment, and science apparatus are examples of the striking and effective objects that can be made by using the techniques described in this chapter. In making these relatively large constructions, children not only receive strong motivation toward conventional learning, but are provided with an opportunity to use the large muscles, to use their abilities in spatial relationships, and to test their motor coordination. They also gain early insights into aspects of vocational education. Frame construction enables children to make large, sturdy items quickly in the classroom, playground, or even in a corner of the cafeteria. Creative work can be begun as early as the first grade, where youngsters have the ability to construct children's furniture and puppet stages. Slow and disadvantaged children may be motivated toward the conventional curriculum in reading and mathematics in their desire to reproduce a prototype or to design something new. Gifted children also delight in being able to design and make experimental and demonstration apparatus.

The frames required to make any desired structure can easily be put together by children in a classroom. This activity requires planning, measuring, and figuring the material sizes needed for a selected structure, providing the child an opportunity to develop in a practical situation the academic skills of mathematics. If a length is not cut properly, what happens? The piece does not fit and the process must be begun over again. The child comes to realize the importance of figuring the sizes of objects accurately and measuring and cutting to the correct length.

It is recommended that common building materials be used to construct the needed frames. Strapping or firring (wood that is 1×2 or 1×3 inches) is reasonably inexpensive and can be bought at any lumberyard. Some teachers prefer to have pine boards ripped to strapping sizes, because pine is easier to work, is less splintery, and holds its shape better. It is suggested that the strapping be cut to varied lengths up to 4 or 5 feet in multiples of 6 inches. These lengths can be cut in a wooden miter box. The use of regular sizes (18, 24, 30, 36, and 48 inches, for example) enables the teacher to reuse the pieces in subsequent construction. All frames, therefore, are made in regular dimensions and the objects to be represented are scaled accordingly. The pieces of wood are fastened together with standard commercial mending plates and corner irons, with gusset plates made by pupils out of Upson board or plywood, and with nuts and stove bolts. Curved frames can be made by using small pieces as segments and fastening them with gusset plates or with nuts and stove bolts. The frames are then covered with appropriate materials and are suitably finished. The results are frequently amazingly clever. The frame method of construction is particularly good for buildings, stages, cages, and other types of structures that are large enough for children to walk into. In fact, this technique allows children to build almost any type of structure. The structures are substantial and involve many principles of sound construction. Frame construction does not require much time or skill, and yet the children can absorb some helpful technical knowledge. Because the results are so realistic, there seems to be a consequent interest in "doing it right." At the conclusion of a unit, the structures can be dismantled and the frames stored neatly and compactly for further use.

It is important to emphasize that frame construction is much more than a recreational experience. The planning requires much detailed mathematical figuring. The constructions can fire a child's imagination and interests. Teachers should take a lead from those commercial enterprises that have profitably taken advantage of children's interest. Places like Frontier Village, Santa's Workshop, and Disneyland in many localities do a thriving business because of their appeal to children's imagination.

Children could very well develop in miniature form segments of similar centers of interest. A clever teacher could devise the making of many outstanding structures to capitalize on children's interests and to further learning. It must always be remembered that the activity is not the core for the school curriculum but an adjunct or vehicle that will carry out some goal of education.

In Figure 9–1, some of the structures that can be built utilizing the technique of frame construction are illustrated.

Procedure

The reader is referred to Chapters 11 and 12 for an explanation of the meaning and use of any type of material or tool mentioned in this and the next chapter.

1. *Prepare Stock for Frames*
   a. Make a sketch or working drawing of the object to be made, showing the necessary dimensions.
   b. Determine the size of the over-all framework to be constructed, represented by the length, width, and height of the structure, as shown in Figure 9–2. Then determine the size of each individual frame. Actual size drawings of each frame can be made on wrapping paper. The drawings can be used to check the accuracy of the strapping as it is cut to length.
   c. Select a piece of strapping that is adequate for the length of the structure. With a miter box cut one end square. Be sure to hold the stock securely against the back of the box. Measure and mark the desired length on the piece of strapping. Start the measurement from the end that has just been cut square. Place the strapping in a miter box and cut to the line. Start cutting as close to the outside of the line as possible. If you have an actual size layout for the frame, check the cut stock with it.
   d. Repeat the preceding operations for every additional piece of strapping that is needed. If the pieces are of different lengths, measure and mark each piece separately. If all pieces are of one size, clamp a length gauge on the miter box. (A length gauge is a block of wood used as a stop, fastened at a distance from the saw blade that is the exact length of the piece to be cut.) Figure 9–3 illustrates how the length gauge is attached to the miter box.
2. *Prepare Gusset Plates:* Gusset plates, recommended for their ease of construction and strength, can be made from Upson board, Masonite, and plywood. Upson board is preferred because it is the least expensive and the easiest to cut, drive nails into, and take apart. Upson board comes in large sheets (4 × 8 feet) and can be procured from any lumberyard.
   a. Select a piece of Upson board.

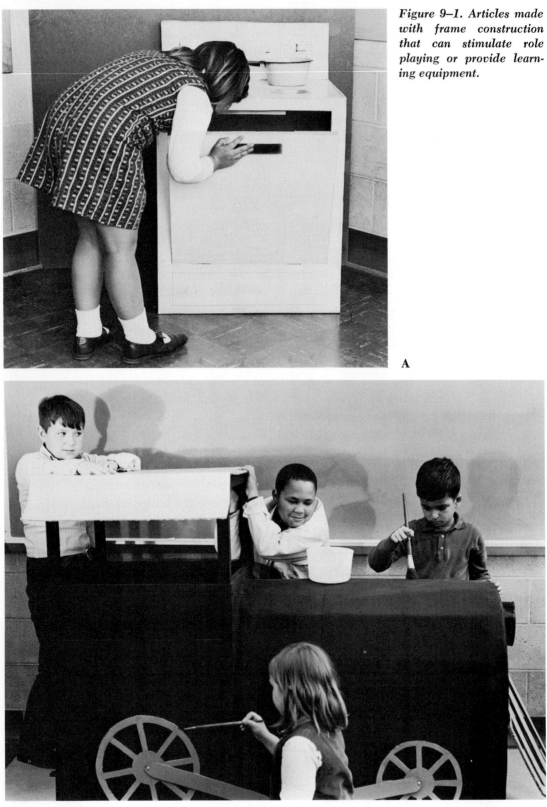

A

B

C

D

F

215

E

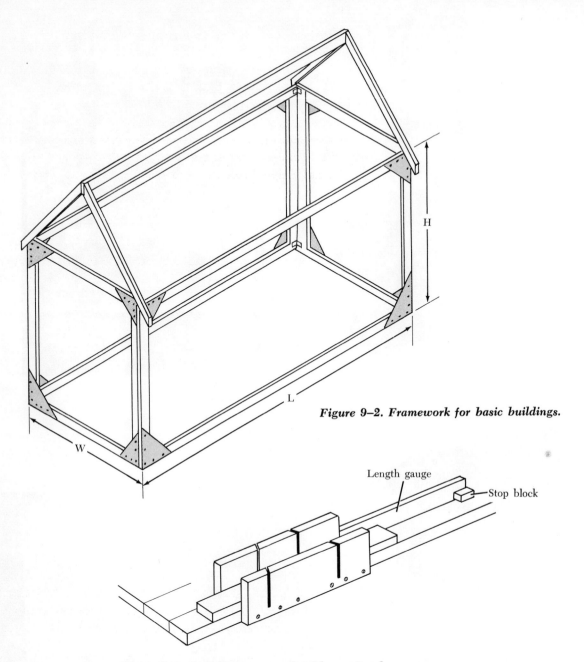

Figure 9–2. Framework for basic buildings.

Figure 9–3. Length gauge used with a miter box.

b. Measure and lay out a 5-inch strip using a ruler and pencil, as shown in Figure 9–4.

c. Measure and lay out a 5-inch square. Select a crosscut saw and cut out the square as shown in Figure 9–4. Be careful not to tear the material.

d. Lay out the gusset plate by drawing a diagonal in the square as shown in Figure 9–4. This divides the square into two right tri-

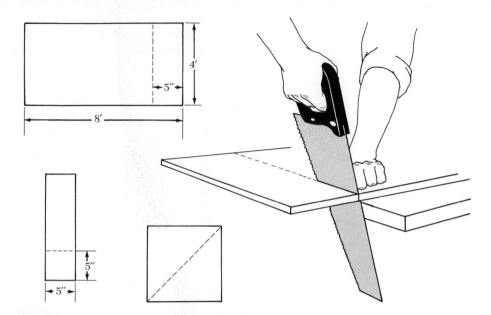

Figure 9–4. Procedure for cutting gusset plates.

angles approximately $5 \times 5 \times 7$ inches. Each of these triangles will form a gusset plate.

 e. Cut the diagonal after securing the square in a vise or clamp on a bench with a handscrew. Saw on the line with a crosscut saw.

 f. Repeat the preceding operations for every additional gusset plate.

3. *Fasten Frame With Gusset Plates:*

 a. Lay out the required rectangles, using four pieces of strapping that have already been cut to the desired lengths. Arrange them on the floor the way they should be fastened together.

 b. Using a clamping jig, clamp the pieces securely in the shape desired. Test with a square and make certain that each corner is a 90° angle. Figure 9–5 illustrates a clamping jig.

 Clamping Jig: A simple clamping jig can be made to assist in nailing frames together.

  (1) Select a piece of strapping that is at least one foot longer than the width of the frame to be nailed together.

  (2) Cut two additional pieces of strapping 6 inches in length.

  (3) Apply glue to one of the wide surfaces of one 6-inch piece of

Figure 9–5. A clamping jig for holding frames in position while securing them.

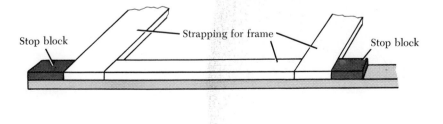

Frame Construction and Its Value in Enriching the Environment

stock. Place this piece of stock onto the wide surface of the longer piece of strapping so that the ends are flush. With 1½-inch, No. 16 wire brads, nail the pieces together.

(4) The second piece can be nailed onto the same surface the desired length from the first block. The length is determined by the size of the frame being constructed. For example, if the frame is 24 inches wide, the distance between the first 6-inch block and the second block will be 24 inches. The distance does not have to be exact, because any extra space can be taken up by using a house shingle as a wedge.

(5) An adjustable jig can be made by attaching the second 6-inch block so that it is moveable. This requires drilling holes about one inch apart through both the base piece and the 6-inch piece of strapping. A nut and bolt can be used to fasten these pieces together. The opening between blocks can be adjusted by removing the nut and the bolt, moving the block to a new position, inserting the bolt, and tightening it with the nut to lock the block in place.

c. Place a gusset plate over each corner. Be sure the edges of the gusset plate are even or flush with the outside edges of the strapping.

d. Nail the gusset plates in position with ¾-inch, No. 16 wire nails. The nails should be driven about three-quarters of an inch away from the edge of the strapping. The nails should be staggered slightly. If they are in one straight line, they are apt to split the strapping.

e. Repeat the preceding operations for every additional frame.

Figure 9–6. Using corner braces to join two frames.

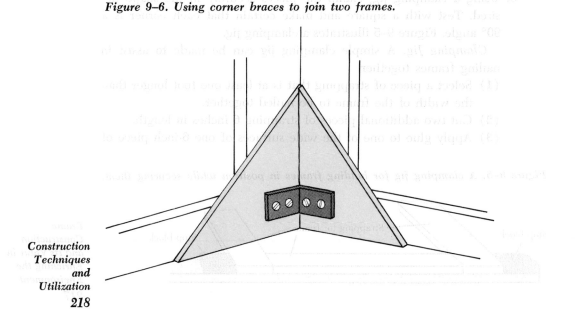

4. *Assemble Frames:*

    a. Arrange the frames in proper relationship to one another. The frames are arranged with the gusset plates facing in.

    b. Lay out and mark the locations for the corner braces. Corner braces are used on the inside of the frames to fasten them. Figure 9–6 illustrates the location of the corner braces. There are two braces in each corner, one at the top, and one at the bottom, located approximately in the center of the strapping. The corner braces are used for 90° angles. If any other angle is desired, the braces can be shaped by clamping them in a vise and bending them to the desired angle.

    c. Locate and mark the centers of the screw holes with an awl or nail.

    d. Select a hand drill and a $\frac{1}{16}$-inch twist drill and drill the required holes $\frac{1}{4}$-inch in depth. Use $\frac{3}{4}$-inch flat head wood screws to secure the corner braces.

    e. Select a screwdriver with a blade tip that is about equal in size to the slot of the screw. Try to drive the screws straight and flush with or slightly below the surface of the corner brace, which has been countersunk for this purpose.

Variations in Frame Construction Techniques

    1. *Door Construction:* Doors are constructed using the same procedures described for building a frame. Figure 9–7(B) illustrates the door for the house in Figure 9–7(A).

       a. Select two pieces of strapping for the door supports A and B.

Figure 9–7. Door (B) will be secured to the frame in house (A).

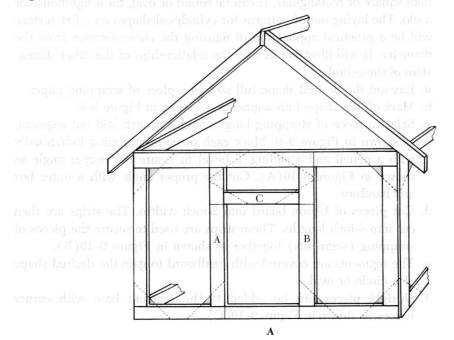

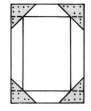

B

A

b. Secure these supports to the frame selected to have the opening for the door. Gusset plates are used to secure the door supports to the frame as shown in Figure 9–7(A). Notice the position of the gusset plates in the drawing. This position is planned to prevent interference with the opening of the door.

c. Select a piece of strapping, C, that will fit between the door supports. Support C is used to establish the door opening, as shown in Figure 9–7(A).

d. The door is hinged to support A with 2-inch butt hinges.

e. The door should be covered with the same material as the rest of the structure.

2. *Window Construction:* Windows can be added to any structure by adding openings to the original frames.

a. Select two pieces of strapping, A and B, that are the height of the frames in which the windows will be placed, as shown in Figure 9–8.

b. Secure supports A and B to the frame using gusset plates and wire nails. Notice the position of the gusset plates in Figure 9–8. This position is used to prevent interference with the window opening.

c. Select two pieces of strapping, C and D, that will fit between supports A and B, as shown in Figure 9–8.

d. Secure the supports C and D to the supports A and B with gusset plates and wire nails. Remember that the position of the gusset plates is important.

e. Shutters and other window decorations can be added to the structure.

3. *Segment Construction:* The desired structure can be some shape other than square or rectangular. It can be round or oval, for a lighthouse or a silo. The laying out of patterns for cylindrical shapes on a flat surface will be a practical application of figuring the circumference from the diameter. It will illustrate as well the relationships of the other dimensions of the cylinder.

a. Lay out the desired shape full size on a piece of wrapping paper.

b. Mark off the shape into segments as shown in Figure 9–9.

c. Select a piece of strapping long enough for each laid out segment, as shown in Figure 9–9. Mark each piece of strapping individually with a pencil and a sliding T bevel to assure the proper angle as shown in Figure 9–10(A). Cut the proper angle with a miter box and handsaw.

d. Cut pieces of Upson board into 2-inch widths. The strips are then cut into 4-inch lengths. These strips are used to secure the pieces of strapping (segments) together as shown in Figure 9–10(B).

e. The segments are covered with cardboard to gain the desired shape of a circle or oval.

f. Upright pieces can be added to the segment base with corner braces, as shown in Figure 9–10(C).

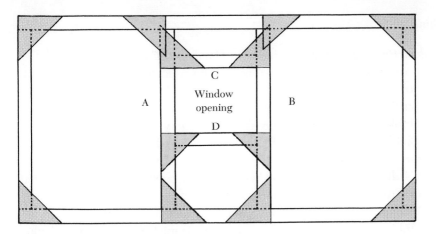

Figure 9–8. Layout for the window opening.

Figure 9–9. Layout for segment construction.

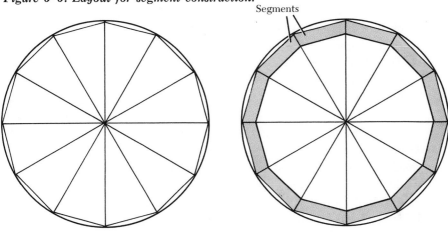

Figure 9–10. Use of a T bevel to lay out angles, straight gusset plates to connect segments, and corner braces to connect uprights.

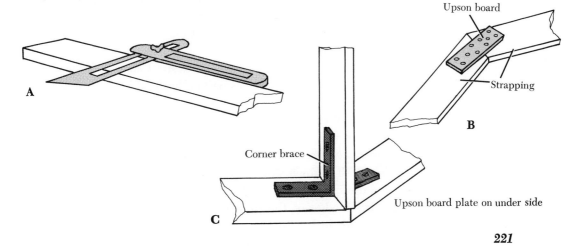

Finishing

1. *Select the Appropriate Material to Cover the Frames:*
   a. Cardboard from large cartons can be used to cover a store, barn, post office, or house.
   b. Burlap can be used to cover a puppet stage or a tent.
   c. Unbleached muslin can be used for scenery.
   d. Chicken wire or hardware cloth can be used for cages.
2. *Color and Add Detail:*
   a. Cardboard can be painted with tempera paints and then shellacked to protect the painted surface.
   b. Burlap can be dyed or purchased in a variety of colors.
   c. Unbleached muslin can be sized with a mixture of water and glue and then painted with tempera paint.
3. *Hinging Frames Together:*
   a. Folding screen hinges should be used when it is important for the frame to fold in either direction. Two 1-inch hinges can be used on frames 6 feet in height and smaller.
   b. Butt hinges can be used on frames that fold in one direction only. Two 2-inch butt hinges can be used on frames 6 feet in height and smaller. On a folding puppet stage 2-inch butt hinges may be used on one side, but on the opposite side it is suggested that 1-inch folding screen hinges be used. This combination will allow the stage to be folded into a narrow package for easy storage.
4. *Dolly Construction:* A dolly (see Figure 9–11) is a low truck with small wheels and is used to add the element of movement to vehicles made from frame construction. To illustrate, a group of children decide to build a train that can move about the classroom. Wheels could be made for the train, but cutting out circles from heavy stock is very difficult even for a trained craftsman. Children could bring in old cart or carriage wheels, but problems of size and fastening could be insurmountable. It is suggested that a dolly be used when movement is important to any vehicle made from frame construction. Wheels can be made from segment construction to hide the dolly wheels and give the vehicle the appearance of moving about on its own wheels. Here is how to construct a dolly:
   a. Cut a piece of ¾-inch plywood to the desired size. A large dolly should be about 2 × 3 feet and a small dolly should be about 1½ × 2 feet.
   b. Purchase a set of casters. For the large dolly use four 2-inch casters; for the smaller use three 1-inch casters.
   c. Secure the casters to the base of the plywood about one inch from the corners with ⅝-inch, No. 8 flat head wood screws. If only three casters are used, locate the front caster in the center about 3 inches from the front edge of the plywood. The dolly is completed and should roll with little effort.
   d. Frames can be secured to the dolly with corner braces.

A

Figure 9–11. Underside view of a dolly and its application to a jeep.

B

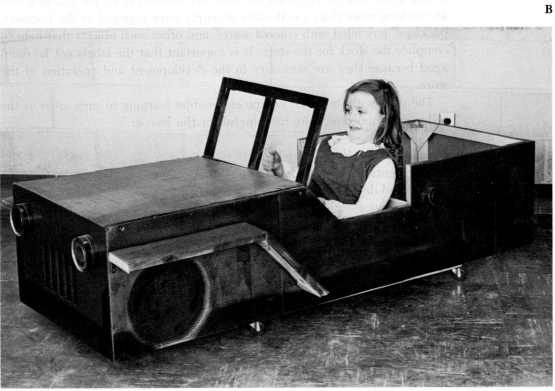

Cardboard Carpentry

Cardboard Carpentry involves children and teachers in using simple hand tools and cardboard to make a variety of toys, models, and equipment for the classroom (Tri Wall Pak, see Chapter 12). The technique allows children in grades one through six to construct sturdy items within the school environment. Many of the items described in this chapter can be constructed with such cardboard carpentry. However, frame construction does allow for greater flexibility in the variety of items that can be constructed. An animal cage, a greenhouse, or a folding puppet stage would be difficult to construct utilizing the techniques recommended in Cardboard Carpentry.

APPLICATIONS

Combined Subject Areas

A STORE

A post office, store, or bank can be constructed that will enable children in the primary grades to have simulated firsthand experiences. Children can perform various activities in relation to the area selected for study. For example, a grocery store is constructed out of frame construction. (See Figure 9–1.) The store is represented by a series of small frames with shelves added to the frames. Props for the store are brought in by the children and are nothing more than a collection of empty cans (opened at the bottom), packages, jars filled with colored water, and other such objects that help to complete the stock for the store. It is important that the labels not be damaged because they are necessary in the development and operation of the store.

The store with its varied equipment enables learning in such areas as the following to become more meaningful for the learner:

Spelling and Vocabulary:
Students develop shopping lists, make signs for the products to be sold, and develop ads for features to be sold.
Mathematics:
Students figure out prices for articles on their shopping list, make change for purchased articles, figure out the cost of one article if multiple items sell for a certain price, and ascertain the total bill.
Reading and Composition:
Information about size and content from labels on packages, cans, and jars can be obtained. Newspaper advertisements can be composed by a group of children, and these can be posted for reading by others.
Social Studies:
Discovering the origin and value of various foods can provide learnings in geography.

Experiments in economics can be worked out. Changes in the stock of the store from an overabundance to a paucity, and variations in the amounts of money the children have can lead to establishing some early understandings of supply and demand.

A STAGE

A puppet stage developed to provide experiences in drama for the primary grades would encourage self-expression through dialogue and would involve several aspects of learning. (See Figure 9–12.)

Language Development:
By combining stage construction (frame construction) with puppet making (papier mâché), children have created the materials for spontaneous language activity. The writing of scripts will be good practice in written expression.

Social Studies:
By staging puppet shows set in various cultures, children can increase their knowledge of people around the world. Historical and anthropological concepts can be brought out through original scripts prepared through research by the pupils.

Figure 9–12. Puppet stage made with burlap-covered frames. Puppets made with styrofoam.

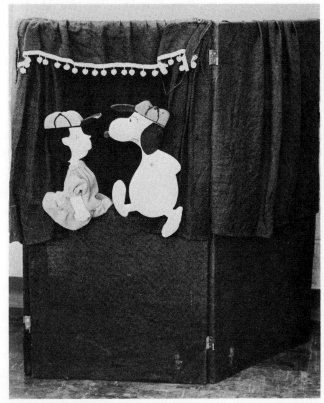

Reading:

Reading skills can be developed through the use of scripts of creative drama to supplement the work-type reading necessary to learn the information needed for the dramas. The ability to use indexes, encyclopedias, and research techniques will be among the many reading skills needed. Oral reading of prepared scripts will be purposeful, and thus fluency and expression will seem natural.

Young children are always fascinated by puppet shows. Acting out fairy tales and other story favorites is a fine reading stimulus.

A CAGE

In Figure 9–1 a simple animal cage that can be constructed by young children using the frame construction technique is illustrated. After the frames are constructed they are covered with hardware cloth. A cage enables the children to have animals in a classroom for observation of their eating and living habits. Children can record the behavior of the animals. Records can be kept of the changes in the animals' appearance as a result of their sleeping and eating habits.

DIORAMAS

In Figure 9–13 a variety of different dioramas are illustrated. These dioramas are constructed out of a wooden frame with a cardboard back and bottom. The back surface is curved and not flat, to give the diorama a more realistic appearance. Appropriate dimensions for a diorama are: length, 36 inches; height, 18 inches; and depth, 18 inches, at its deepest point.

The diorama enables children to develop material that describes their

Figure 9–13. Dioramas made with a variety of materials and techniques illustrate concepts to be explained by children in verbal presentations.

A

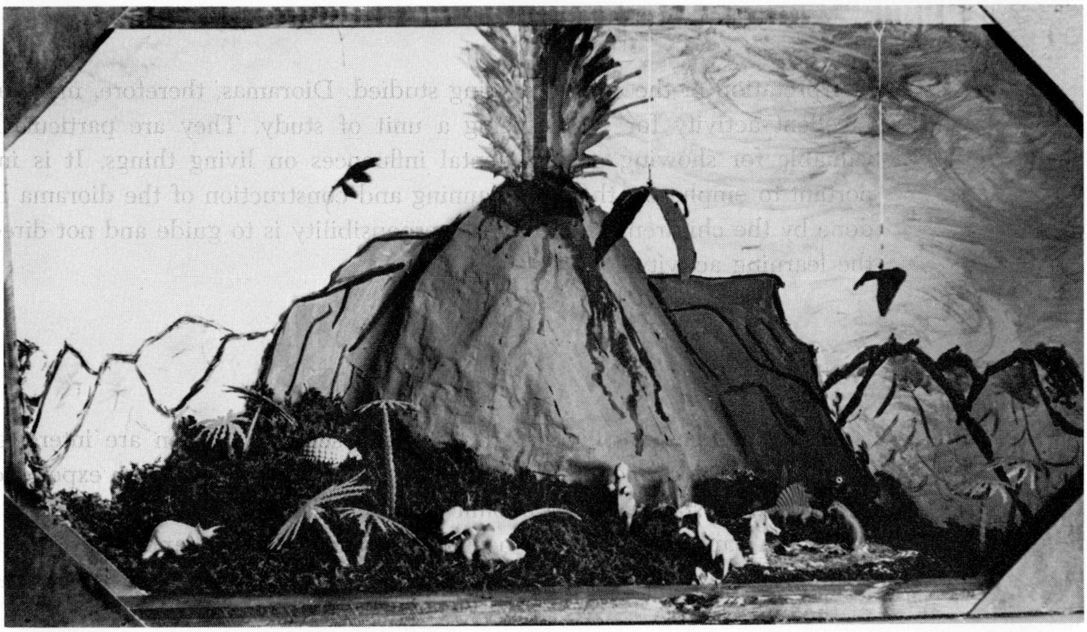

B

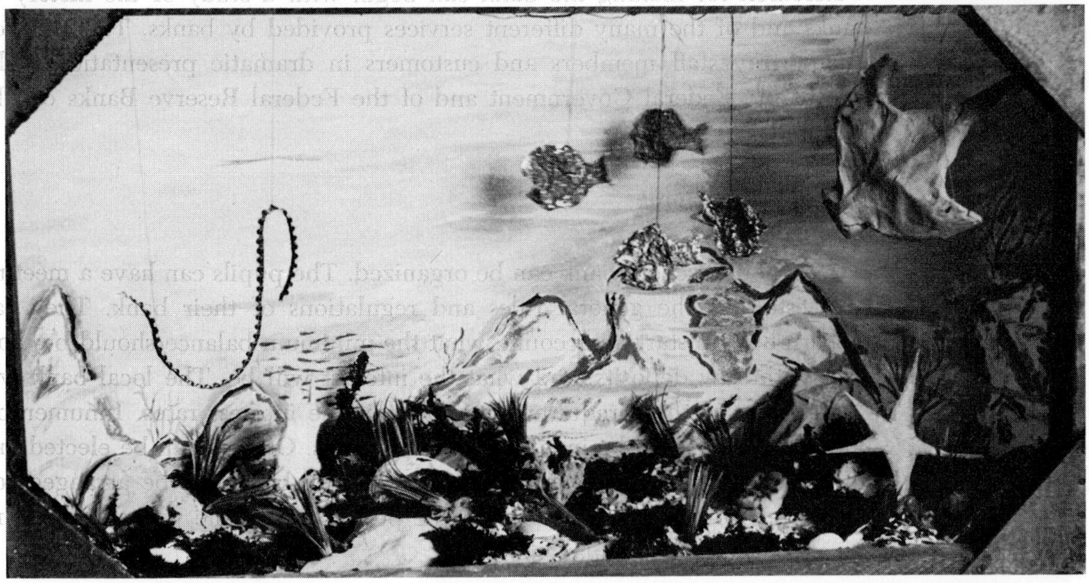

C

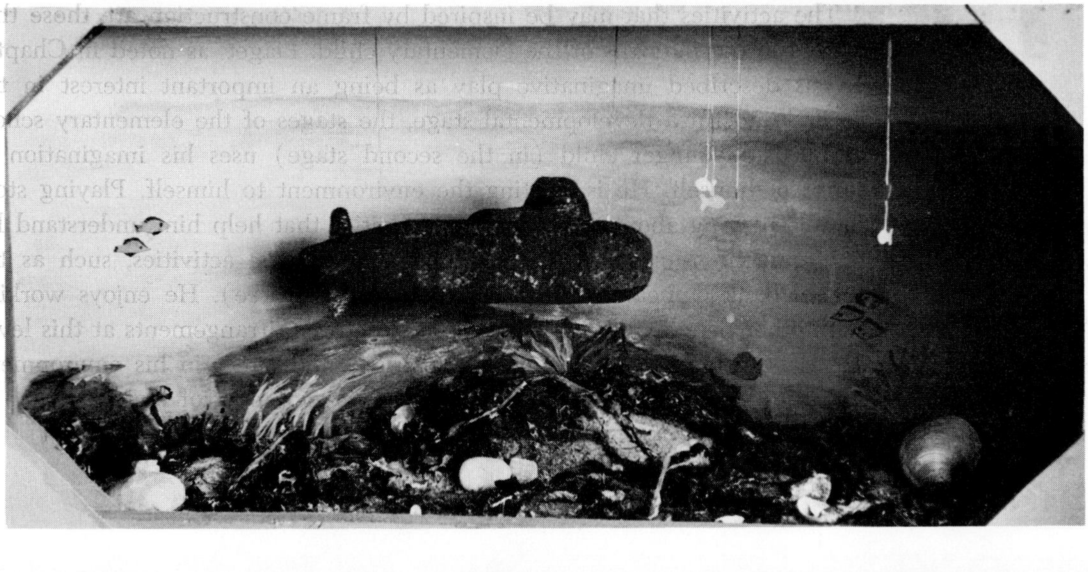

D

interpretation of the concepts being studied. Dioramas, therefore, make an excellent activity for summarizing a unit of study. They are particularly valuable for showing environmental influences on living things. It is important to emphasize that the planning and construction of the diorama be done by the children. The teacher's responsibility is to guide and not direct the learning activity.

BANKING

In any grade, from kindergarten to high school, children are interested in the workings of money in our economy. Each child needs the experience and the understanding of economic transactions, whether large or small. A classroom bank can fulfill this need by providing for firsthand experience in handling money in banking transactions. It can be constructed in a corner of the classroom.

Research for making the bank can begin with a study of the history of banks and of the many different services provided by banks. The children can portray staff members and customers in dramatic presentations. The role of the Federal Government and of the Federal Reserve Banks can be explored.

The School Bank:

An actual school bank can be organized. The pupils can have a meeting to establish the general rules and regulations of their bank. They can learn how to start an account, what the minimum balance should be, how to withdraw deposits, and what the interest will be. The local bank will set many of these requirements and pay the interest rates. Innumerable computations will be involved in this process. Officers can be elected and duties assigned. Supervision by a community bank can be arranged for, and record forms secured. With the permission of the parents, the bank can be put into regular operation.

The activities that may be inspired by frame construction are those that appeal to the interests of the elementary child. Piaget, as noted in Chapter 1, has described imaginative play as being an important interest in the second and third developmental stage, the stages of the elementary school child. The younger child (in the second stage) uses his imagination in terms of himself. He is relating the environment to himself. Playing store or role playing about the home are activities that help him understand his environment. More formalized drama and realistic activities, such as the school bank, appeal to the older child (stage three). He enjoys working with other people and following more structured arrangements at this level. He is beginning to expect order and cause and effect in his environment, because this stage is characterized by the development of logic.

CONCLUSION

Frame construction derives its values from two sources: (1) It provides a prop or realistic setting for dramatization, role playing, and simulated game situations, thus stimulating the imagination and providing excellent practice in oral language and in human and social relations. (2) It becomes a tool for learning, (a) in the form of the diorama, summarizing scientific or social relationships; (b) in the form of the cage, giving a home to an animal to be studied; or (c) in the form of the greenhouse (see Figure 9–14), providing the environment for growing plants.

The ease with which the construction can be accomplished, and the realistic results, can make this activity a true inspiration to children, particularly as a stimulus to various language activities.

LEARNING ACTIVITIES

1. Evaluate the activities suggested in this chapter for using frame construction in the classroom. Compare the teaching of the same concepts without the devices that could be developed with frame construction.

Figure 9–14. A scientific environment for plants can be provided through a greenhouse, which can be constructed for indoor or outdoor use.

2. Describe how one device made out of frame construction could be used to stimulate verbal learning in a number of subject areas.
3. List items that could be prepared ahead of time and placed in a storage chest for use in frame construction.
4. With a group of children plan and make a puppet stage using frame construction techniques.
5. With a group of fellow students design and construct teaching materials that could be used to enrich the learning activities in one of the following areas:
   a. The home
   b. Community
   c. Living things
   d. Transportation
   e. Role playing
6. Construct a piece of furniture or equipment out of frame construction for a classroom.
7. Compare cardboard carpentry with frame construction.
8. Develop with a group of children a plan for making an animal cage. Describe the assignments that would be given to each child.
9. Make an inventory of your community to see which materials could be obtained free of charge for use in frame construction.
10. Develop a list of materials needed by a classroom teacher to embark on a project in frame construction. Give the approximate cost of each item.

REFERENCES

BARCOCK, DAVID R. "Cardboard Carpentry New Craft for Teachers." *Instructor,* **79**:99–101 (November 1969).

GERBRACHT, CARL, AND BABCOCK, ROBERT J. *Industrial Arts for Grades K–6.* Milwaukee: Bruce, 1959.

HAMMOND, JAMES J., et. al. *Woodworking Technology.* Bloomington, Ill.: McKnight and McKnight, 1961.

ROTH, ELEANOR. "Cardboard Carpentry New Craft for Children." *Instructor,* **79**:101–102 (November 1969).

SHARKEY, ANTHONY, AND NAIMAN, ADELINE. *Cardboard Carpentry.* Newton, Mass.: Education Development Center, Inc., 1968.

TEEL, DEAN A. "Creating With Wood." *Instructor,* **78**:54–55 (October 1968).

CHAPTER 10

Solid Block Construction
and Its Implication *for* Learning

The school curriculum can be enriched through the replication of materials that can depict a period in time. Small-scale model buildings are sometimes desirable in connection with studies of the community, the farm, colonial life, transportation, or the westward movement. Props for puppet shows developed to dramatize history, ethnic groups, or children's literature can be constructed. Models can assist the teacher in explaining how homes, factories, office buildings, and other types of structures have changed over the years. Homes around the world can be constructed, as shown in Figure 10–1, and the basic features and characteristics studied with emphasis placed on the geographical determinants that dictate the types of roofs, sizes and shapes of buildings, construction materials, and general design. The evolution of the various forms of transportation can be studied by children as they create models of those of early times, and children can be stimulated to use their imagination in making models of the vehicles of the future.

Solid wood models can be easily constructed by children in a classroom. Standard building materials can be cut to specified lengths and arranged in a variety of forms, similar to the way in which children use building blocks in everyday play. In this case children have the added experience of partially making the blocks with which they are to build these model buildings.

A

Figure 10–1. Models of homes around the world. Research for these models indicates to the child environment and resources that are considered in home building.

B

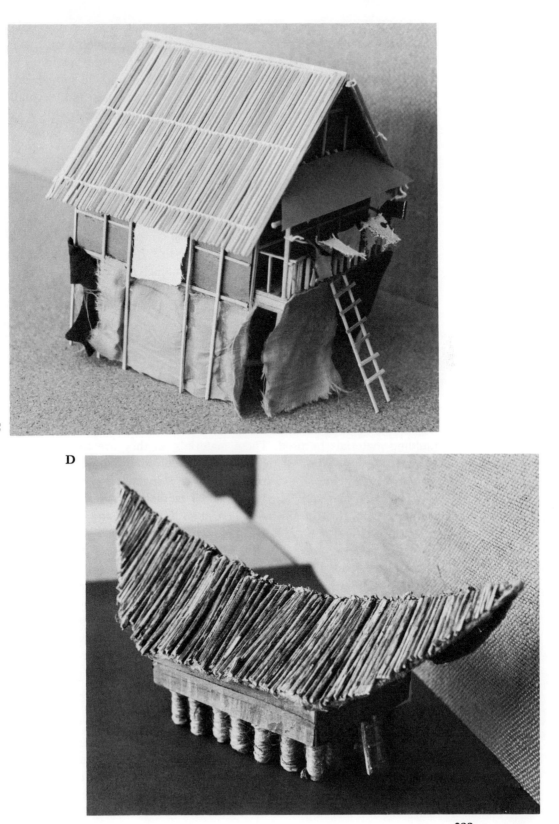

C

D

233

Solid block construction is more than a manipulative experience isolated from the academic skills taught to children. Scaling a building or a vehicle requires a workable knowledge of proportions and fractions; children need to draw plans for the buildings; figure out shapes, sizes, and proportions of the building units; and determine methods of fastening and decorating. These activities afford the child an opportunity to measure with a ruler, figure out measurements, lay out geometric shapes, and use simple hand tools. These actions provide practice and training in hand-eye coordination and large- and small-muscle development essential to safe living.

Children are fascinated by miniaturization. Doll houses, building blocks, electric trains, erector sets, and model planes and boats are all very intriguing to children. Because of this interest, model making is a popular activity in the school curriculum at all levels. Unfortunately, model making and its educational implications are often lost because teachers are not familiar with the simple constructional techniques needed.

All the skills involved in the making of the models suggested in this chapter are within the ability range of elementary-aged children. These building processes require children to think about scaling, proportion, and balance, in the area of mathematics. They call for high level planning skills in developing a well-coordinated sequence of designing, measuring, laying out, drawing, painting, cutting paper, cutting wood, pasting, gluing, and finishing. They demand determination, craftsmanship, and discipline in working out the finished product.

To simplify the process of construction, it is recommended that standard building materials be used. These materials, as they are classified, have a size relationship. Wood of the following dimensions, 1×2-inches, 1×3-inches, 2×2-inches, 2×3-inches, and 2×4-inches, is commonly referred to as building material. The conventional method of specifying lumber dimensions is to give the thickness first, then the width, and then the length. In the preceding, a 1- $\times$ 2-inch board is a board 1-inch thick $\times$ 2 inches wide, and a 2- $\times$ 4-inch is a board 2 inches thick $\times$ 4 inches wide. (As a matter of record these are not true dimensions. They are the dimensions before machining the board to relative smoothness. The actual size of a 2- $\times$ 4-inch is $1\frac{5}{8} \times 3\frac{5}{8}$-inches and a so-called 1- $\times$ 2-inch board is actually $1\frac{3}{16}$-inch $\times$ $1\frac{5}{8}$-inches. Because a whole number is easier to compute than a fraction, the boards are represented as being full size.) Materials of various sizes can be purchased at a lumberyard and cut into blocks of workable sizes.

Scaling

A simple scheme for scaling these blocks to size is to represent one story by the 2-inch thickness of the common 2×4. The average height of one story is 8 feet; therefore, under this plan 2 inches equals 8 feet. The scale is 1 inch = 4 feet. A board $2 \times 4 \times 4$ inches would represent a building one story or 8 feet high $\times$ 16 feet wide and 16 feet long. A 2- $\times$ 3- $\times$ 8-inch block would represent a one-story building 8 feet high, 12 feet wide and 32 feet long. If the desired scale is not known and must be determined from a postcard, picture, or illustration, the following procedure is recommended: measure the distance from the foundation to a point where the roof meets the side walls. Determine the number of stories and consider that each story is eight feet high. The building can be scaled accordingly. In Figure 10–2, a one-story building, it will be found that the height of the story equals one-half inch; therefore, the scale used in determining the size of the structure is ½-inch = 8 feet. The length of the barn, 2½ inches without the ell, is therefore projected to be 40 feet. If these measurements are transformed, as indicated by the scale 1 inch = 4 feet, it is determined that a 10-inch long block is needed for the base of the barn.

Approximate shapes in good proportion are usually all that are necessary to construct a replica of some desired structure. General details can be added by painting or stenciling, pasting cutouts on the surface, or by a covering of properly decorated paper or cardboard.

Making Model Buildings

1. *Procedure for Constructing the Base:*
    a. Determine the specifications of the building or unit to be constructed.
    b. Select and lay out 2- × 4-inch stock for the base of your structure. Check the ends of these pieces for relative squareness. If necessary, lay out a square end with a try square and pencil.
    c. If a commercial miter box, as shown in Figure 10–3(A), is not available, clamp a wooden miter box to a bench by means of a C clamp or hand screw, as shown in Figure 10–3(B).

Figure 10–2. Model for using the scaling procedure.

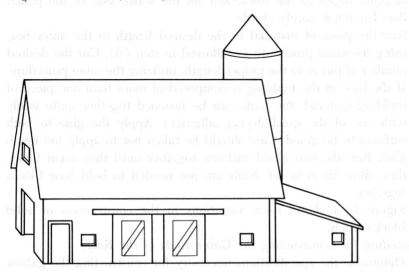

Solid Block
Construction
and Its
Implication
for Learning

235

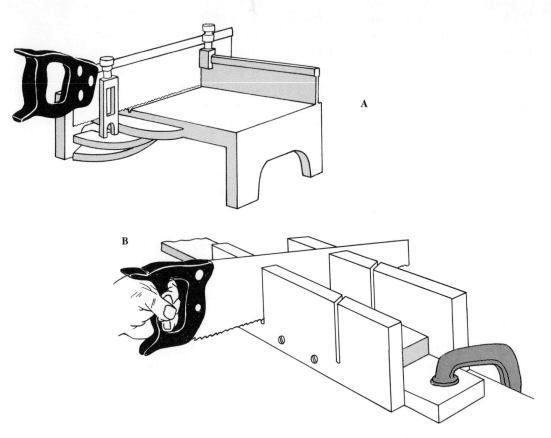

Figure 10–3. A commercial and a homemade miter box.

   d. Cut the piece of 2- $\times$ 4-inch material by placing it in a miter box
   with the squared lines just inside the saw teeth and, with the saw
   at right angles to the stock, saw on the waste side of the pencil
   line, leaving it barely visible.

   e. Saw the piece of material to the desired length in the miter box,
   using the same procedure as followed in step (d). Cut the desired
   number of pieces to the proper length, utilizing the same procedure.

   f. If the base of the building is composed of more than one piece of
   building material, the parts can be fastened together quite easily
   with one of the quick-drying adhesives. Apply the glue to both
   surfaces to be glued. Care should be taken not to apply too much
   glue. Rub the two glued surfaces together until they seem tacky,
   then allow them to set. Nails are not needed to hold base blocks
   together.

   g. Figure 10–4 shows some variations in the construction of solid
   block models.

2. *Procedure for Constructing the Gable Ends of the Roof:*

   a. Determine the specifications necessary for constructing the gables.

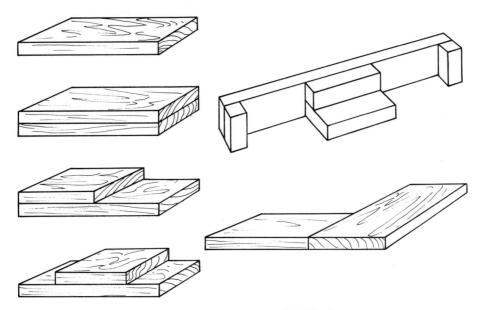

Figure 10–4. Arrangement of base blocks for solid block structures.

These specifications will be determined by following the instructions under the section on scaling a building and by referring to your drawing.

b. Select appropriate stock (for example, 1- × 3-inch pine or fir strapping) for the gable section of the building. Check the ends of the selected stock for relative squareness. If necessary, lay out a square end with a try square and pencil.

c. Square the stock in the miter box. Check steps (c) and (d) under Section 1, Procedure for Constructing the Base.

d. Lay out the gables. The gables are usually laid out in the form of a square and cut on the diagonal, as shown in Figure 10–5(A). Gables of different shapes can be obtained by cutting smaller or larger triangles and joining them into a gable end, as shown in Figure 10–5(B).

e. If the desired cut is a 45° angle, adjust the miter box to make a 45° angle cut. Place the material in a position to allow the saw to cut on a diagonal. Proceed by cutting the material. Other shapes will require that the saw be set at different angles or that a coping saw be used.

f. To make a right angle cut, readjust the saw to a 90° angle. Place the piece of material under the saw and cut on the line.

g. Repeat steps (e) and (f) until the appropriate number of gables are constructed.

h. Glue the gable ends in their appropriate positions, being careful that the ends and face edge of the base are flush, as shown in Figure 10–6. When gluing stock together without the use of nails

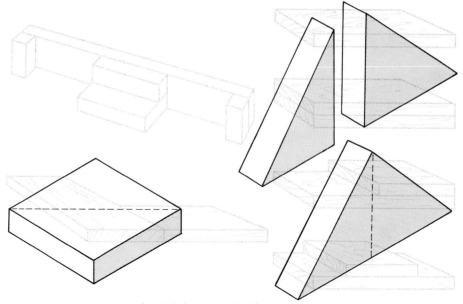

A   B

Figure 10–5. Laying out and cutting gables.

or clamps, it is recommended that the pieces be rubbed together and then allowed to set. It is also recommended that nails not be used to hold the gables, because they are difficult to drive and may split the wood. The glued joint will be strong enough for most classroom activities.

3. *Procedure for Decorating the Building:*

    a. The sizes and ends of the structure are usually covered with cardboard or construction paper. Other materials can be utilized to give the desired effect, such as twigs, dowels, or straw.

    b. Select the desired materials for the ends and sides of your structure.

    c. Lay out the cardboard or construction paper using a pencil, square, and ruler. Leave a small flap on the end pieces, as illustrated in Figure 10–7. The flap will enable the securing of an even and closed joint at the corners.

    d. Lay out doors and windows on the side and end pieces, using India ink, crayon, or water colors to give the desired features.

    e. Cut out all pieces, being sure to cut on the lines.

    f. Glue all pieces in their proper places with a quick-drying glue. Apply glue to the wooden base and then press the cardboard or construction paper in place.

    g. Repeat steps (e) and (f) until the various structures or gables are constructed.

4. *Procedure for Constructing the Roof:*

    a. Select cardboard or other desired materials for the roof. Straw, grass, or twigs can be utilized for the desired roof effect. Cardboard makes a good base for securing these materials.

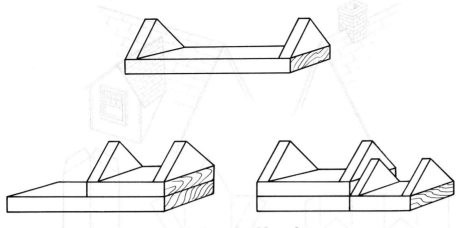

Figure 10–6. Positions of base blocks and gable ends.

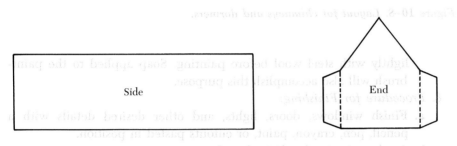

Figure 10–7. Layout for side and ends of model.

b. Lay out the desired shape and dimensions of the roof, allowing for overhang on the gables and eaves. With a pair of scissors or a paper cutter, cut out the desired shape being careful to cut on the lines.

c. Glue the roof to the gables with a quick-drying glue. Apply the glue to the edges of the gables, being careful not to use too much.

5. *Procedure for Constructing a Chimney:*

a. Chimneys that protrude from the peak or from the side of a roof can be laid out, cut, and folded into desired shapes and fastened with masking tape. The same procedure applies to dormers. Figure 10–8 illustrates this procedure.

b. Select cardboard or construction paper and lay out the chimney and/or dormer. See the drawing for correct dimensions.

c. With a pair of scissors, cut along the outside of the solid lines of the pattern just made.

d. Make proper folds and fasten edges together with masking tape, glue, or rubber cement.

e. Locate the chimney and/or dormers in their proper position and secure them with masking tape.

f. Because masking tape is coated with wax, it should be rubbed

Solid Block Construction and Its Implication for Learning

239

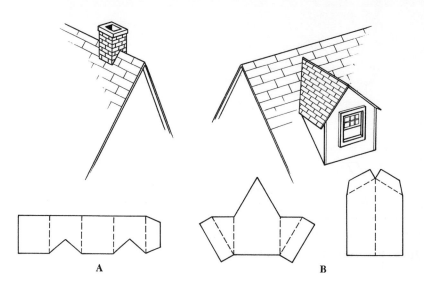

Figure 10–8. Layout for chimneys and dormers.

lightly with steel wool before painting. Soap applied to the paint-brush will also accomplish this purpose.

6. *Procedure for Finishing:*

    a. Finish windows, doors, lights, and other desired details with a pencil, pen, crayon, paint, or cutouts pasted in position.

    b. Apply paint to the desired surfaces.

    c. Check the structure for neatness and unwanted marks.

Making Models and Cutouts of Irregular Shapes

IRREGULAR MODELS. Models of tanks, trucks, automobiles, and ships require unusual shapes. (See Figure 10–9.) To construct these objects odd-shaped pieces of lumber should be used along with some simple hand tools. The following procedure can be used:

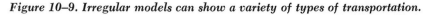

Figure 10–9. Irregular models can show a variety of types of transportation.

A

B

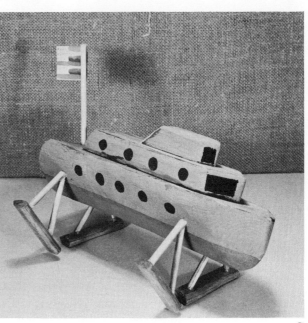

C

D

E

*Solid Block
Construction
and Its
Implication
for Learning*
241

1. Select and glue blocks together to obtain the gross shapes.
2. Rough out the stock to the desired shape. Roughing is accomplished by using a handsaw to cut out the approximate shape. (See Figure 10–10.) Sometimes small blocks cut with a handsaw can be glued together to obtain the rough shape.
3. Using a serrated-tooth file or rasp, round off these cuts to the contours needed. The serrated-tooth file or rasp can be used to change a square piece of wood to any given shape without any previous cutting with a handsaw. Its disadvantage is that it requires a long time to obtain a finished product.
4. Use a gouge to assist in the cutting operation.
5. Smooth the surface with a file and sandpaper.
6. Finish the surface with paint or other decorative materials.

PICTURE CUTOUTS FOR PANORAMAS. People, animals, buildings, and other objects can be incorporated into a natural panorama by using pictures cut from a variety of sources. Cutouts require less skill and time than solid block construction to develop a table community, farm, historical village, or buildings of a foreign country. This technique can be used by children who do not possess the psychomotor skills needed to construct a solid block model. The following steps describe the procedure needed to construct picture cutouts:

1. Select the pictures needed for the panorama:
   a. These pictures can be cut from magazines, newspapers, books, and catalogs.
   b. Pupils can draw and color pictures of buildings, people, animals, and other objects needed to complete the panorama.
2. Select the backing material for the pictures. Hardboard, cardboard, and plywood can be used.

Figure 10–10. Steps in cutting out an irregular shape.

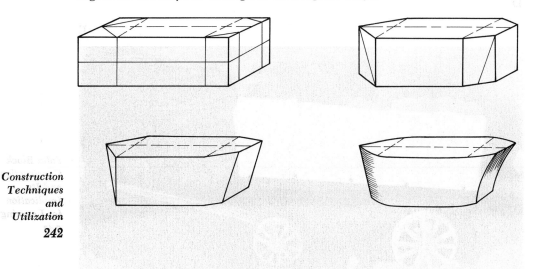

3. Glue the pictures to the backing material. Make sure that the pictures are flat and smooth.
4. Interesting effects can be obtained by cutting the pictures and backing to conform to the contour of the trees, hills, and sky of the picture selected. (See Figure 10–11.) Figure 10–12 illustrates cutouts without the background cut to conform to the contour of the landscape.

Figure 10–11. Panorama. Background is cut to conform with the landscape.

Figure 10–12. Panorama without background cut away.

5. The picture cutout needs a base to enable it to stand on a flat surface. The base block is made from a piece of wood ¾ × 1 × 2 inches.
6. On the base block, locate and mark-off the center of one face surface. This part of the block is the largest surface area.
7. At the base line of the cutout, locate and mark the center.
8. Apply glue to the face of the block. Place the base block with the glued surface against the center of the base line of the cutout and move the block back and forth to work the glue into both surfaces to increase holding power. Allow the glued joints to dry.
9. Now the picture cutout is ready to be placed in the panorama.

APPLICATIONS

Language Arts

LANGUAGE DEVELOPMENT. Classroom activities dealing with the construction and manipulation of actual objects or models provide a natural way for children to develop language skills. They become so engrossed in the activity that they not only lose self-consciousness, but have immediate, tangible, interesting ideas relative to what they have constructed to impart to other members of the class.

It does not matter that the activity, such as those described subsequently, is associated with another subject area. The interest and involvement of the pupil in the activity generates the language experience. In the primary grades, a pupil might describe a familiar portion of his environment, which he has reconstructed as part of a community project. At the intermediate level a controversial subject, such as a community redevelopment model, could engender debate with all its attendant marshaling of facts and persuasive reasoning. The following activities could be a part of almost any three-dimensional representation that is utilized in a subject area:

1. Letters written for professional advice on the topic
2. Oral and written plans and messages within and between committees
3. Oral and written reports or summaries
4. Final recommendations as a result of an experiment or demonstration
5. Technical data related to the construction of a model evolved from research on existing facilities. Experiences with proportions and with transferring dimensions from existing facilities to a model

Mathematics

SCALING. The construction of models requires that pupils learn to scale a building, vehicle, or other object from the actual structure or from a picture found on a postcard or in a book. Pupils can construct model buildings by actually measuring the original structure and then scaling these measurements to fit a classroom sand table. Or, they can develop their scale from a small illustration.

Building any model from solid block construction requires extensive use of the ruler for measuring. It requires a realistic use of many mathematical concepts, notably ratio and proportion.

Social Studies

TRANSPORTATION. Trucks, tanks, ships, covered wagons, airplanes, and other types of vehicles can be constructed using the techniques described in this chapter. An examination of the vehicles illustrated in Figure 10–9 shows how variously-sized blocks of wood can be combined to create a great variety of modes of transportation. Solid block construction allows pupils an opportunity to duplicate various modes of transportation from the past and present. It also allows pupils an inexpensive medium in which to create models of various types of transportation of the future. These models could be used in dioramas or layouts in studying transportation.

THE COMMUNITY. Another activity utilizing solid block could be a layout of a community. This could be done at two levels.

At the primary level the immediate school environment can be reconstructed on a large table. The model will have all the streets laid out on a plywood or a Masonite base. Stores, playgrounds, and houses will be located and marked off. Each child in a class will make a picture cutout of his home. He will also make a 1-inch cube to hold his picture. Groups of students will work together planning and constructing schools, stores, playgrounds, and other facilities needed to complete the school area. Small cars, trucks, and other vehicles can be used to illustrate traffic and safety problems in the area. Stop lights can be constructed.

SAFETY. Concepts in safety and geography can be built. Children can manipulate their 1-inch picture cube showing others in the class the safety procedures that they must consider on their way to and from school. Members of the group can be asked to check one another for correct crossing signs, safety signs, signal lights, and the use of geographic terms related to direction. Because children in a group will come from different directions, a variety of safety considerations will be exposed in a very realistic and meaningful way.

GEOGRAPHY. Georgraphic terms appropriate to the age level can be reinforced as the group writes or tells the direction to and from school. Words such as north, south, east, west, bridge, hill, river, stream, swamp, and others can be used in describing directions. Children can also describe the types of homes they live in and features of the buildings in the community.

COMMUNITY PLANNING. At the intermediate level, young people should be readily aware of some of the needs and potentials of their community. They might try a project on community redevelopment. The techniques described in this chapter enable pupils to put ideas for their community into concrete form. In planning a scale model of a redevelopment area within a community, pupils start to realize the problems related to rebuilding a section of a city or town.

PRESENTATION OF THE PROBLEM. The class is presented with the problem of what changes should be made in their community.

Defining the community and determining its needs are the first important steps in this problem. Planning maps can be secured from the town hall or the local planning board, which specifically define the community. Needs of the community should be in accordance with the demands of its residents and the available resources.

The planning maps and master plans will give pupils clues to the specific characteristics of the land available and the facilities planned for the community. The desires of the residents for redevelopment can be secured through a questionnaire randomly distributed to residents. Such questions as the following might be asked:

1. What buildings are of historical value to the community?
2. What sections of the community need to be rebuilt and why?
3. What types of facilities are needed by the community? Recreation? Schools? Shopping areas? Industry?
4. What is the best style of architecture for the community?

Pupils should take walks or bus rides through the community to observe problem areas. They can use these firsthand experiences to ascertain their conception of the needs of the community.

Professional Advice:

1. A *realtor* could make suggestions in relationship to property needs for housing, medical facilities, industry, shopping, and recreation.
2. An *architect* could explain the problems related to the design of structures and landscaping.
3. A *construction contractor* could help determine the building costs.
4. An *economist* could tell what redevelopment could mean to the economy of the community.
5. A *city officer* could explain the difficulties of the community in raising money for the project.
6. A *city planning* group could discuss the finished projects.

Activities:

1. Pupils could conduct a survey of the community to determine if there are any serious problems in housing, traffic, recreation, or congested business districts.
2. Pupils could construct scale models that accurately show the historical landmarks of the community.
3. Pupils could make topographical maps of the area that houses their school population.

Figure 10–13. Neighborhood model.

4. Pupils could construct models of sections of the community to represent the present. (See Figure 10–13.)
5. Graphs, charts, diagrams, and murals should be made to tell the story of street plans, buildings, and family life. These activities require the use of the techniques described in other sections of this text as well as those in this section. For example, graphs and charts require the use of layout tools, whereas diagrams and murals may require the information described in the chapter on layout and sketching techniques.
6. A final layout and construction of the ideal community of the future could be built. An audiotape recording could be made to explain the reasons why the ideal community looks as it does.

MODEL VILLAGES. In studying American or world history and geography, models of villages of the past or of other countries could help children understand different ways of living and environmental effects on people. Figures 10–14 and 10–15 represent examples of this activity. Figure 10–16 is an example of how different types of dwellings can be used to probe economic and cultural influences.

It has been previously pointed out that psychologists agree that it is important for children to have experiences with objects and materials instead of just reading or hearing about them. The importance of providing children with the opportunity to work in group activities that free them from their egocentrism and allow them to interact has also been stressed.

Solid Block Construction and Its Implication for Learning

Figure 10–14. Model of Mystic Seaport, Stonington, Conn.

Figure 10–15. Models that indicate occupations in early America.

A

B

Figure 10–16. These models can be used to stimulate verbal discussion of the reasons for the differences in the homes.

In working with models and panoramas, children engage in group activity. Most of the learning activities are group projects. The individual either makes one contribution to a planned group project (for example, one building for a model village), or he works directly with a group (for example, doing finishing work on a farm scene). By practicing smooth working relationships, children are learning respect for their own work and respect for others. They learn to handle difficult situations of human interaction by analyzing difficulties with the teacher's help and by working out solutions that involve the accommodation of others' viewpoints and compromise. They learn to generalize about effective human relationships by utilizing the many episodes that occur when people work together and depend on one another as topics for discussion and analysis under the guidance of the teacher. Such learning is suited to the elementary grades because it includes children in the developmental stage when peer relationships are important for the first time. In the activities needed for the thorough community-planning project, children of the intermediate grades receive valuable firsthand experience in community life. They meet and talk to residents, community workers, and elected officials. They come to grips with real problems and are challenged to present viable solutions. They must use the high-level skills of conceptualizing, generalizing, synthesizing, and problem solving. They are stimulated in verbal learning at the highest level through their contacts with maps, charts, and community models.

CONCLUSION

Solid block construction is an excellent technique for making models. Its use in the elementary classroom provides interest and challenge to the children. With the use of standard-size lumber or blocks and the common finishing techniques made possible with paint, paper, glue, and other simple ingredients, a great variety of construction and reconstruction is available to the pupils. The techniques are easy enough so that they do not get in the way of learning; yet the making and using of the models in their settings provide striking visual and tactile expressions of various concepts and processes important in the education of children.

LEARNING ACTIVITIES

1. Prepare a purchase list of the materials needed by a classroom teacher to embark on a project of solid block construction. Consider the finish as well as the building materials. Give the approximate cost of each item.
2. Describe a typical scene from each major period in our history. Tell how it could be constructed in solid block.
3. Select three pictures of well-known buildings of the world. If you were making solid block models of these buildings what scale would be appropriate for each structure?
4. With some other students in class construct a model of one of these:
   a. Historical place in the United States such as Greenfield Village or Sturbridge Village.
   b. Transportation in past, present, or future.
5. Select a section of your community and with some other students in class plan to redevelop this area. Make a model of the present area and a second one of how it would look after redevelopment.
6. With a group of first-grade children, construct a model of their neighborhood using the panorama technique described in this chapter. Remember, children can draw their own homes or they can be cut from magazines.
7. With some other students in the class select a group of homes around the world that will depict some economic and geographic factors about the country. Have each member of the group construct one building and develop a list of materials that were used in the building because of its geographic location.
8. Develop a plan for using solid block construction in the following situation:
   a. Area of study: historical point west of the Mississippi.
   b. Size of group and grade level: twenty-five fourth-graders.
   c. Describe how you would introduce this activity.
   d. List and describe the activities for each child.
   e. Estimate the length of time the activity should take.
9. Inventory the community for free building materials that could be used by children to construct models out of solid block construction. Check industrial plants, cabinet shops, and lumberyards for building ma-

terials. Make sure you have a list of correct names of the materials needed.

REFERENCES

HAMMOND, JAMES J., et al. *Woodworking Technology.* Bloomington, Ill.: McKnight and McKnight, 1961.

HILLER, CARL E. *From Tepees to Towers: A Photographic History of American Architecture.* Boston: Little, 1967.

KOSKEY, THOMAS A. *Creative Corrugated Cardboard.* San Francisco: Fearon, 1954.

NELSON, LESLIE. *Instructional Aids.* Dubuque, Iowa: William C. Brown, 1958, pp. 49–58.

THOMAS, MURRAY R., AND SWARTOUT, SHERWIN G. *Integrated Teaching Materials.* New York: Longmans, 1960, pp. 433–446.

PART THREE

Tools, Materials, *and* Supplies

This final section is designed to familiarize the reader with the tools and materials mentioned throughout the book. In Chapter 11 the various tools will be described and their use, not only as instruments but also as examples of scientific principles, will be explained. The opportunity of allowing children to demonstrate the physical laws that the tools, as simple machines, exemplify will be pointed out to the teacher.

The final chapter will also seek to assist the teacher and principal in cutting the costs of an activity program through:

1. Construction of useful articles that will be needed in the program
2. Making materials that can be used to produce models and devices
3. Suggested economies in collecting materials:
   a. purchasing low-cost materials
   b. soliciting donations from the home and from businesses
   c. utilizing scrap materials
4. A system of storage that is convenient and economical

Consideration is given to safety, an important aspect requiring careful planning and watchful eyes.

Finally, help is given in suggesting sources of supply for the tools and materials that must be purchased.

CHAPTER 11

Hand Tools *and* Their Relationship *to* Learning Activities

Tools represent an extension of the human hand. We all know they are used frequently throughout life. Every man and woman finds occasion to use a tool daily. Children, therefore, are gaining skills of lifelong value when they become familiar with using tools. Basic scientific principles can also be illustrated through hand tools. Each tool represents a simple machine or a combination of the machines. The concept of mechanical advantage can be clearly grasped through the use of tools. Children are usually exposed to simple machines but are seldom shown how these machines contribute accuracy, efficiency, speed, and sometimes safety in the performance of tasks.

In this section illustrations of the tools recommended for the elementary classroom, the principles of their operation, and explanations of their use are presented. Specific recommendations of size and quantity appropriate to the elementary level are also given. In the last part of this section the writers describe how to build two pieces of basic equipment, the miter box and workbench. Of course, these can be purchased ready-made, but a considerable saving of money is possible if they are constructed in the classroom.

SIMPLE MACHINES AND THEIR RELATIONSHIP TO TOOLS

When primitive man first put one end of a log under a heavy boulder and pushed on the other end to start it rolling, he was inventing one of our important machines, the lever. The discovery of this machine showed man that work could be made easier to perform. This represented a giant step toward the taming of the wilderness and the improvement of civilization.

The lever is only one of the simple machines used by man to simplify his work. Others include the wheel and axle, gears, pulleys, the inclined plane, the wedge, and the screw. These simple machines are found individually or in various combinations in the hand tools described in this chapter. Machines serve man in three essential ways:

1. They multiply force.
2. They multiply speed.
3. They change the direction of a force.

Tools are classified into three categories: testing and layout tools, driving tools, and cutting tools. An understanding of the classification of a tool should help provide some insight into the basic principle by which that tool assists the individual to gain mechanical advantage. All tools, except the testing and layout tools, are examples of the simple machines. (See Figure 11–1.)

Machines Change the Form, Direction, or Amount of Energy

Fundamentally, a machine is a device that transforms energy from one form to another. For example, an engine changes the chemical energy of gasoline into mechanical energy, whereas turbines change mechanical energy into electrical energy.

A machine can change the amount of force. A bit brace changes the limited force of the arm and back muscles into enough force to bore holes of various sizes into a piece of soft or hard wood.

A machine can also change the direction in which a force pushes or pulls. When the handle of a hand drill is turned in one direction, the twist drill turns in a different direction.

Machines can be used to change speed. The rear wheel of a bicycle goes around much more rapidly than the pedals moved by the feet.

LEVERS. Leverage is applied in the operation of many hand tools requiring an increase and control of force. Every lever has a bar and a pivot called a fulcrum. The hammer (when driving nails), scissors, and the wheelbarrow represent the three types of levers with regard to the relative position of the force, the object to be moved, and the fulcrum. Tinner's snips, vise handles, hammers, and pliers are examples of the lever. Chisels, planes, saws and other tools are combinations of levers and wedges.

INCLINED PLANE. Every time you walk up a ramp you are making use of

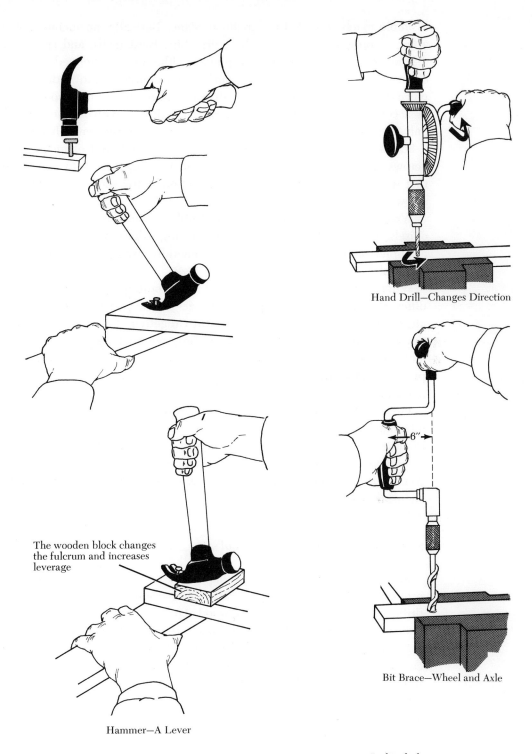

Hand Drill—Changes Direction

The wooden block changes the fulcrum and increases leverage

6"

Bit Brace—Wheel and Axle

Hammer—A Lever

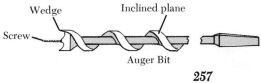

Wedge

Screw

Inclined plane

Auger Bit

Figure 11–1. Simple machines as exemplified in hand tools.

257

a simple machine called the inclined plane. Basically, an inclined plane is a flat, sloping surface. Auger bits, drill bits, twist drills, and spiral screwdrivers are examples of inclined planes. Although the inclined plane saves effort or force, it does not save work. For example, a screw driven into a piece of wood with a spiral screwdriver requires the same amount of work as a common screwdriver. The spiral screwdriver, with its inclined plane, only decreases the amount of time needed to drive the screw home.

Screw. The screw is a simple machine, a special kind of inclined plane. Screws are often used to change a small turning force into a large force that works in a straight line. The application of the screw is found in hand screws, vises, and clamps.

Wedge. The wedge is actually a double inclined plane. Knives, planes, chisels, gouges, files, saws, and the cutting edges of drills and bits are examples of the wedge. Wedges are generally used to split, divide, or cut material.

Wheel and Axle. The wheel and axle combination consists of several different parts: a crank and a shaft, or several wheels of different sizes attached to each other so that they turn together. Leverage is obtained in the wheel and axle by the art of twisting, winding, or cranking in such a manner that force is distributed in a circular motion around a fixed point or pivot. Hand drills, bit braces, and screwdrivers are examples of the wheel and axle.

Pulley. The pulley is basically a wheel that turns easily on an axle. The advantage of a pulley is that it changes the direction of the force needed to move an object. One or more pulleys in a frame is called a block. A group of pulleys connected with a rope or chain is called a block and tackle. This combination of pulleys not only changes direction but also increases mechanical advantage.

Selection of the Appropriate Tool

Mechanical advantage is an important consideration in selecting the proper tool for a particular operation. For example, a ¼-inch hole can be drilled or bored into a piece of wood. Drilling requires using a hand drill and a ¼-inch twist drill, whereas boring requires the use of a bit brace and a ¼-inch auger bit. One of the questions that arises is which tool will accomplish the job with efficiency and accuracy. A test of both tools will indicate that the bit brace and auger bit are the correct hand tools for this job.

SAFETY

Tools were developed to aid man in his work. Safety in their use is therefore important, lest they become a detriment rather than an asset.

Safety is accomplished through proper care, understanding, and respect for the tool.

The teacher needs to use judgment when presenting children with information related to safety. Perhaps a good rule to follow is to give enough instruction to eliminate danger of injury, damage to the tools, or excessive spoilage of the materials. Supplementary information can be supplied as difficulties arise. It is important to emphasize that the degree to which tools are beneficial or detrimental in the fabrication of an object or item depends on the pupil's use of tools.

Considerations in Using Tools

It is difficult to overemphasize the importance of good tools and their relationship to safety. The first consideration in tool safety is the purchase of tools of good sturdy quality. Some individuals think that because children will mishandle tools and replacement will be necessary, the tools purchased for use with young children can be inexpensive and of lesser quality than those used by adults. This is faulty reasoning. Name brand tools that are strongly constructed of durable materials will absorb the punishment dealt them by inexperienced hands to a greater degree than inexpensive tools. They will outwear cheaper tools; but, more important, they are safer to use.

For example, the blade on an expensive crosscut saw or ripsaw is less apt to bend and twist out of shape than is the blade of a cheaper saw. A saw with a twisted or bent blade is more difficult to use because it will bind in the saw kerf. The twisted or bent blade also makes cutting a straight line more difficult. When the saw sticks or binds in the saw kerf, the operator usually increases the force applied to the cutting stroke. The increased force decreases the control the operator has over the cutting tool and can result in a serious injury.

A second consideration is the importance of selecting the correct tool for a particular task. Each tool has been designed and tested to perform a certain operation. The wrong tool for a task creates unnecessary difficulties and even frustrations as the operation is performed. Therefore, the teacher must be concerned with whether the tools selected are appropriate to the nature of the work being done. For example: (1) Tinner's snips should not be used to cut wire or nails because of the danger to the operator from flying scraps and the likelihood of spoiling the cutting edge of the tool. (2) Screwdrivers should not be used for prying objects apart because of possible damage to the blade and tip. Also, the screwdriver may slip and cause injury.

The third consideration is the condition of the tool. A loose handle increases the difficulty in controlling a tool when performing a task. Because of the limited motor skills and coordination of young children, a loose handle could result in an injury to the operator and/or damage to the materials. Tools should be checked and pupils warned that loose parts—

such as blades, handles, screws, or nuts—are dangerous. They should be instructed to check with the teacher before using a tool that is in poor condition.

Tools with dull cutting edges are more dangerous than sharp ones. A knife with a dull cutting edge requires greater force on the cutting stroke. The increased force usually results in the pupil's trying to think of new ways to hold the tool or material to gain the needed strength to cut the material. Personal injury may occur if the pupil uses the tool incorrectly or awkwardly. An example is cutting toward the body rather than away from it when using a knife.

The proper tool in good condition in the hands of a skillful craftsman is the goal to keep in mind. Boys and girls in the process of developing manipulative skills have enough to concentrate on when conditions are good. Therefore, every effort should be made to supply the pupils with appropriate tools of superior quality. Pupils, in turn, should learn to use tools with respect, to keep them clean, to set them down carefully when not in use, and to store them in an assigned place.

Safety Rules

The following rules should be understood by the pupils before embarking on any program requiring the use of tools.

1. Always cut away from the body when using a knife.
2. Keep hands away from the front of a sharp-edged tool while the tool is in use.
3. Watch the thumb when using it as a guide in crosscutting or ripping.
4. Test the sharpness of tools on a scrap piece of stock.
5. Keep tools away from the edge of a bench or a table.
6. Make sure all handles, blades, and other parts are secure.
7. Use tools only for their intended purpose and then properly.
8. Be careful when handling long pieces of materials in a classroom.
9. Carry only one tool at a time. Watch out for others when carrying sharp or pointed tools.
10. Walk cautiously when carrying tools or moving about where others are using tools.
11. Report any accidents, however slight, to the teacher.

The following criteria should be considered when selecting tools for an activity program:

1. The number of tools should be adequate for the planned program.
2. Tools should be purchased with the physical capacities of the children in mind.
3. If only a limited number of tools can be purchased, it is advisable to

buy a variety of tools (one of each type), rather than a number of one type.

4. Name brand tools, or those that are substantially constructed, should be purchased over inexpensive or poorly constructed tools.

Tool Storage

Storage of tools is one of the most important considerations to any program that involves the use of tools. Proper storage reduces damage to tools and prevents loss. Because classrooms are not built with a storage facility for tools, the teacher must plan an adequate place to store them. If one set of tools is going to be used in more than one classroom, this factor has to be kept in mind also. The following suggestions should be considered in planning for tool storage facilities:

1. The cutting edges of the tools should be protected from hitting other tools or surfaces.
2. The accessibility of tools is an important consideration. Pupils should be able to take tools from storage with ease and without danger to the individual or tool.
3. Each tool should fit into a definite place. One tool for one spot facilitates checking tools at the end of a work session.
4. If the tools are used by another class, a movable panel or tool chest should be considered. If each class has its own set of tools, a permanently fastened panel may be the answer.

PLANNING A TOOL PANEL. When laying out a tool panel, it is a good practice to arrange tools according to their use or classification. Such a logical arrangement makes it easy to locate needed tools. Screwdrivers, hammers, bit braces, hand drills, and nail sets should be clustered in the same general area; the cutting tools, such as saws, knives, auger bits, and twist drills, will make up another cluster.

Tools can be hung on a panel using homemade or purchased tool holders. Some tools, such as screwdrivers, nail sets, and bits, require only a piece of wood attached to the tool board, as shown in Figure 11–2.

A variety of hooks, clips, and holders is available commercially for holding tools, as shown in Figure 11–2. Some of these clips and holders can be used on a plywood panel, whereas others need to be used on a pegboard.

Silhouettes can be painted on the panel to guide pupils in returning tools to their proper places. Labels placed on the panel will assist pupils in learning the correct names of the various tools.

A tool chest can be used for storage as a last resort. Tool chests are not practical because tools are hard to find and because it is difficult to keep the cutting edges from hitting each other. It also limits the number of children that can be selecting a tool at one time. If a tool chest needs to be

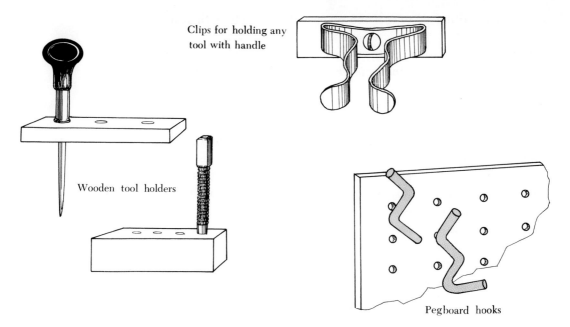

Clips for holding any
tool with handle

Wooden tool holders

Pegboard hooks

Figure 11–2. Types of holders for tools.

used because of expediency, the teacher should probably man the tool box to prevent injury.

STORAGE SPACE. The techniques and activities recommended throughout this text require some type of storage area. The space needed for this purpose will vary according to the complexity of the program. The success of the program depends to a great extent on some kind of organized system of storage. Poor storage facilities may result in a situation that is almost impossible to control. The writers suggest that materials be obtained or purchased with these factors in mind. Many types of storage racks and cabinets are available that can help the classroom teacher minimize this problem.

Getting Out Stock

Getting out stock means selecting, laying out, and cutting material appropriate to the job at hand.

PROCEDURE

1. Determine the kind of stock, dimensions, and other necessary data for the project to be fabricated. A plan or drawing of the activity to be undertaken can assist in determining the materials needed.

2. Check the scrap storage container for needed materials. Many times satisfactory material is available there without cutting large stock.

3. If you cannot find suitable material in the short-piece container, go to the material storage area. Check kind and grade of stock, and check dimen-

sions. Examine the stock for flaws, defects, or blemishes, and determine if they will interfere with the use of that material for the particular activity at hand. Select the stock that will result in the least amount of waste.

4. Make proper considerations for color, texture, figure, grain, and other qualities, and be sure each piece is best suited for the purpose it is to serve.

5. Lay out your stock, keeping in mind all necessary considerations of waste, defects, strength, beauty, and the like. The stock should be large enough to allow for rough cutting. Pupils should be required to get the teacher's approval before cutting any stock.

6. Stock should be properly supported and care taken to avoid over-cutting lines, tearing, bending, or otherwise damaging stock or tools and equipment. Use the proper tools, and be certain the cut is accurate.

7. Unused materials should be stored in the proper place in a safe, neat, and appropriate way.

8. All tools should be returned to their proper place.

RECOMMENDED TOOLS FOR CHILDREN'S USE

The tools most commonly required in an elementary school program are described in this section. Special recommendations for their purchase and directions for their use are also given.

Ruler

In technical literature the ruler is usually called a rule. In this text it is referred to as a ruler because this term is common in school practice.

PRINCIPLE OF OPERATION. The ruler is used for duplicating and testing a standard unit of measure.

SPECIFIC RECOMMENDATION. A 2-foot bench ruler and a yardstick, both marked off in sixteenths of an inch, are desirable.

USE. The ruler is used to provide for accurate transference of measurements and layout distances on materials.

Using the Ruler

1. Develop skill in reading a ruler. Know the location of measurements such as the following: $\frac{5}{16}$, $\frac{7}{16}$, $\frac{9}{16}$, $\frac{11}{16}$, $\frac{13}{16}$, and $\frac{15}{16}$.
2. Hold the ruler on edge when laying out or making measurements. Mark the distance with a pencil. Do not make a dot, but use a line perpendicular to the ruler to indicate the measured point.

Try Square

PRINCIPLE OF OPERATION. The right angle of a square is used in testing the squareness of adjacent surfaces.

SPECIFIC RECOMMENDATION. A try square with a 6-inch blade should be used.

USE. To test the squareness of adjacent surfaces, draw guidelines and lay out stock.

Using the Try Square

1. To test adjacent surfaces, hold the handle of the square against the side of the board, as shown in Figure 11–3(A).
2. To test a surface for flatness, hold the blade tightly against the surface as shown in Figure 11–3(B).
3. To make a line with a try square and pencil, hold the handle of the square against the edge of the board with the left hand, and slide the square along the board until the edge of its blade is located in the desired position.

T Bevel

PRINCIPLE OF OPERATION. A set angle is used in testing the angle of adjacent surfaces.

SPECIFIC RECOMMENDATION. A T bevel with an 8-inch blade should be used.

USE. A T bevel can be used to lay out, test, and transfer angles other than those that are 90°.

Using the T Bevel

1. Figure 11–4 illustrates how a protractor is used to set a T bevel to the desired angle.
2. The T bevel is used in the same way as a try square, but is not a substitute for it. Figure 11–4 shows how the T bevel is used for checking or transferring angles.

Figure 11–3. Testing for squareness (A) and flatness (B).

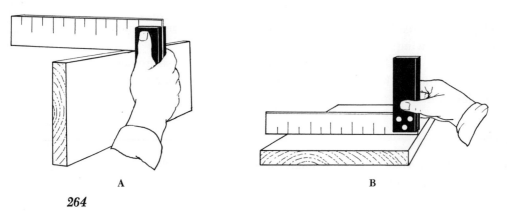

A   B

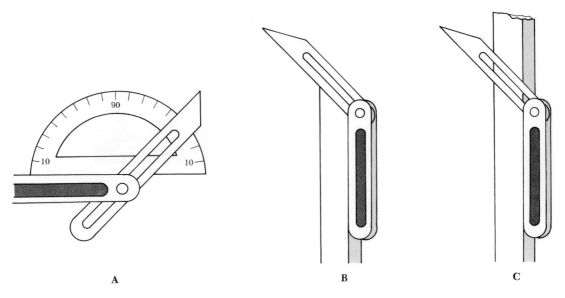

Figure 11–4. (A) and (B) show methods of setting the T bevel. (C) shows the transferring of the desired angle to the stock.

Scratch Awl

PRINCIPLE OF OPERATION. The tip of the scratch awl works on the principle of the wedge, while the handle acts as a wheel and axle.

SPECIFIC RECOMMENDATION. A scratch awl with an overall length of 6½-inches should be used.

USE. The scratch awl can be used for starter holes in wood before using the twist drill, wood screws, or nails. It can be used to punch small holes in leather, thin metals, or plastic containers. It is also used to mark metal surfaces.

Using the Scratch Awl

1. Locate the position of the hole and mark with a plus sign (+).
2. Place the tip of the awl at the center and force the awl into the wood with a twisting motion. Care should be taken not to use the awl on thin wood or too near the edge, because it forces the wood fibers apart.
3. Small holes can be punched in some materials by hitting the wooden handle of the scratch awl with the flat of the hand.

Crosscut Saw

PRINCIPLE OF OPERATION. The teeth of the crosscut saw cut on the principle of a knife and chisel.

SPECIFIC RECOMMENDATION. A crosscut saw 20 inches in length with eight points to the inch should be used.

Hand Tools and Their Relationship to Learning Activities

265

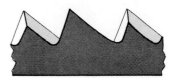

Side View of Crosscut Saw Teeth

Top View of Crosscut Saw Teeth

Figure 11–5. Diagrams of the crosscut saw teeth.

USE. The crosscut saw can be used to cut with or across the grain; however, the teeth of the crosscut saw are designed to cut across the grain or at an angle to the grain. (See Figure 11–5.)

Ripsaw

PRINCIPLE OF OPERATION. The teeth of the ripsaw cut on the principle of a chisel.

SPECIFIC RECOMMENDATION. A ripsaw 20 inches in length with eight points to the inch should be used.

USE. The ripsaw is used to cut with the grain. (See Figure 11–6.)

Using a Saw

1. Lay out a guide line to follow when cutting with a handsaw. A straight edge should be used along with a pencil or knife.
2. Narrow pieces (4 inches and under) can be cut to length in a miter

Figure 11–6. Diagrams of the ripsaw teeth.

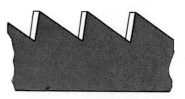

Tools,
Materials,
and Supplies

266   Top View of Ripsaw Teeth

Side View of Ripsaw Teeth

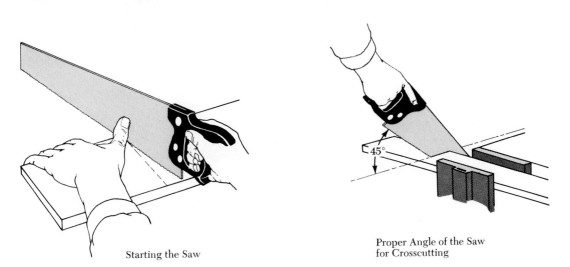

Starting the Saw

Proper Angle of the Saw
for Crosscutting

Figure 11–7. Position of a crosscut saw at the start and during the actual cutting.

box or held in a vise. Wide boards are cut to length by placing the boards on a stool or chair.

3. Figure 11–7 illustrates the position of the crosscut saw when cutting to length.

4. Stock can be cut to width with a ripsaw.

5. Guide the edge of the saw with a guide block or the knuckle of the left thumb. Start the saw with two or three light, upward strokes to engage the saw teeth.

6. Once the teeth are engaged, a few short strokes will deepen the groove so that the left hand can be removed. It is important to take full-length strokes and apply arm and body pressure when cutting.

7. Keep on the line. Short strokes and a slight twist of the handle can be used to get the saw back on the line.

8. When the cut nears the end, the operator should hold the piece with the left hand, as shown in Figure 11–8.

Figure 11–8. Supporting the board while finishing the cut.

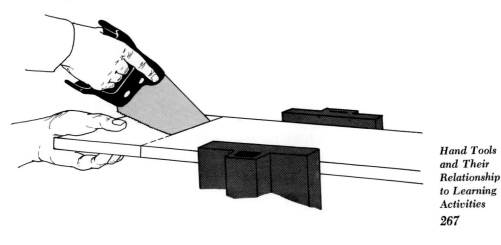

*Hand Tools
and Their
Relationship
to Learning
Activities*

267

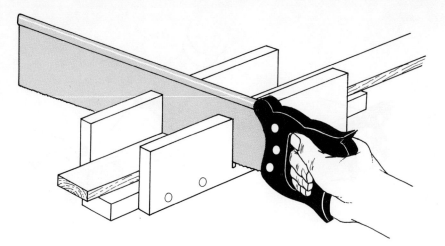

Figure 11–9. Using a backsaw in a miter box.

Backsaw

PRINCIPLE OF OPERATION. The backsaw uses the same principle as the cross-cut saw.

SPECIFIC RECOMMENDATION. A 14-inch, No. 4 backsaw should be used.

USE. The backsaw is used for fine work: cutting molding, angles, and the like; it also can be used in a wooden miter box. It has fine crosscut teeth and a thin blade that is reinforced with a steel rod along its back. The steel backing prevents the backsaw from twisting. Figure 11–9 illustrates its use with a wooden miter box.

Coping Saw

PRINCIPLE OF OPERATION. The coping saw uses the same principle as the ripsaw.

SPECIFIC RECOMMENDATION. The frame size should be $\frac{3}{16}$- $\times$ $\frac{3}{8}$-inch, accommodating all $6\frac{1}{2}$-inch pin end or lock loop end blades.

USE. A coping saw is used to cut notches and curves that would be difficult to cut with any of the other handsaws.

Using the Coping Saw. Because the teeth of the coping saw blade face the handle, the saw cuts when it is pulled toward the operator. (See Figure 11–10.)

Procedure for Cutting Interior Sections

1. Drill a $\frac{1}{4}$-inch hole in the waste section of the material to be cut out.
2. Remove one end of the blade by unscrewing the handle of the coping saw and applying pressure to the frame.
3. Slide the blade through the hole and replace the saw blade in the frame. Once the blade is secured sawing can be started. (See Figure 11–11.)

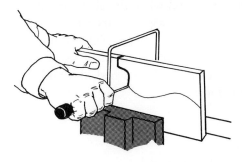

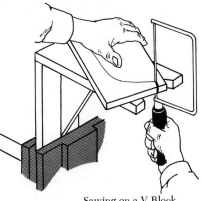

Sawing on a V Block

Figure 11–10. Using the coping saw for exterior cuts.

*Figure 11–11. Using the coping saw
for interior cuts.*

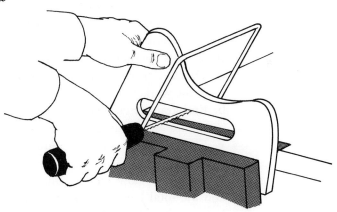

Files

PRINCIPLE OF OPERATION. The teeth of a file or rasp work on the principle of the cutting wedge.

SPECIFIC RECOMMENDATION

Type	Shape	Size
Cabinet file	half round	10″
Cabinet rasp	half round	10″
Wood file	half round	10″
Second cut mill	flat	10″
File card		

File handles should be purchased for all files to protect the operator from injury from the tang of the file. A file card is a special wire brush used to clean files.

*Hand Tools
and Their
Relationship
to Learning
Activities*

269

Uses. Files are used to remove burrs and sharp edges from metals. They are also used to remove large amounts of material when the shape or space will not allow cutting with a sharp-edged tool. A rasp is coarser than a file. Cabinet files and cabinet rasps are half round in shape. Their radius is larger than that of regular half-round files and half-round wood rasps, and they are thinner. Their teeth are finer than those of the wood files and the wood rasps, and they leave an excellent finish.

Shaping with a File or Rasp

1. The size and shape of the file are determined by the surface to be worked. Flat or convex edges of a piece of wood should be filed with a flat surface, whereas concave shapes should be filed with the rounded surface. The rasp is used to rough out the desired shape, and the file is used for a smoother cut.
2. Secure the stock in a vise. Grasp the handle of the file with the right hand, and the tip with the fingers of the left hand.
3. The file is pushed away from the operator when slight downward pressure is exerted. The file is then lifted off the surface on the return stroke and another forward stroke is taken.
   a. Concave surfaces require that the file must be held at right angles to the work.
   b. End grain or curved surfaces require that the file be held diagonally to the stock to avoid cutting grooves and flat spots in the surface.
   c. Flat or convex surfaces require holding the file in the direction of the surface.
4. Long, rather slow and rhythmic strokes should be used when filing, and the total length of the file should be used. Squealing and squeaking sounds indicate that the stock is being held incorrectly in the vise.

Hand Plane

PRINCIPLE OF OPERATION. The blade of a plane works on the principle of a cutting wedge.

SPECIFIC RECOMMENDATION. An 8-inch smooth plane is required.

USE. This tool planes the surface of material straight and smooth.

ASSEMBLING AND ADJUSTING. The assembling and adjusting of a plane is not difficult if the procedures are followed.

Assembling

1. If the plane-iron blade needs sharpening, the teacher should seek the help of a qualified person (industrial arts teacher or consultant).
2. Place the plane-iron cap on the flat side of the plane-iron with the screw in the slot. Figure 11–12 illustrates the position of the plane-iron cap and plane-iron for purposes of assembling the two together.

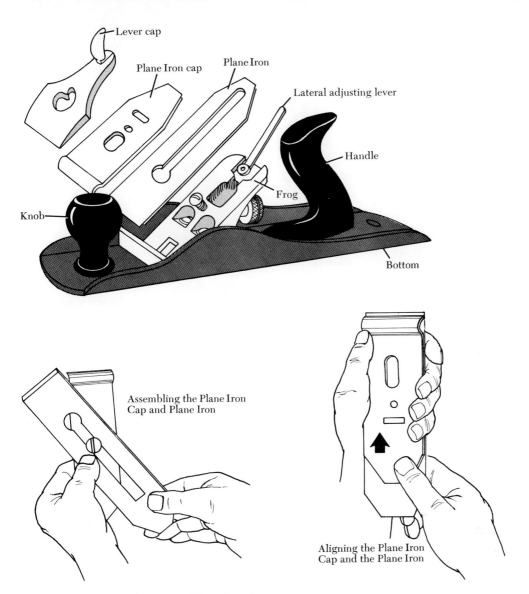

Figure 11–12. Steps in assembling the plane.

Lever cap

Plane Iron cap

Plane Iron

Lateral adjusting lever

Handle

Frog

Knob

Bottom

Assembling the Plane Iron
Cap and Plane Iron

Aligning the Plane Iron
Cap and the Plane Iron

3. Adjust the plane-iron cap. It should be about $\frac{1}{16}$-inch from the cutting edge of the blade for average work. It should never touch the cutting edge of the blade. Fasten the cap by tightening the screw with a screwdriver.

4. Place the assembled plane-iron and cap in the plane by placing the plane-iron with its level side down on the frog. Check to make sure that the plane-iron is placed properly on the lateral adjusting lever.

5. Place the lever cap over the plane-iron assembly, making sure the screw slides properly in the slot.

6. Push down on the cam located on the lever to secure the entire assembly. If the cam does not adjust freely, recheck the assembly.

*Hand Tools
and Their
Relationship
to Learning
Activities*

271

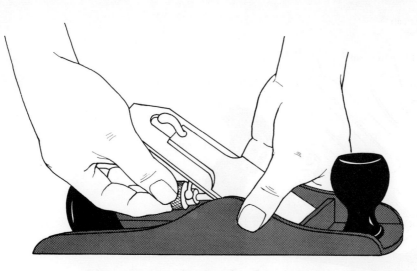

Figure 11–13. Adjusting the plane for cutting depth.

ADJUSTING

1. The cutting edge of the plane-iron should be parallel with the bed of the plane. This can be regulated by moving the lateral adjusting level.
2. The depth of the cut is regulated by manipulating the adjustment nut to the right or left until the desired depth is obtained. (See Figure 11–13.)

USING A HAND PLANE

1. *Planning a face true and smooth:*
   a. Select the face with the least number of imperfections.
   b. Draw an arrow indicating the direction of the grain.
   c. Clamp the board end-to-end between two pieces of stock; one piece (A) should be thinner than the piece being planed, as in Figure 11–14. The stock should not be clamped edge-to-edge, because the pressure across the grain will cause the material to bend. If it were planed flat in this position, the board would spring to a curved position when the pressure was released.
   d. Adjust the plane-iron to cut a fine shaving. Plane off any high corners on the board and then plane just enough to clean the surface. Remember, when starting to plane, to bear down on the knob at the front of the plane. When the entire plane is on the surface, bear down equally on both the knob and handle. As the front of the plane begins to pass off the board, relieve the pressure on the knob.
   e. Test the surface frequently with a try square or the edge of a plane.
2. *Planing an edge true with the face:*
   a. Fasten the board securely in the vise with the better of the two edges up.

b. Grasp the handle of the plane with the right hand. The thumb of the left hand is placed on the base of the knob, while the fingers are placed on the bottom surface of the plane. Fingers in this position can slide against the face surface and aid in keeping the plane parallel and steady.

c. Take full-length strokes, keeping in mind that pressure is applied to the knob at the start of each stroke and on the handle at the end of the stroke.

d. Sight down the edge to check for squareness and straightness as the surface is being planed. With a try square, check the squareness of the working face with the edge.

3. *Cutting or planing an end:*

a. When the end grain is not going to show, the end can be squared by cutting the end off in a miter box.

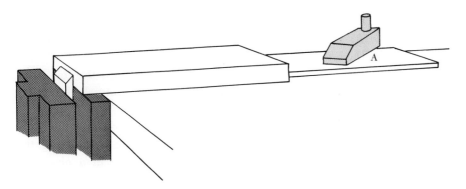

Figure 11–14. Positioning stock for planing the face of a board.

b. When the end grain is going to show, the end should be cut straight and then planed. Plane from an edge half the distance across the end; then plane the remaining distance from the opposite edge. If end grain is planed across the entire width, end fibers will split and chip. Grasp the plane as for edge planing, but keep the plane at an angle with the end of the stock. Planing in this position gives a shearing cut across the wood fibers.

c. Test for squareness with a try square.

Bit Brace

PRINCIPLE OF OPERATION. The bit brace works on the principle of the wheel and axle.

SPECIFIC RECOMMENDATION. A bit brace with an 8-inch swing, ball bearing head, and semibox ratchet should be used.

USE. The bit brace is used for holding and driving auger bits.

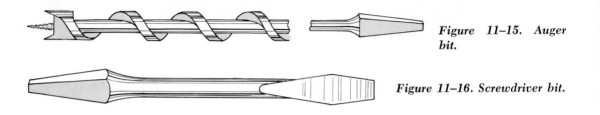

Figure 11–15. Auger bit.

Figure 11–16. Screwdriver bit.

Auger Bit

PRINCIPLE OF OPERATION. The auger bit works on the principles of the cutting wedge and the inclined plane.

SPECIFIC RECOMMENDATION. A complete set of thirteen bits, ranging in size from ¼- inch to 1-inch by $\frac{1}{16}$-inch, is required.

USE. The auger bit is used for boring holes in wood, Masonite, and Upson board. (See Figure 11–15.)

Boring a hole

1. Select the correct size bit for the hole to be bored and secure it in the jaws of the bit brace.
   a. To open the jaws of the chuck hold the chuck with the left hand and turn the handle with the right hand in a counterclockwise direction.
   b. Place the shank of the auger bit between the jaws of the chuck.
   c. Tighten the shank of the auger bit in the chuck by holding the chuck with the left hand and turning the handle in a clockwise direction.
2. Secure the stock in a vise, or clamp the stock to a bench. If the stock is clamped to a bench, add a piece of scrap stock between the good stock and the bench.
3. Mark the center of the hole with a nail or an awl. Place the point of the bit in the hole. Hold the bit brace and auger bit so that they are at right angles to the surface, and with the right hand turn the handle in a clockwise direction, while applying a downward pressure to the head.
4. Check for straightness as the hole is being bored. A try square can be used to check for squareness. A second way of checking is by sighting from two directions at right angles to each other.
5. To prevent splitting the bottom of the hole, bore until the point of the bit comes through the surface. Reverse the stock and place the point of the bit in the small hole and bore through. Another method is to back the material with a scrap block of wood and bore right through the good stock into the scrap block.
6. Boring a hole to a predetermined depth is called stop boring. It is accomplished in two ways. A stop block can be made by boring a hole

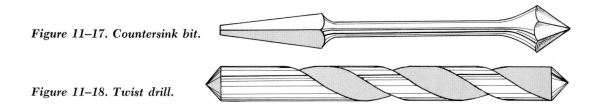

Figure 11–17. Countersink bit.

Figure 11–18. Twist drill.

in a block of wood and placing it on the bit to cover the part that is not needed in the measurement. The other method is to mark the bit at the correct depth with masking tape. The former is the safer method.

7. Holes can be bored at many different angles; therefore, it is important to keep the bit at the desired angle until the hole is completed.

Screwdriver Bit

Principle of Operation. The screwdriver bit works on the principle of the wheel and axle.

Specific Recommendation. A ⅜-inch screwdriver bit for slotted screws should be used.

Use. The screwdriver bit (see Figure 11–16), is used to gain mechanical advantage in driving screws.

Countersink Bit

Principles of Operation. The countersink works on the principles of the cutting wedge and inclined plane.

Specific Recommendation. A ¾-inch countersink bit with brace shank should be used.

Use. The countersink (see Figure 11–17) is used to taper a hole to the same shape as the head of a flat head wood screw.

Hand Drill

Principle of Operation. The hand drill works on the principles of the wheel and axle and the inclined plane. The teeth of the gear train utilize the principle of an inclined plane.

Specific Recommendation. Use a drill with a chuck capacity of from 0 to ⅜-inch.

Use. A hand drill is used to hold and drive a twist drill.

Twist Drill

Principles of Operation. The twist drill works on the principles of the inclined plane and the cutting wedge.

SPECIFIC RECOMMENDATION. A complete set ranging from sizes $\frac{1}{16}$- to $\frac{1}{2}$- by $\frac{1}{64}$-inch.

USE. To make small round holes in wood, metal, plastic, and other materials use a twist drill. (See Figure 11–18.)

1. Select the correct size twist drill and secure it in the jaws of the hand drill.
   a. To open the jaws of the chuck hold the chuck with the left hand and turn the crank handle with the right hand in a counterclockwise direction.
   b. Place the shank of the twist drill in the center of the jaws of the chuck.
   c. Tighten the shank of the twist drill in the chuck by holding the chuck with the left hand and turning the crank handle in a clockwise direction.
2. Secure the stock in a vise, or clamp the stock to a bench, adding a piece of scrap stock between the good stock and bench.
3. Locate the center of the hole and mark it with an awl or a nail. Place the point of the drill in the marked hole and adjust it to a perpendicular position. With the right hand, turn the crank handle and apply pressure to the frame handle. (See Figure 11–1, page 257.) Remember to check that the drill is held in the correct position when drilling.
4. Drilling a hole to a predetermined depth is accomplished with the same procedures as for stop boring. (See Auger Bit, step 6.)
5. Holes can be drilled at a variety of angles. Nails with their heads removed can be used to drill holes in soft materials. Finishing nails or brads can be used to drill into two pieces of wood to hold them together. Drill until the chuck is close to the wood, loosen the drill, and drive the nail the rest of the way with a hammer.

Tinner's Snips

PRINCIPLE OF OPERATION. The handles work on the principle of the lever, the pin acting as the fulcrum or pivot for the handles and the blades. The blades work on the principle of two cutting wedges.

SPECIFIC RECOMMENDATION. Straight lip snips with a 3-inch cut and overall length of 12½-inches should be used.

USE. Tinner's snips are used to cut metal 22 gauge or lighter. (The gauge refers to the thickness of the metal.) They can also be used to cut curved board or chicken wire. Snips should not be used to cut nails, wire, or screws.

Using Tinner's Snips

Tools, Materials, and Supplies

1. Hold the Tinner's snips as shown in Figure 11–19, and keeping the cutting edge at right angles to the work.

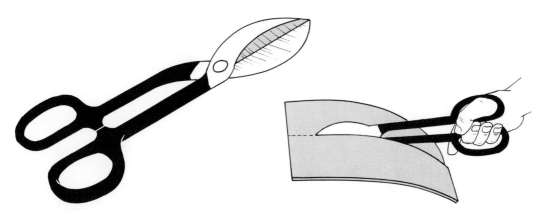

Figure 11–19. Tinner's snips and position of the hand for holding snips.

2. Open the blades of the snips as wide as possible and insert the metal. The metal should contact the angle formed by the open blades.
3. Apply hand pressure to the handles and cut to within ½-inch of the end of the blade. Open the blades and repeat the cutting operation.
4. When cutting corners or notching, use the points of the blades.
5. Irregular shapes and inside or outside curves are first cut in the rough to about ⅛-inch from the line, and then are cut directly to the line. The thin edge of metal will curl out of the way leaving a smooth edge.
6. To cut an internal opening, drill a hole in the waste material large enough to start the point of the snips.

Claw Hammer

PRINCIPLE OF OPERATION. The claw hammer works on the principle of a lever.

SPECIFIC RECOMMENDATION. A hammer weighing ten ounces should be used.

USE. A claw hammer should be used to drive and withdraw nails.

Driving Nails

1. Plan the placing of the nails carefully. Nails should be located three-quarters of an inch from the end or edge of a board. When nails are placed closer, a pilot hole slightly smaller than the diameter of the nail should be drilled through the top board to prevent splitting. Knots and defects should be avoided when nailing material together.
2. Hold the hammer handle at the end and stand so that the nail can be sighted for straightness. Hold the nail until it is secure in the material.
3. Hit the nail flat on the head. Start with light taps and increase the force as the nail penetrates the stock. Decrease the force of the blow as the head of the nail approaches the surface.

4. Finish nails are usually set below the surface, whereas other types of nails are driven flush with the surface.
5. Bent nails or nails that tend to follow the grain should be withdrawn and a new start should be made.

Pulling Nails

1. Place the claws of the hammer under the head of the nail and apply pressure to the end of the hammer handle.
2. As the handle approaches right angles to the surface, the nail becomes harder to withdraw. A block of wood can be used to change the fulcrum and make the nail pulling easier. A block of wood can also be used to prevent marking the surface.

Hand Screw Clamp

PRINCIPLE OF OPERATION. The handle of the hand screw works on the principle of the wheel and axle. While the jaws are adjusted by a screw action, the jaws grip and hold material by a lever action.

SPECIFIC RECOMMENDATION. Two of each of the following sizes are required:

Length of jaw	Opening
4″	2″
6″	3″
8″	4½″

USES. Hand screws are used to apply pressure to surfaces fastened with glue, nails, or screws. They are used also to aid in securing materials in position for work.

Using Hand Screws

1. Jaws are adjusted for size opening by simultaneously revolving the two spindles. (See Figure 11–20.)
2. Compression is applied by tightening the inside spindle. Jaws must be kept parallel in the compression operation to obtain uniform pressure. If the outside spindle is tightened too much, compression results at the ends of the jaws, causing them to dig into the material.

Screwdriver

PRINCIPLE OF OPERATION. The screwdriver works on the principle of the wheel and axle.

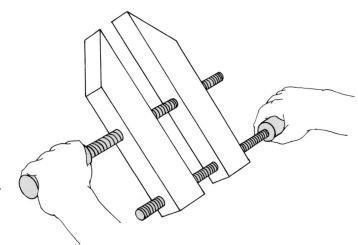

Figure 11–20. Hand screw clamp.

SPECIFIC RECOMMENDATION. The blade length should be 6 inches, diameter $\frac{3}{16}$-inch, and the tip $\frac{1}{4}$-inch.

USE. Screwdrivers are used to drive and withdraw screws.

Using the Screwdriver

1. Make a hole with a nail or drill of sufficient size to allow the screw to be partially inserted into the surface.
2. Apply the tip of the screwdriver to the slit in the screw head; holding the screwdriver at right angles to the surface, rotate the screwdriver clockwise until the head is flush with the surface. (See Chapter 12, for the section on wood screws.)
3. To withdraw screws, reverse the motion until the screw is loose.

Pliers

PRINCIPLE OF OPERATION. The handles work on the principle of the lever, the pin acting as the fulcrum or pivot point for the handles and the jaws.

SPECIFIC RECOMMENDATION. A pair of 6-inch combination pliers and a pair of 5-inch side cutters are required.

USES. Side cutters are used to cut wire and to hold the end of wire for bending and twisting. Combination pliers have many uses. They can be applied to hold material and to tighten screw eyes.

Workbench

In Figure 11–21, a simple workbench that can be built by children for use with their constructional activities is illustrated. The materials needed are inexpensive and easy to work with. It can be converted into such equipment

Hand Tools and Their Relationship to Learning Activities

279

Figure 11–21. The workbench with vises in position.

Figure 11–22. Converting the workbench into a plant stand.

as a plant stand or a science table. (See Figure 11–22.) The bench can be taken apart for easy storage.

1. Lay out the legs to their full size on a piece of wrapping paper. (See Figure 11–23.) The height of the table will depend on the age of the group it is being built for, 24, 26, or 30 inches.
2. Select four pieces of 3-inch strapping, for the crosspieces. With a sliding T bevel, set the angle for the top and bottom cuts. (See Figure 11–23.)
3. Set the T bevel against the strapping and mark a line along the blade.
4. Cut along the line with a crosscut saw. A wooden miter box could be made with the desired angle so that all legs could be cut to that angle.
5. Glue and screw the two pieces of strapping together for both sets of legs. Use 1-inch, No. 8 flat head screws and countersink the screw heads.
6. Select eight pieces of 3-inch strapping, 16 inches in length. These pieces are to be used as fillers (see Figure 11–24) to make the legs the same thickness. All angles should be laid out with a sliding T bevel.

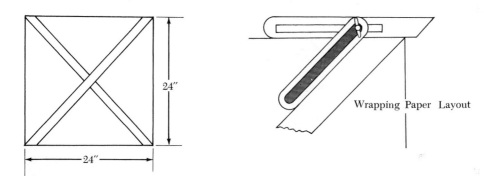

Figure 11–23. *Laying out the legs of the workbench on wrapping paper and transferring angles.*

Figure 11–24. *(A) Adding fillers to insure the uniform size of legs. (B) Staggering the position of screws for strength.*

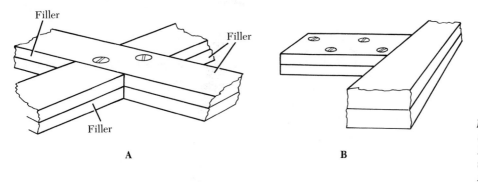

A   B

7. Glue and screw (1-inch, No. 8 flat head screws) the filler pieces in place. Stagger screws, four to a section. (See Figure 11–24.)

8. Select four pieces of 3-inch strapping, 24 inches long, for the caps of the bottom and top of each leg. (See Figure 11–25.)

9. Glue and screw the top and the bottom caps to the crosspieces. The legs are completed and ready for sanding.

10. Select two pieces of 3-inch strapping, 46½ inches long, for the side supports of the bench.

11. Select two pieces of 3-inch strapping, 54 inches long, for the cross supports.

12. Cut out a ¾-inch notch on the legs at the top, as shown in Figure 11–25(B). The notch is cut with a crosscut saw or backsaw along line X.

13. Select four corner braces 1½ inches × 1½ inches × ½-inch. Locate the position of the four corner braces. (See Figure 11–26.)

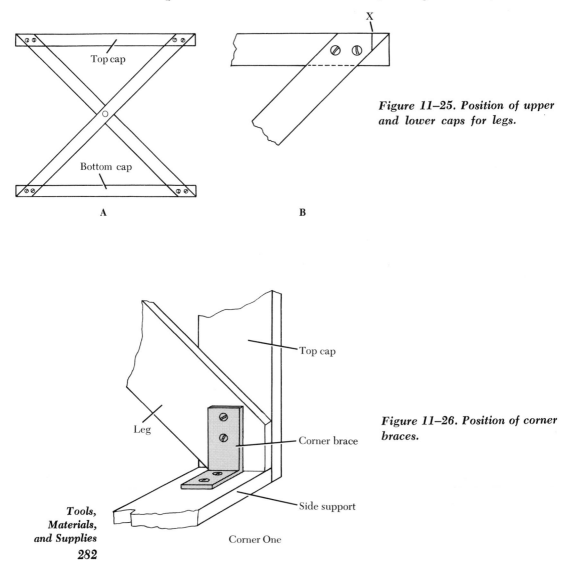

Figure 11–25. Position of upper and lower caps for legs.

A

B

Figure 11–26. Position of corner braces.

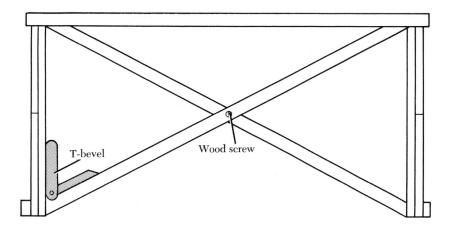

Figure 11–27. Checking angles for the cross supports with a T bevel.

14. After the two side supports are secured to the legs with the corner braces, locate and lay out the cross supports. Making sure that the legs are straight and, using a T bevel, transfer the angle for the cross supports. (See Figure 11–27.)
15. Secure the cross supports in place with a corner brace at the end of each support. At the intersection of the cross supports, secure the two pieces of strapping with a 1-inch, No. 8 flat head wood screw.
16. Select a piece of ⅜-inch plywood 2 × 4-feet for the top of the bench. Screw the top to the side supports and to the top caps of the legs with 1-inch, No. 8 flat head wood screws. Be sure to countersink the heads of the screws.
17. Sand the bench with 2/0 sandpaper and shellac it.

Woodworker's Vise

There are a number of vises on the market that can be used with young children. A small one can be obtained that can be attached to tables, saw horses, and benches up to 2¼ inches thick. The workbench described here can be equipped with a small vise.

How to Construct a Wooden Miter Box

The wooden miter box (see Figure 11–28) can be used to cut narrow stock to length and to an angle. Most wooden miter boxes are constructed with a 45° and a 90° cut; however, wooden miter boxes can be constructed for any desired angle.

1. Cut two pieces of hardwood for the sides of the miter box; one 17 inches × 4 inches × ¾-inch and a second 17 inches × 5 inches × ¾-inch.

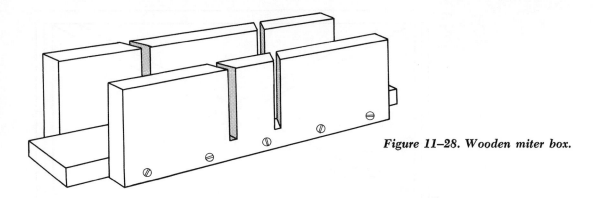

Figure 11–28. Wooden miter box.

2. Cut a piece of hardwood for the base, 20 inches × 4 inches × ¾-inch.
3. Lay out the two sides, as shown in Figure 11–29(A). On side (1) measure three-eighths of an inch from the bottom edge and draw a center line. Measure three-eighths of an inch from the bottom edge and draw a center line similarly on the other side piece.
4. Mark locations for nails by measuring 1 inch from the end for the first nail and 3¾ inches across the center line for the others. Mark both side pieces, as shown in Figure 11–29(B).
5. Mark nail locations with an awl.

Figure 11–29. Layouts for the sides and bottom of a miter box.

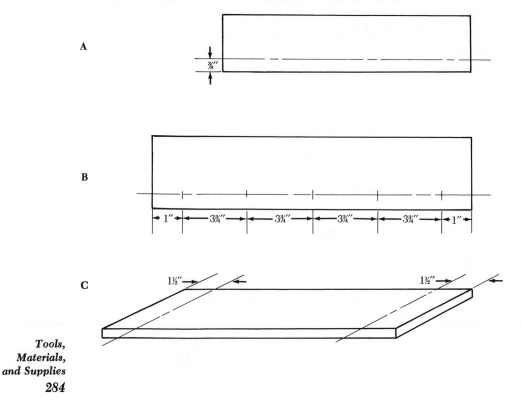

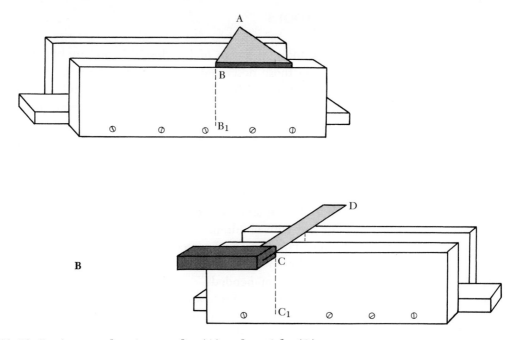

Figure 11–30. Laying out slots for angular (A) and straight (B) cuts.

6. Drill the five holes in each side with a hand drill and a $\frac{1}{16}$-inch twist drill.
7. On the base piece, 20 inches $\times$ 4 inches $\times$ $\frac{3}{4}$-inch, mark off a distance 1½ inches from the both ends, as shown in Figure 11–29(C).
8. Apply glue to one edge of the base between these lines.
9. Nail side (1) to the base with 6-d common nails. Repeat steps (8) and (9) for side (2). Remember that side (2) extends below the base.
10. Make a cardboard template with a base and height of 5 inches and a 45° angle. Lay out the lines for a 45° cut, as shown in Figure 11–30(A). Place one edge of the cardboard against the outer edge of the side and draw a line A–B along the diagonal edge with a pencil.
11. Using a try square draw two perpendicular guidelines from points A and B of the diagonal line to the base of each side, (A–A_1; B–B_1).
12. Clamp the miter box in the vise, and with a crosscut saw, cut line A–A_1; cut B–B_1 down to the base point. Care should be taken to keep the saw straight and on the line.
13. With a try square and a pencil, mark off a line at right angles to the side of the miter box across the top edges at a point that will not interfere with the 45° cut. With a pencil line, connect point C–D with the base of each side, as shown in Figure 11–30(B). These lines are designated C–C_1 and D–D_1.
14. Repeat step (12) for cutting lines C–C_1 and D–D_1.
15. The miter box can be used to cut 45° and 90° angles.

Hand Tools and Their Relationship to Learning Activities

SECONDARY TOOLS

The following tools, although highly desirable and useful, are somewhat less essential than those described earlier in the chapter.

THREADING KIT *(Tap and Die)*: The kit consists of a tap for cutting threads in a piece of wood and a die for cutting threads on a wooden dowel. Children can make their own nuts and bolts with the kit.

SABER SAW. A saber saw is an electrical hand-held tool that can be used to cut straight lines or complex curves. It is actually a portable jig saw and can be used for the same operation.

C CLAMPS (OR CARRIAGE CLAMPS.) C clamps can be used to hold small pieces of material for gluing or cutting. Four-inch C clamps are the appropriate size for use with children.

ROUND PUNCH. Punches can be used to cut holes in metal or cardboard and can be purchased in a variety of diameters. A ¼-inch and ¾-inch diameter punch is recommended.

SURFORM TOOLS (PLANE, FILE, AND POCKET). Surform tools can be used to smooth, shape, or form wood, plastic, leather, Keene's cement, soft metals, and fiber composition boards. They cut more easily, work faster, and last longer than other conventional surface forming tools. The writers recommend one of each type.

NAIL SET. A nail set is used to drive and set finishing nails. Nail sets come in a variety of sizes. The size is determined by the diameter of the tip. A ³⁄₃₂-inch nail set is recommended.

BRAD DRIVER. A brad driver is a special tool that can be used to drive and set brads. It is available in one standard size and is excellent for driving ½-inch and ¾-inch wire brads into soft materials.

CHISELS AND GOUGES. Chisels and gouges are used in chipping, trimming, and carving. The chisel has a straight blade, whereas the gouge is a chisel with a curved blade. A ⅜-inch and ¾-inch chisel and gouge are recommended.

CARVING TOOL SET. Carving tools are chisels and gouges with variously shaped cutting edges. A set usually includes a straight chisel, a skew chisel, a straight bent chisel, a parting tool, a straight gouge, and a veining tool. The set is excellent for children to use when carving small objects.

CONCLUSION

In order to insure a smoothly run program that includes the advantages of construction activities, the classroom should have certain pieces of basic equipment. Tool panels, or in some cases tool chests, should be a part of the equipment. They should contain

Tools, Materials, and Supplies

| 4 Claw hammers | 2 Pairs of pliers |
| 2 Screwdrivers | 2 Try squares |

1 T bevel
2 Bit braces (one set of auger bits)
2 Hand drills (one set of twist drills)
2 Crosscut saws
2 Ripsaws
1 Backsaw
3 Coping saws

1 Hand plane
1 Pair of Tinner's snips
6 Hand screw clamps
4 Woodworking vises
1 Screwdriver bit
1 Countersink bit
1 File card
2 Scratch awls

The following tools are listed in the order in which they should be added to the original list. This order is flexible and the program should determine these needs.

1. Surform tools
2. Carving tool set
3. Chisels
4. Saber saw
5. C clamps

6. Round punch
7. Threading kit
8. Nail set
9. Brad driver

Once these are part of the classroom equipment, provision should be made for their care and maintenance, and safety rules for their use should be formulated and adopted by all. As the tools are being used, the children should be taught the principles on which they operate and the optimum methods of use. The handling of tools is not only a means to interesting educational construction, but is also a habit of lifelong value, a reinforcement of scientific principles, and an experience in sharing and working together.

LEARNING ACTIVITIES

1. Plan a science experience using the following tools as illustrations of how simple machines are used to assist the craftsman.
   a. Bit brace
   b. Claw hammer
   c. Screwdriver
   d. Hand drill
2. Compare the mechanical advantage gained by using a bit brace with a 6-inch sweep with one that has a 12-inch sweep. Develop a science lesson that utilizes the various tools to illustrate the concept of mechanical advantage.
3. Select a particular tool and describe its evolution. Explain how this same procedure could be used with a group of children as a research project. Describe in detail the advantages or disadvantages of this type of activity.
4. Develop a booklet on how to use a specific tool for a child with low reading ability; be sure to use words that need to be reinforced.

5. Select a group of similar tools, or the same tools in different sizes and quality. Experiment with their use and then write a summary of the values and shortcomings of each.
6. Survey the literature on early childhood education related to creative activities or play. This literature will indicate the importance of allowing children to work with tools and material. Why is there a feeling that preschool children should be allowed to use these tools and materials and not elementary school children?

REFERENCES

FEIRER, JOHN L. *Industrial Arts Woodworking* (2nd ed.). Peoria, Ill.: Chas. A. Bennett, 1960.

FEIRER, JOHN L. *Woodworking for Industry*. Peoria, Ill.: Chas. A. Bennett, 1963.

GERBRACHT, CARL, AND BABCOCK, ROBERT J. *Industrial Arts for Grades K–6*. Milwaukee: Bruce, 1959.

GRONEMAN, CHRIS H., AND FEIRER, JOHN L. *General Shop*. New York: McGraw Hill, 1954.

HAMMOND, JAMES J., DONNELLY, EDWARD T., HARROD, WALTER, AND RAYNER, NORMAN. *Woodworking Technology*. Bloomington, Ill.: McKnight and McKnight, 1961.

MATTIL, EDWARD L. *Meaning in Crafts*. Englewood Cliffs, N.J.: Prentice-Hall, 1965.

CHAPTER 12

Materials *and* Supplies *for the* Classroom

The techniques and activities suggested in the previous section were developed with an emphasis on the teacher's and child's exploration of different types of materials to express an idea or develop a concept as shown in Figure 12–1. The main objective of this chapter is to familiarize the reader with a variety of materials and their possible sources.

The amount of material accumulated for use by any one classroom is limited by budget, by storage space, and by safety factors. It should be possible to keep on hand certain basic materials, such as wood, paints, modeling ingredients, wire mesh, and containers, and to plan to acquire others as needed. It is also feasible to have a large cupboard or chest to place bits and pieces of a wide variety of substances not generally considered constructional equipment but useful in many ways imagined by the children. Some suggestions for this storehouse and a list of more basic materials are presented at the end of this chapter.

Much of the material needed in an elementary school classroom can be secured free of charge from local business establishments and industry. The enterprising teacher, assisted by the pupils and parents, will have little trouble procuring a large variety of materials. In fact, some teachers have reported that they have been overwhelmed with replies after sending home requests for various supplies.

When a special type of material is needed, the teacher should be very

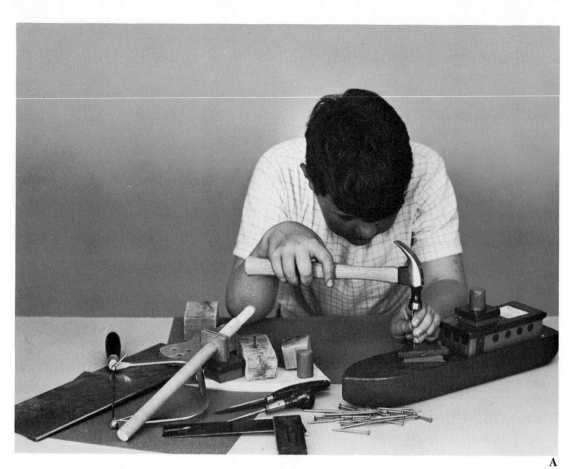

A

Figure 12–1. Pupils exploring with materials.

specific in describing it and the quantity required. A story that brings this point into focus concerns a class with a student teacher. They had decided to represent a segment of the local community in solid block construction. The activity was in the planning stage on a Friday afternoon. The student teacher and the children discussed the materials that would be needed to build the various models and the manner of grouping them properly. One pupil suggested that a large table was needed to hold the finished models. The children exclaimed that a ping pong table would be excellent for the purpose. The planning session was brought to an end with the close of school. On Monday morning two children arrived at school with their parents and two ping pong tables. One parent explained that he and his son had spent the whole weekend constructing the table, because it was needed by the class.

This story illustrates the embarrassment and chagrin that can result from inadequate communication among teacher, children, and parents. Requests should be specific and delegated. The story also illustrates how willing and eager parents are to help teachers in almost any type of activity.

B

Acquisition of Material

The list at the end of the chapter could be used to suggest and select what might be appropriate for purchase or for soliciting from home and community. The more important and versatile items are listed first in each category. Many of the items belong in the "bits and pieces" collection already mentioned. Some objects can be borrowed for temporary use.

If possible a budget should be allotted for materials and supplies. Before the school year begins, the teacher should purchase basic supplies, especially those that are not available in the community. A portion of the budget should be reserved for purchases needed as the program progresses. Much thought should be given to what can be obtained without cost, both at the beginning of the year, and as the plans of teacher and pupils unfold.

Industry and the business community can be approached both for the donation of materials and for suggestions of where material can be inexpensively purchased. Parents too can be requested to donate. A letter should accompany any request explaining how much material is needed and how it will be used by the children.

Storage

The teacher should remember that storage of materials is an important aspect of a smoothly run program. Therefore, before purchasing or requesting any materials, the teacher should consider where they will be kept. If the program is going to allow children to use materials to solve their problems and to express their creativity, these materials must be available for their use.

Cardboard boxes are useful for storage. Some cardboard boxes come with covers like those found on foot lockers. These make excellent containers. A list of the materials in each box can be marked clearly on the outside. Children can then readily select the box that has the materials needed and, when finished with the material, can return it to the appropriate place. In some instances small boxes (shoe, cigar) can be filled with assorted materials and stored in the larger boxes. The answer to the storage problem depends on the type and size of the classroom.

MATERIALS NEEDED

Teachers should be familiar with materials suitable for the elementary classroom. An understanding of the properties, sizes, uses, and special considerations of the basic materials is necessary in order to plan adequately for a diversified program within the limits already mentioned.

Occasionally it is possible to make the material that will be used to construct learning devices. By combining common, inexpensive supplies, a raw material can be prepared that is just as suitable as an expensive commercial product. One example of this homemade material is substitute clay.

SUBSTITUTES FOR CLAY

There are four excellent substitutes for clay and plasticene that children can use to create interesting figurines and instructional materials. These are the following:

Sawdust clay
Salt-cornstarch clay
Salt-flour clay
Cornstarch-baking soda clay

These mixtures can be used just like clay for modeling a variety of items or objects. One of the following techniques can be used to model any one of these clays:

Pinch Method

The pinch method is the easiest procedure to use when forming simple figurines or objects. The desired shape is actually pinched out of a ball of clay. This technique requires that a piece of clay be pinched, pulled, or pushed in any way that seems to bring out the desired shape.

Coil Method

The coil method utilizes coils of clay to form bowls, plates, animals, and people. The coil method is more difficult than the pinch method because it requires pushing the clay together to form a uniform piece of material. Two coils placed together will not stick as if they had been glued unless material from each coil is worked together with the touching coils. Some sophisticated objects can be modeled using this technique.

Slab Method

The slab method is similar to rolling out pie crust dough. A ball of clay is placed on a hard surface and rolled out with a rolling pin. The thickness can be controlled by rolling the clay between two sticks of the same thickness. Objects can be cut out of the slab with a knife or cookie cutter. Dishes, boxes, and other items can be constructed with this technique. It requires cutting the desired shapes and fitting them together like pieces of wood.

USES IN THE CURRICULUM

These clays can be used to cover hardware cloth or chicken wire that has been shaped to illustrate land formations, or they can be modeled into land formations by using the pinch, coil, or slab methods. (See Figure 12–2.) They give children an opportunity to work with proportions in a real situation. The child must actually measure for himself 1 cup, one-half cup, one-third cup or one-quarter cup to gain his objective. He is not faced with a verbal or an abstract problem, but with one that has interest and meets one of his needs—that of making a material that can be modeled. The child also has an opportunity to see what happens when the improper proportions are used. The writers have seen salt-cornstarch clay that would not harden after weeks, because the instructions for making the mixture were not followed. They also have seen sawdust clay that could not be modeled because the mixture lacked enough water. However, they have also been gratified by the excitement that results when children make their own mixture from the raw materials and then model their material into an interesting object.

Figure 12–2. Sawdust clay model to show conservation in agriculture.

Each of these clays is made according to a simple recipe using common ingredients. Besides creating a new material, children gain experience in science and mathematics concepts through making substitute clays.

Sawdust Clay

Sawdust clay is a very durable material, because the finished object is like a piece of pressboard. (See Figure 12–3 and 12–4 for applications.)

Ingredients	Materials
Sawdust (about one pail full)	Plastic dishpan
Water	Sieve (piece of screening)
Wheat paste (wallpaper) or flour	
Glue (white)	

294

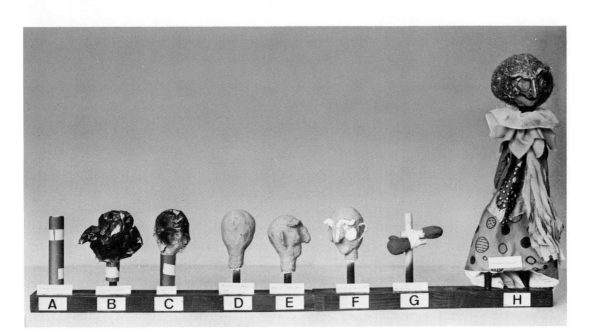

Figure 12–3. Steps in making a puppet from sawdust clay: A. Roll paper. B. Crush paper for the base shape. C. Tape crushed paper to secure shape. D. Cover base shape with sawdust clay. E. Add features to the puppet head. F. Paint features. G. Model hands from sawdust clay. H. Make clothing for the puppet.

Figure 12–4. Figurines made with sawdust clay.

1. Place the sieve over the dishpan.
2. Take a handful of sawdust and place it on the sieve and sift the sawdust through the screen. The finer the sawdust, the smoother the finished object will be.
3. Lift the sieve from the pan and throw away those particles that would not go through the screening.
4. Repeat steps (1), (2), and (3) until the desired amount of sawdust is sifted. The sifted sawdust should be checked for sticks or large particles. It must be of a fine texture.
5. Mix the sifted sawdust with wallpaper paste, using ten parts of sawdust to one part of paste. These ingredients should be mixed while dry, making sure that the wheat paste is evenly distributed.
6. Add water to the mixture a little at a time. Keep stirring while adding water until the mixture can be rolled into a ball. Be careful not to add too much water. Water should not drip from the mixture when squeezed.
7. The mixture is ready for modeling. It can be mixed as many as six hours before it is used if the storage container is covered with a damp cloth.

DRYING THE FINISHED PROJECT

1. Place a piece of wire screening on top of the open end of a cardboard box. Allow the object to dry on the wire screening so that the air can get to all sides. If the finished object is placed on a piece of cardboard where the base is not allowed to dry, the surface will mildew and may even generate a sour smell.
2. Turn the finished object over and around every day to assist the drying process. It will take from two to three days for the sawdust clay to dry.
3. When the surface is dry, it can be left rough or sanded smooth with sandpaper.
4. The surface can be painted with tempera, water colors, or oil paint.

Cornstarch–Baking Soda Clay

Ingredients	Materials
1 cup cornstarch	Saucepan
2 cups baking soda	Spoon
1¼ cups cold water	Cloth
Food coloring	Source of heat (hot plate)

PROCEDURE

1. Mix cornstarch and baking soda in a saucepan until thoroughly blended.

Tools, Materials, and Supplies

296

2. Add cold water to the mixture. If color is desired add a few drops of food coloring.
3. Place the saucepan and ingredients over a medium heat for about four minutes. Stir constantly until the mixture thickens to a moist mashed-potato consistency.
4. Remove from the saucepan onto a damp cloth and allow to cool. Knead mixture for several minutes.
5. The mixture is ready for modeling.
6. Finished objects will usually harden in forty-eight hours.
7. The finished object can be painted with tempera or water colors, then dipped into clear shellac, sprayed with clear lacquer, or brushed with clear nail polish.

Salt–Cornstarch Clay

Ingredients	Materials
1 cup of table salt	Double boiler
½-cup cornstarch	Spoon
¾-cup of water	Source of heat (hot plate)

Figure 12–5. Figurines made with salt-cornstarch clay.

1. Mix the salt, cornstarch, and water thoroughly in the top part of the double boiler. Food coloring can be added if color is desired.
2. Place the whole boiler, with water in the lower part, over a low heat. Stir the mixture constantly. In about two or three minutes it becomes so thick that it forms a lump.
3. Remove the mixture from double boiler to a piece of waxed paper or aluminum foil and allow it to cool.
4. When the mixture has cooled sufficiently to be handled it should be kneaded by hand for several minutes, after which time it is ready to be modeled. The mixture can be stored in waxed paper for several days before it is used.
5. This mixture is very good for modeling puppet heads, small figurines, and flat pieces. It hardens to the consistency of stone. (See Figure 12–5, p. 297.)
6. Finished items can be painted with tempera or water colors and then dipped into shellac, sprayed with clear lacquer, or coated with clear nail polish.
7. One box of salt with the proportionate amounts of cornstarch and water will make enough of the mixture for at least eight children to model average-sized objects.

Figure 12–6. Geometric shapes modeled from salt-flour clay.

Salt–Flour Clay

Ingredients	Materials
1 cup flour	Saucepan
¾ -cup salt	Spoon
1 cup water	Source of heat (hot plate)

PROCEDURE

1. Put the salt in the saucepan and heat until it is piping hot; then remove it from the heat.
2. Put the flour into the saucepan with the salt and mix the ingredients together.
3. Add the salt and flour mixture to the water gradually and stir thoroughly. Food coloring can be added if color is desired.
4. Place the saucepan over low heat. Stir the mixture constantly, being sure to scrape the mixture up from the bottom of the pan as it is being stirred.
5. When the mixture has thickened and appears crumbly and dry, scrape it from the saucepan onto a piece of waxed paper or aluminum foil, and allow it to cool enough to be handled. Knead the mixture for two or three minutes. It is now ready to be worked.
6. The finished object can be painted with any type of paint. (See Figure 12–6 for applications.)

WOOD

It is valuable to have a basic understanding of common lumber. Standing trees, which are potential building materials, are called timber. When they are cut down, they are still known as timber, but when they are sawed and planed they are called lumber until they are made into finished products. Trees grow as a series of long, close-grained cells that form a compact but porous material. Because of this growth structure, wood is able to accommodate finishing materials and to hold nails, screws, glue, and other fasteners.

Each type of wood possesses its own unique properties and characteristics. Lumber cut from the same section of a tree will often differ in color, grain, and figure.

Botanical lumber is classified as hard or soft, depending upon the specie of tree from which it is cut. Deciduous or broad-leafed trees produce hardwoods, whereas softwoods come from coniferous or needle-bearing trees. The botanical classification has no relationship to the degree of hardness or softness of the lumber. For example, balsa is the lightest and one of the softest of all woods; however, its botanical classification is hardwood. Many softwoods are actually harder than some classified as hardwoods. Pines, firs, and other evergreens are softwoods; whereas maples, oaks, elms, poplars, and the fruit trees are the hardwoods. Softwoods comprise 80 per cent of all lumber and are used for building. Hardwoods are used for beautifully finished items such as furniture or flooring.

Woods are difficult to identify by chemical analysis. They are identified by the physical characteristics of color, grain, figure, and sometimes by odor or taste.

Lumber is milled from trees by different techniques depending on the grain pattern or certain desired characteristics. After the lumber is milled, it is dried for use. It is either air dried or kiln dried. Drying is the process of removing moisture from the milled lumber to reduce the warping or cupping effects of the material.

Lumber is purchased either by the board foot or the linear foot.

THICKNESS. Any board under 1 inch is considered to be 1-inch thick. Commercially, lumber is milled to the following thicknesses: $\frac{3}{8}$-, $\frac{1}{2}$-, $\frac{5}{8}$-, and 1 inch; and then surfaced on two sides to $\frac{1}{4}$-, $\frac{3}{8}$-, $\frac{1}{2}$-, $\frac{3}{4}$-, or $1\frac{3}{16}$-inch, respectively.

WIDTH. Any board that is less than a whole number of inches is figured as the next higher whole number. Lumber is milled to 3-, 4-, 5-, 6-, 8-, 10-, and 12-inch width. If a $4\frac{1}{2}$-inch board is ordered, it is figured as a 5-inch board.

LENGTH. Length is usually measured in feet. One of the following formulas can be used in computing board feet. Dimensions in inches can be calculated by

$$\frac{T'' \times W'' \times L''}{144} = \text{board feet}$$

Length in feet can be calculated by

$$\frac{T'' \times W'' \times L'}{12} = \text{board feet}$$

Boards, manufactured board (plywood, pressed wood, and Upson board), are sold by the square foot. Molding, trim, firring, and 2×4 stock are sold by the linear foot.

Soft Pine

There are four different types of soft pine: Ponderosa, Idaho White, Sugar, and Northern. They all come from trees that have needles 3 to 5 inches in length in clusters of three.

PROPERTIES

Ponderosa has a soft texture and close grain, and is unexcelled for smooth finishing. It has less tendency than most woods to split when nailed.

Idaho White has a soft texture, varying in color from nearly white to a pale reddish brown. It has excellent screw and nail-holding power.

Sugar pine is a creamy white and darkens with age and produces a soft-grained texture. It is strong for its weight and very easy to work with tools.

Northern pine is close grained, of fine texture, and is white or pale ivory in color. It is not affected by atmospheric changes.

Uses

1. *Ponderosa* is used for light construction requiring close-fitting joints.
2. *Idaho White* is used for general woodworking.
3. *Sugar pine* is used for woodcarving, cabinet work, and pattern work.
4. *Northern pine* is used for doors, sashes, blinds, and matches.

Market Analysis

1. *Sales Units:* Pine can be purchased by the board and linear foot.
2. *Shapes:* Boards, planks and structural timber.
3. *Sizes:* All standard sizes.
4. *Grades:* Available in all standard softwood grades.

Pressed Wood (Hardboard)

Pressed wood is manufactured from wood chips that are transformed into fibers under high steam pressure. The fibers are then pressed in a heated hydraulic press to form sheets.

Properties. Pressed wood is equally strong in all directions because it has no grain pattern. Although it is very brittle, it does not split, splinter, crack, shrink, or swell as a result of weather as lumber does. It can be worked readily with hand tools and can be held with nails, screws, nuts and bolts, and glue. Pressed wood can be finished with paints and varnish.

Uses. Commercially, pressed wood is used for the backings of cases, cabinets, subflooring, and jigs and templates. In schools it can be used for templates and jigs and for miscellaneous parts in various teaching materials.

Sales Units. Pressed board can be purchased in sheets. Tempered and untempered pressed board are smooth on one side and have a screen impression on the opposite side. The tempered pressed board has a harder surface than the untempered and is best for exterior use.

Sizes. Tempered and untempered are available in $\frac{1}{16}$-, $\frac{1}{8}$-, $\frac{3}{16}$-, $\frac{1}{4}$-, and $\frac{5}{16}$-inch thickness and sheets 1×4 feet, $1\frac{1}{2} \times 4$ feet, 3×4 feet, 4×6 feet, 4×8 feet, and 4×12 feet.

Firring

Properties. Firring is a soft wood with high load-bearing strength. It has shock resistance, stiffness, and bending strength. Firring can be worked readily with hand tools and will hold nails, screws, and glue reasonably well.

Uses. Commercially, firring is used for supporting ceiling tile, for fillers between cement walls, and for making plywood. It is used in frame construction to build houses, barns, puppet stages, and simple work benches.

Sales Units. Firring can be purchased in the following dimensions:

1. *Width:* 2 and 3 inches
2. *Length:* 8, 10, 12, 14, and 16 feet
3. *Thickness:* 1 inch

    The actual size will be less for the width and thickness than the size ordered. A 2-inch piece of firring is only $1^{11}\!/_{16}$ of an inch in width and only three-quarters of an inch in thickness.

HARDWARE

A supply of hardware is necessary for the use of wood and similar materials in the program. The common articles needed, the fastening and strengthening agents, are described here and recommendations for a seasonal purchase are made.

Nails

Uses. Nails are used to fasten materials together when driven into or through the pieces of material.

Shapes. Nails can be purchased with the following types of heads and wire diameter:

1. *Common nails:* Large in diameter with a wider head than other nails. (See Figure 12–7.)
2. *Box nails:* Similar to common nails except that the wire diameter is smaller and heads are thinner
3. *Wire nails:* Similar to box nails except that the wire gauge is different
4. *Finishing nails:* Slender nails with a small head that can be set below the surface. (See Figure 12–8)
5. *Wire brads:* Similar to finishing nails but smaller in size

Sizes. The sizes of common, finish, and box nails are specified by the term penny (d), prefixed by a number, such as 8d or 16d. Figures 12–7 and 12–8 illustrate the sizes of common and finish nails.

The sizes of wire brads and wire nails are specified by length and wire gauge. The wire gauge represents the size of the diameter of the nail. As the gauge number increases, the diameter of the nail decreases; for example, a 1-inch, No. 16 wire nail or wire brad is larger than a 1-inch, No. 20 wire nail or wire brad.

Sales Unit. Common, finish, and box nails can be purchased in any desired quantity, small or large, but are usually sold by the pound. Wire nails

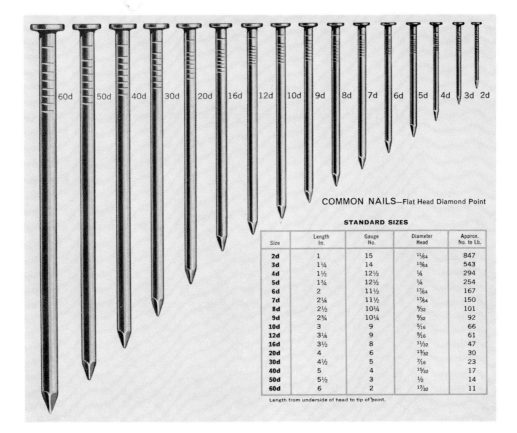

COMMON NAILS—Flat Head Diamond Point

STANDARD SIZES

Size	Length In.	Gauge No.	Diameter Head	Approx. No. to Lb.
2d	1	15	11/64	847
3d	1¼	14	13/64	543
4d	1½	12½	¼	294
5d	1¾	12½	¼	254
6d	2	11½	17/64	167
7d	2¼	11½	17/64	150
8d	2½	10¼	9/32	101
9d	2¾	10¼	9/32	92
10d	3	9	5/16	66
12d	3¼	9	5/16	61
16d	3½	8	11/32	47
20d	4	6	13/32	30
30d	4½	5	7/16	23
40d	5	4	15/32	17
50d	5½	3	½	14
60d	6	2	17/32	11

Length from underside of head to tip of point.

Figure 12–7. Common nails two-thirds actual size. (By permission of the United States Steel Corporation.)

and wire brads are usually sold in ¼-pound, ½-pound, and 1-pound packages.

RECOMMENDED PURCHASE. Common, finish, box, and wire nails should be kept in different sizes so that all necessary sizes will be available in some type of nail for different activities. One ¼-pound package of each of the wire brads, sizes ½-inch, No. 18; ¾-inch, No. 18; 1-inch No. 20; and 1½-inch, No. 20.

Wood Glue

USES. Glue is an adhesive used to fasten wood, paper, plastic, metal, or other materials. A good glue will cement joints and parts together so that the glued part will be stronger than the wood itself.

SALES UNIT. Synthetic resin glue, or white glue, is available in ¼-pint, pint, quart, and gallon containers.

RECOMMENDED PURCHASE. Synthetic resin glue should be purchased in gallon containers.

FINISHING NAILS—BRAD HEAD, DIAMOND POINT, KUPHED

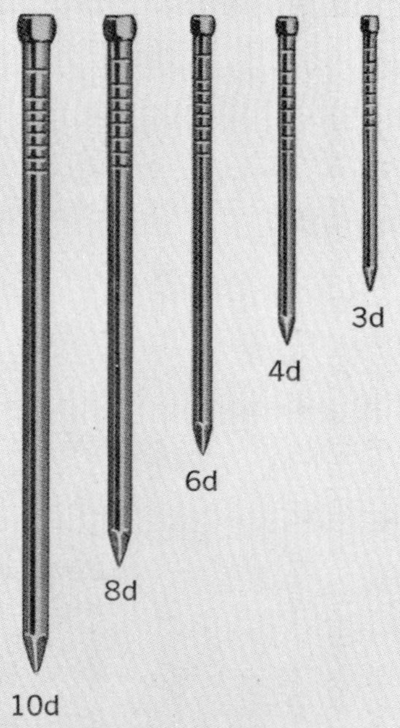

STANDARD SIZES

Size	Length In.	Gauge No.	Diam. of Head Gauge No.	Approx. No. to Lb.
3d	1¼	15½	12½	880
4d	1½	15	12	630
6d	2	13	10	288
8d	2½	12½	9½	196
10d	3	11½	8½	124

NON-STANDARD SIZES

Size	Length In.	Gauge No.	Diam. of Head Gauge No.	Approx. No. to Lb.
2d	1	16½	13½	1,473
5d	1¾	15	12	535
7d	2¼	13	10	254
9d	2¾	12½	9½	178
12d	3¼	11½	8½	113
16d	3½	11	8	93
20d	4	10	7	65

Length is overall.

Kuphed (Cup Head) style on non-standard sizes above, to accommodate nail set, can be furnished on request.

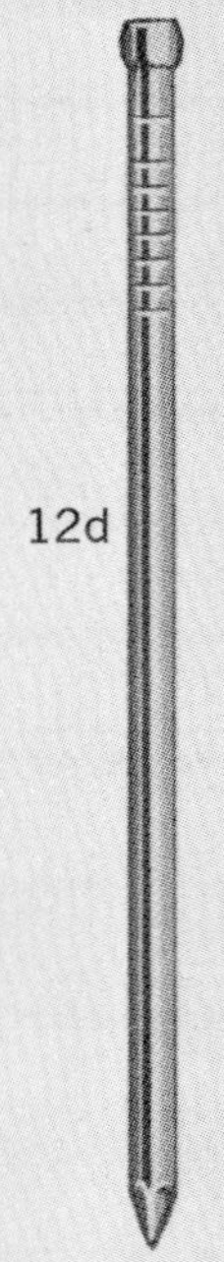

Figure 12–8. Finishing nails in actual size. (By permission of the United States Steel Corporation.)

1. Test the surfaces to be glued for the correct match. Glue will not compensate for spaces between surfaces. The tighter the surfaces fit together, the better the joint or surfaces glued together will hold.
2. Number the surfaces to be jointed. If permanent strength is needed, clamps should be used and a dry run performed. Then glue should be applied and the joint allowed to set under pressure. When clamps are not available or needed, surfaces can be rubbed together and then allowed to dry. This type of joint is not as strong as one glued under pressure, but it is adequate for use in constructional activities in the elementary schools.
3. With a brush or stick, apply the glue in a thin layer to the surfaces to be joined together. Resin glues dry fast, so work quickly.
4. If clamps are used, protective blocks should be placed between the jaws and the surface being glued. Paper inserts should be used between surfaces to prevent the protective blocks or the jaws of hand screws from sticking unintentionally. Apply pressure with the clamps to tighten the joint. Make sure that the work is flat and square. Some joints can be nailed or screwed together after glue is applied. The nails or screws will act as clamps and pull the joint together.
5. Excess glue should be wiped from the surface with a damp paper towel at once before the glue hardens.
6. Allow the glued object to set. The material can be handled after one hour.

Rubber Cement

Because the properties and uses of rubber cement are so commonly known, little will be said about them here. However, it should be pointed out that for holding materials temporarily, rubber cement should be applied to only one surface, and the surfaces should be pressed together while the glue is still wet. To hold two surfaces together permanently, rubber cement should be applied to both surfaces and allowed to dry before the surfaces are placed together. One of the advantages of rubber cement is that when it dries, unwanted spots can be rubbed off the surface without leaving any marks.

Wood Screws

USES. Screws are used to fasten materials together when greater strength is desired than can be obtained from a nail joint. Materials screwed together can be separated without damage to either member.

SHAPES. Screws can be purchased with flat, oval, and round heads. (See Figure 12–9.)

SIZES. Screws are manufactured in lengths from ¼-inch to 5 inches and with a wire gauge that ranges from 0 to 24. The wire gauge of a screw

Materials and Supplies for the Classroom

305

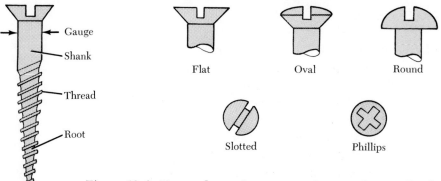

Gauge

Shank

Thread

Root

Flat

Oval

Round

Slotted

Phillips

Figure 12–9. Nomenclature for screw and types of screw heads.

represents the size of the diameter of the shank, as shown in Figure 12–9. As the gauge number increases, the diameter of the shank increases, for example, a No. 6 screw has a smaller shank diameter than a No. 8 screw.

Sales Units. Screws can be purchased in any desired quantity, small or large, but the smaller quantities (less than a full box) cost more in proportion than the larger amount.

Recommended Purchase. Assorted sizes should be purchased, between ½ to 1½ inches in length, with slotted, round, and flat heads.

Fastening with Wood Screws

1. Select the correct size screw.
   a. *Type of head:* Flat head screws are used where the head is to be flush with the surface. Round head and oval head screws are used where it is not objectionable for the heads to show or remain above the surface. (See Figure 12–10.)
   b. *Length:* Approximately two-thirds of the screw should enter the second piece of material
   c. *Gauge number:* The gauge size increases with the strain and the size of materials being screwed together.
2. Lay out the positions of the screws not closer than one-half inch from the end or edge of the material when possible. Screws are arranged in a straight line for appearance and staggered for strength.
3. Drill a hole in the first piece the size of the shank diameter. (See Figure 12–10.) Test for proper sizes by drilling a hole in a piece of scrap stock. These holes are called shank holes.
4. Soft woods do not require any hole in the second piece of material. Hard woods—maple, oak, birch, and walnut—require that a hole be drilled in the second piece of material. Locate the position of these holes by marking through the holes in the first piece with an awl.
5. Drill the holes in the second piece to a length equal to that of the penetration of the screw and a diameter equal to the root of the screw. These holes are called pilot holes.

6. Countersink for the head of the screw when using flat or oval head screws. (See Figure 12–10.)

7. Soap or wax applied to the threads of the screw will assist in the driving of screws into hard woods.

8. Select the proper screwdriver. The blade tip should be as wide as the diameter of the screw head and should fit the slot of the screw snugly.

9. Place the pieces together and insert the screws in the holes. Drive screws by holding the screwdriver in the palm of the right hand with the fingers and thumb around it. Keep it at right angles to the surface of the material and in a straight line with the screw. Turn the screwdriver in a clockwise direction. Guide the screw, and at the same time, hold the end of the screwdriver in the screw slot with the thumb and the index finger of the left hand.

10. If the screw slips out of the slot it will gouge the surface or damage the screw slot.

11. Stop turning the screw when the two pieces are held firmly together and the head is seated.

Stove Bolts and Carriage Bolts

Uses. Stove bolts and carriage bolts are used to fasten the various parts of an object together where strength is a requirement. They also can be used where it is desired to dismantle the finished object and use the parts over again in another activity. Wing nuts can be used with bolts to permit tightening or loosening with only the fingers. Stove bolts can be used to fasten

Figure 12–10. Screws in final position and steps in the preparation of stock for securing with screws.

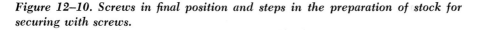

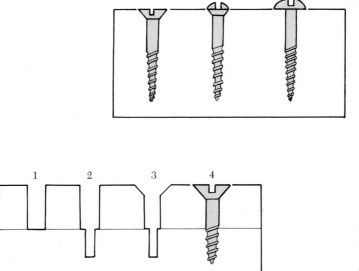

1. Shank

2. Pilot

3. Countersink

4. Screw in position

almost any material in which holes can be drilled, whereas the squared shank on the carriage bolt limits its use to soft surfaces, such as wood, that will allow the square shank to be drawn into the material as it is tightened.

SHAPES. Stove bolts are available with either flat heads or round heads, both heads having slots like those of wood screws. Carriage bolts have a rounded head without a slot. They are further distinguished by a square section on the shank just below the head.

SIZES. Stove bolts are manufactured in lengths from ½-inch to 6 inches and in the following diameters ⅛-, ³⁄₁₆-, ¼-, ⁵⁄₁₆- and ⅜-inch. For general purposes, bolts up to 1 inch in length should be ⅛-inch in diameter; bolts from 1 to 2 inches in length should be ³⁄₁₆-inch in diameter; bolts from 2 to 3 inches in length should be ¼-inch in diameter; and bolts 3 to 4 inches in length should be ⁵⁄₁₆-inch in diameter. Carriage bolts are manufactured in lengths from ¾-inch to 6 inches in the following diameters ¼-, ⁵⁄₁₆-, ⅜-, and ½-inch.

RECOMMENDED PURCHASE. Stove bolts should be purchased in assorted sizes between ½-inch to 4 inches in length. Carriage bolts should be purchased in assorted sizes between 2 to 4 inches in length.

Corner Braces

USES. Corner braces are used to hold two or more pieces together or to strengthen a weak joint. They are used in frame construction to hold two or more frames together. They should be secured with screws that fill the countersunk hole and fit flush with the surface for maximum strength.

SIZES

Side Lengths	Size Width	Screw Size
1"	½"	¾" × No. 6
1½"	½"	¾" × No. 6
2"	⅝"	¾" × No. 8
2½"	⅝"	¾" × No. 8
3"	¾"	¾" × No. 9
3½"	¾"	¾" × No. 9

RECOMMENDED PURCHASE. A 1½ × ½-inch corner brace can be used for most of the activities fabricated by children.

Hinges

USES. Hinges are used to construct a joint that allows one or both members to move. A door is an example of a joint formed with hinges that allow only one member to move. The puppet stage illustrated in Chapter 9 can be folded like an accordian requiring both members of the joint to move.

Butt Hinges

Length of Joint	Width Open	Screw Size
1″	1″	½″ × No. 3
1¼″	1¹⁄₁₆″	⅝″ × No. 4
1½″	1⅜″	⅝″ × No. 5
1¾″	1⁷⁄₁₆″	⅝″ × No. 5
2″	1⁹⁄₁₆″	¾″ × No. 6

Double-Action Screen Hinges

Size or Wood Thickness	Length of Joint
¾″	1¾″
⅞″	1¾″
1″	1⅞″
1⅛″	1¾″
1¼″	2″

RECOMMENDED PURCHASE. Most of the constructed items requiring hinges in an elementary school will use 2- × 1⁹⁄₁₆-inch butts. Some special items, such as the puppet stage will require 1- × 1⅞-inch double-action screen hinges.

Sandpaper

USES. Sandpaper is a coated abrasive that is used to smooth or polish a surface. Sanding a surface smooth is very important in finishing any surface.

TYPES AND SIZES OF SANDPAPER. The abrasive surface on a sheet of sandpaper is manufactured from flint quartz, garnet, silicon carbide, and aluminum oxide. The grit (degree of coarseness) varies with the type of paper: flint paper, extra fine to extra coarse; garnet paper, 6/0 (very fine) to 2 (coarse). Sandpaper comes in various forms: sheets, belts, tapes, disks, and rolls.

RECOMMENDED PURCHASE. Flint sheets 9 × 11 inches in size with a grit of fine, medium, and coarse in packages of fifty sheets. For some situations, The Handy Pack, fifteen 4½- × 5-inch sheets in assorted grits is acceptable.

USING SANDPAPER

1. For economical and efficient use, the large sheets (9 × 11 inches) should be torn into four parts, first by tearing them in half the long

Materials and Supplies for the Classroom

way and then by tearing each piece in half again. The tearing operation is performed by placing the sandpaper grit side down against the edge of the bench with one half hanging over and tearing by pulling down on the edge of the paper.

2. On flat surfaces sandpaper should be used with a block of wood. Sanding without a proper sized block can cause damage to the surface and result in sandpaper being wasted.

3. When using sandpaper to smooth any surface, the sanding should always be in the same direction as the grain. Sanding across the grain produces scratches on the surface.

4. A sanding block can be used for sanding convex shapes. When sanding concave shapes, the sandpaper can be wrapped around a short dowel or a piece of broomstick.

5. When sanding small curves and corners, a small piece of folded sandpaper can be used.

6. Sandpaper can be used to smooth the edges of cardboard, linoleum, pressed wood, plaster, Keene's cement, and sawdust clay.

Hardware Cloth

Hardware cloth is a galvanized wire screening that can be used to fabricate an animal cage or other objects requiring a screened surface. It can be purchased in rolls or by the running foot at most hardware stores. The size is determined by the mesh, or the number of squares per inch. For example, hardware cloth with four squares per inch would be ¼-inch mesh. It comes in meshes that vary from one to four squares per inch, widths that vary from 24 to 48 inches, and lengths up to 150 feet. The size mesh will depend on the purpose for which the hardware cloth is needed. An animal cage could require a fine or large mesh depending on the size of the animal. An animal with paws that can fit between the mesh could be injured by catching his leg.

Chicken Wire

Chicken wire is a wire screening that can be used as a base for various kinds of models. It differs from hardware cloth in the shape of the openings and the flexibility of the material. Because of its flexibility, it makes an excellent base for papier mâché objects. Chicken wire can be cut to the desired shape with a pair of Tinner's snips and formed or sculptured by hand. The mesh is determined by the size of the opening rather than the number of squares per inch. Chicken wire with a 1-inch mesh is excellent for shaping and forming. It can be purchased at most hardware stores in rolls that are 150 feet in length and vary in width from 24 to 48 inches.

Wood Dowels

Dowels are cylindrical pieces of wood that are usually manufactured from birch or maple. They are used for spindles, shafts, axles, and other such objects. Wood dowels are available in the following diameters: $\frac{1}{8}$-, $\frac{3}{16}$-, $\frac{1}{4}$-, $\frac{5}{16}$-, $\frac{3}{8}$-, $\frac{7}{16}$-, $\frac{1}{2}$-, $\frac{9}{16}$-, $\frac{5}{8}$-, $\frac{3}{4}$-, $\frac{7}{8}$-, 1 inch and in various other diameters up to 3 inches. They usually are sold in 36-inch lengths. A variety of dowels with different diameters is recommended.

SPECIALIZED MATERIALS

As the activity program grows, children may want to experiment with a wider variety of materials. Styrofoam, cardboard, cement, or metals offer possibilities if they can be put in the budget or otherwise procured.

Styrofoam

USES. Styrofoam is a light, pure white material that can be readily cut into a variety of shapes. Puppets, models, and decorations can be fabricated or sculpted from styrofoam with a few simple tools.

SHAPES AND SIZES. The following information includes some of the shapes and sizes in which stryofoam can be purchased:

Description	Sizes of diameters
Balls	$\frac{3}{4}$", $1\frac{1}{8}$", $1\frac{1}{2}$", 2", 3"
Egg shapes	$2\frac{1}{2}$" $\times$ $3\frac{1}{4}$" and 3" $\times$ $4\frac{1}{4}$"

	Width	Length	Thicknesses
Sheets	12"	36"	$\frac{1}{4}$", $\frac{1}{2}$", 1", 2", 3", 4"
Dowels	$1\frac{1}{2}$"	12"	

RECOMMENDED PURCHASE. A variety of sizes and shapes give the program greater flexibility; however, styrofoam is expensive, so the funds available will govern to some extent what should be purchased. Sheets 12 $\times$ 36 $\times$ 1 inch and balls $1\frac{1}{8}$ inches and 2 inches in diameter are very useful in any activity program.

WORKING WITH STYROFOAM

1. A coping saw, knife, and sandpaper are all the tools needed to shape styrofoam. However, a hot wire is the quickest and most effective way of cutting styrofoam. This tool can be purchased or fabricated, but it is not essential.

2. Styrofoam surfaces can be glued together with a synthetic resin glue (white glue) or a special plastic adhesive for foam plastics. Certain types of glue will dissolve styrofoam.

3. The surface of styrofoam can be decorated with tempera paints, water colors, oil paints, and spray paints. However, care must be taken to make sure that the paint will not dissolve the styrofoam.

Tri-Wall Pak

Uses. Tri-Wall Pak is a triple-wall corrugated cardboard used to make objects and instructional materials, such as toys, mobiles, sculpture models, and classroom equipment. It has been used extensively for cardboard carpentry. Children and teachers can work the material with the basic hand tools described in Chapter 11.

Sizes. Sheet Sizes are 42×54 inches, 4×5 feet, and 4×6 feet.

Recommended Purchase. The writers suggest that you send for information from, Tri-Wall Containers, Inc., One Dupont Street, Plainview, New York.

Keene's Cement

Keene's cement can be used to make and mold instructional devices. It also can be used to make lamps, ash trays, powder boxes, and other such objects. Keene's cement can be worked with all the basic hand tools. It can be cast in rubber and sand molds. Keene's cement can be intermixed with colors to present a finish that has the appearance of marble. It can be painted with water colors, tempera, and oil paints and protected with lacquer or varnish. The advantage of Keene's cement over plaster of Paris is that it takes longer to harden. Keene's cement hardens in about twenty-four hours. It can be purchased by the pound or in 100-pound bags. (See Figure 12–11 for application.)

Plaster of Paris

Plaster of Paris can be used to make castings in rubber and sand molds. It can be worked with a knife and sandpaper. The finished object can be painted with water colors and coated with lacquer or varnish for a lasting finish. Plaster of Paris hardens in a matter of minutes.

METALS

The activities suggested in Chapters 3 through 10 require very little use of metals. One reason for this is their high cost; another is the danger of injury from sharp edges. But if children are careful, they can use some

Figure 12–11. Keene's cement model that demonstrates the water cycle.

metals in their endeavor to learn about the characteristics and properties of materials. Tin or aluminum cans are useful for many activities. The following metals can be purchased and used effectively by children in an activity program.

Aluminum

Aluminum is a silvery white, nonferrous metal of a medium degree of hardness. Aluma, from which aluminum is made, is one of the substances that makes up the clay of bauxite. It is separated from the clay in electric furnaces.

PROPERTIES

1. *Physical:* Aluminum is light in weight and relatively strong. It is a good conductor of heat and electricity and is silvery in color.
2. *Chemical:* It resists corrosion and has high resistance to atmospheric activity.
3. *Mechanical:* Aluminum has elastic strength, yet it is easily formed and shaped. It has high malleability and ductility, but becomes hardened when worked.

USES. Aluminum foil is used for tooling, and heavier-gauged sheet stock is ideal for metal craft work. Commercially, aluminum is used as a sheet metal, casting metal, forging metal, or can be pressed or rolled into forms for air, highway, rail, and water transportation units, structural and electrical building, industrial equipment, household equipment, and packaging.

*Materials and
Supplies for
the Classroom*

1. *Sales units:* Single units by sheets or linear feet in rolls, rods, and bars
2. *Shapes:* Sheets, rods, tubing, bars, and angles
3. *Sizes:* All standard metal sizes
4. *Grades:* Graded by the percentage of alloying metals present for desired characteristics

Copper

Copper is a reddish brown, nonferrous metal that appears abundantly in nature. Good copper is 99 per cent pure.

PROPERTIES

1. *Physical:* Light in weight, but heavier than aluminum, it has a high coefficient of expansion, hardens with age, and is reddish in color.
2. *Chemical:* It resists corrosion, but tarnishes rapidly.
3. *Mechanical:* It is easily formed and shaped, welded, or soldered. Can be annealed and hardened. It becomes hardened when overworked.

USES. Copper foil is used for tooling, whereas heavier-gauged sheet stock is ideal for metal craft work. Commercially it is used, because it conducts heat and electricity, for nails, tubing, tanks, utensils, containers, decorations, and accessories.

MARKET ANALYSIS

1. *Sales unit:* Single units by sheets or linear feet in rolls
2. *Shapes:* Sheets, rods, tubing, and bars
3. *Sizes:* All standard metal sizes
4. *Grades:* Soft or cold rolled

Galvanized Iron

Galvanized iron is a silvery grey metal with an iron or steel ferrous core and a fine nonferrous coating.

PROPERTIES

1. *Physical:* Light in weight and fairly strong, with a bright, silvery, spangled appearance
2. *Chemical:* Rust resistant without painting
3. *Mechanical:* Easily bent, formed, and shaped; high ductility; comparatively soft for ease in rolling and soldering

Uses. Galvanized sheets can be used to make a tray for an animal cage or the base for a plant table. Commercially, galvanized iron is used extensively in general sheet metal work and in the heating and ventilation trade almost to the exclusion of all other metals.

MARKET ANALYSIS

1. *Sales unit:* Single sheets or bundles with from two to ten sheets in a bundle, depending on the size and gauge
2. *Shapes:* Only in sheet stock
3. *Sizes:* Manufactured in various thickness, widths and lengths
4. *Grades:* Tight coat or loose coat zinc

FINISHING MATERIALS

The final satisfying step in the construction of any object is the finishing. At this point, the object is turned from material into a representation of an idea or concept. It takes on color and character. It provides one of the chief sources of interest and satisfaction for children. They enjoy bright attractive colors and the individual touches they have conceived. Because this is the last operation in fabricating any object, teachers should be well informed regarding its hazards and pitfalls. Frustration and disappointment in the last stages of a process are hard for children to bear and would defeat the purpose of the activity.

Those finishing materials most commonly used by children of elementary school age are tempera paints, water colors, poster paints, latex paints, spray paints, shellac, and lacquer.

Tempera, poster, and water colors can be used to paint wood, paper, cardboard, substitute clay models, and styrofoam. These paints only add color to the surface; they do not protect it. One or more coats of shellac are required to protect the surface from constant handling and moisture. For example, a figurine made from sawdust clay can be decorated by using water colors, but if the object is to remain attractive it must be coated with shellac or lacquer. Layers of shellac and lacquer can be built into a finish that can compare to a glazed piece of clay.

Tempera paints can be applied to a large surface with a sponge rather than with a paint brush.

Latex paints (interior and exterior) makes an excellent finishing material for objects that require a tough, durable, opaque finish. Latex paints can be purchased in a wide variety of colors. However, the writers suggest that because almost every paint job completed around the house results in a certain amount of extra paint, children's homes are a free source of the material. If parents will donate it, a ready supply can be on hand for use in the classroom. Latex paint is an excellent finishing material for children's use because it dries quickly, it can be thinned with water, and brushes (and children) can be cleaned with ordinary soap and water. This means that no extra cleaning solvents need to be purchased.

Spray paints are available in a variety of colors and can be used on metals, woods, and other materials. They require no brushes; and, with a little experimenting, some interesting results can be obtained. Children can produce unusual effects by combining colors in spray painting. Areas can be protected with cardboard while the exposed area is sprayed; then the cardboard can cover the painted area while another color is sprayed. Combinations that fuse together are the result. Spray paint, however, is very expensive, both in price and in amount wasted.

Shellac is a transparent coating that can be applied by brush or sprayed with an aerosol can. Shellac is an excellent material for sealing or protecting a surface. However, it will turn white if exposed to moisture. Brushes must be cleaned with denatured alcohol. Brush cleaning that requires solvents presents a problem for some young children, but with proper controls they can handle the task.

Lacquer can be purchased in a variety of colors or as a clear transparent solution that can be applied by brush or sprayed from an aerosol can. Water or moisture will not affect the lacquer finish as it does a shellac finish. Brushes should be cleaned with lacquer thinner.

There are a number of clear wood sealers that are used to finish paneling and floors. These finishes can be purchased in a variety of trade names and make excellent substitutes for shellac and lacquer. Like latex paints, these materials could probably be obtained from children's homes.

Some of these finishing materials are fire hazards and should be stored in fireproof containers. Shellac and lacquer should not be stored in plastic containers; if possible they should be stored in a metal storage cabinet.

Paint brushes can be purchased in a variety of sizes and shapes. Flat brushes are used for general work and can be obtained in sizes ranging from ½-inch to 4 inches. Artist's brushes are available in sizes smaller than ½-inch. Oval brushes and round brushes are used for special purposes such as painting trim and sashes.

SOURCES OF TOOLS, MATERIALS, AND EQUIPMENT

The classified telephone directory can be used as an excellent guide to sources for tools, materials, and equipment in one's immediate area. Some of the headings that will be of assistance are

Artists Materials	Lumberyards
Arts and Crafts Supplies	Paint and Painters Supplies
Hardware Supply Stores	Printing Supplies

The writers have found in their own programs that a number of catalogs can be very helpful in locating the desired supplies needed in an activity program. These catalogs list the tools, materials, and equipment; the various sizes; a brief description of the item; and, in many cases include a picture. The following catalogs are excellent for locating tools, materials, and equipment:

Beckley Cardy
1900 N. Narragansett Ave.
Chicago, Ill. 60639

Macpherson Leisure Crafts
941 East Second St.
Los Angeles, Calif. 90012

Brodhead Garrett
4560 East 71st St.
Cleveland, Ohio 44105

Milton Bradley Company
43 Cross St.
Springfield, Mass. 01101

Gledhill Bros., Inc.
20 Chestnut Ave.
Jamaica Plain, Boston, Mass. 02130

Patterson Brothers
15 Park Row
New York, N. Y. 10038

J. L. Hammett Co.
Hammett Place
Braintree, Mass. 02184

Materials and Supplies

The following list could be used as a reference when ordering materials or as a guide to the type of materials that can be requested from parents, industry, or the business community.

I. *Cloth*

unbleached cotton	rickrack
felt	leather scraps
cotton scraps	leather lacing–gimp
wool scraps	old ties
burlap	old felt hats
old nylons	old trousers
old socks	old coats
cotton balls or batton	bias tape
ribbon–bows	woven tape

II. *Wood*

2 × 4's (all sizes)	popsicle sticks
plywood (all thicknesses)	toothpicks
spools (small and large)	sawdust
dowels (birch or maple), different diameters	wooden balls
wooden crates	wood scraps (all types)
pine scraps	wooden clothespins
Masonite scraps	wooden handles (broom, etc.)

III. *Wire*

insulated wire
wire hangers
chicken wire
steel wool

pipe cleaners
hardware cloth
screening

IV. *Paints*

tempera
oil paints
felt markers
water base paints
oil base paints
shellac

varnish
lacquer
thinners–paint, etc.
water colors
Latex paints

V. *Hardware*

screws
nails
nuts and bolts
straight pins
safety pins
snaps
gate hooks
corner braces

iron plates
hinges
tacks–all kinds
screw eyes
rubber bumpers
wing nuts and bolts
brass paper fasteners
brads

VI. *Yarn*

cotton
wool

loops
tinsel rope

VII. *Metals*

aluminum
copper
galvanized iron

tin cans
aluminum cans
tin plate

VIII. *Paper*

construction paper–all colors
oak tag–all colors, basically
    manila
paper bags
newspapers
brown wrapping paper–mural
    paper
newsprint
index cards
napkins
Kleenex
crepe paper
tin foil
straws
paper cups

drinking straws
stencil paper
waxed paper
paper towels
wallpaper
paper doilies
old greeting cards
envelopes
shirt cardboards
paper plates
cardboard dowels (from
    hangers)
cardboard tubes
corrugated cardboard

IX. Containers

baby food jars
milk cartons
soap containers
plastic containers (all sizes)
Styrofoam containers
fruit containers
salt and oatmeal boxes
egg boxes
suit boxes
hat boxes
shoe boxes
candy boxes
cigar boxes
match boxes

tobacco cans
coffee cans
fruit juice cans
muffin tins
cake tins
pails
cookie sheets
mixing bowls
dishpans
saucepans
spoons
measuring cups
measuring spoons
double boiler

X. Miscellaneous

glue
rubber cement
cements (plastic)
wheat paste
flour
cornstarch
baking soda
salt
food coloring
sugar lumps
vegetables
pine cones
sea shells
flower pots
glitter
beans
marbles
shirt stays
buttons
corks
macaroni
swizzle sticks
ping pong balls
mousetraps
old toys (wheels or motors)
needles
pins
batteries
broom
dustpan
mop
rolling pin
leather scraps
masking tape

old candles
tiles–plastic, asphalt, and
    ceramic
clay
styrofoam (all sizes)
glass tubing
sand
straw and hay
human hair
display motors
old clocks
sponges
paint brushes
sandpaper
emery cloth
ink
pipe cleaners
soap–bar and powder
cellophane tape
single-edge razor blades
crinoline
sequins
balloons
nail files
pencils
crayons
chalk
rubber bands
clothesline
ink pad
matchsticks
feathers
foam rubber
magazines

old light bulbs
rubber jar rings
unusual shells and pebbles
unusual rocks
artificial flowers
old calendars

cotton thread
embroidery thread
string–heavy and light
old jewelry
hot plate

CONCLUSION

This chapter was devoted to a description of some of the materials that can be utilized by children and teachers to enrich the learning process. Many of these materials can be used very effectively as experiments in learning about the physical, chemical, and mechanical properties of a material. Instead of reading about these properties, children can actually manipulate materials to learn what is meant by high resistance to atmospheric conditions, good holding power, or high malleability and ductility. This activity would represent an excellent example of changing from an abstract stimuli to the use of an experience with concrete materials and a completely new type of stimuli. For example, in explaining the mechanical properties of copper it is stated that copper hardens if it is overworked and that it can be annealed. A child could take a piece of copper and start working it with a hammer. To his amazement he would find that the surface got hard and also brittle, that it stretched, and that if annealed it got soft again.

Children can learn to distinguish between what is meant by characteristics and properties of a material in a very practical situation. They can work with soft and hard woods and discover that some hardwoods are actually softer and easier to work than some soft woods.

The classroom that has a large variety of materials has established an opportunity that will allow children to explore their environment. A small amount of materials limits the child's opportunity to invent and create objects and items that can help him understand the material world. A teacher who understands the characteristics and properties of materials and plans for their availability and use can speed the children on an important program of discovery based upon learning styles. It will be difficult for the program to function if the teacher does not understand some of the characteristics and properties of the materials and supplies so important to such a program. These materials can help children unfold a whole new approach to learning in that they allow them to invent a learning style that meets their individual needs.

LEARNING ACTIVITIES

1. Plan a science experience that would utilize some of the materials suggested in this chapter to assist you in developing the following concepts with children:

    a. Properties: physical, mechanical, and chemical

    b. Characteristics

2. Plan some experiences for children that would illustrate how different types of materials could be used to enrich the learning task in the following areas:

    a. Art

    b. Language Arts

    c. Mathematics

    d. Geography

3. Survey your community for possible sources of free materials that could be used with children to assist in their instructional program.

4. Collect some catalogs that could be used to assist you in ordering equipment, tools, and materials. Write the specifications for ordering the following materials:

    a. Hardware cloth

    b. Screws

    c. Glue

    d. Metal for copper tooling

    e. Sheet of plywood

    f. Common nails

    g. Finish nails

5. Survey the literature on British primary education related to how children should be allowed to invent and explore with equipment, materials, and tools. Do you agree or disagree with this point of view? Defend your answer.

6. Develop some activities utilizing substitute clay that could be used to enhance learning in the following areas:

    a. Social Studies

    b. Art

    c. Mathematics

REFERENCES

GERBRACHT, CARL, AND BABCOCK, ROBERT J. *Industrial Arts for Grade K–6.* Milwaukee: Bruce, 1959.

HAMMOND, JAMES J., DONNELLY, EDWARD T., HARROD, WALTER, AND RAYNER, NORMAN. *Woodworking Technology.* Bloomington, Ill.: McKnight & McKnight, 1961.

LARK-HOROVITZ, BETTY, LEWIS, HILDA, AND LUCA, MARK. *Understanding Children's Art for Better Teaching,* Columbus, Ohio: Charles E. Merrill, 1967.

MATTIL, EDWARD L. *Meaning in Crafts.* Englewood Cliffs, N.J.: Prentice-Hall, 1965.

McFEE, JUNE K. *Preparation for Art.* San Francisco: Wadsworth, 1961.

INDEX

DATE DUE

OCT 2 9 1976			
OCT 6 '78	OCT 10 '78		
OCT 31 '78	OCT 30 '78		
GAYLORD			PRINTED IN U.S.A.